Writers will say, Why am I not so well read? Expositors, why didn't I see it all like that too? And readers will join in unanimous praise for a great feast of biblical truth made so digestible, garnished with so many apt illustrations and always focused on the God of all grace. I have lost count of the times I stopped reading to pray and praise – and I have certainly lost count of the number of tit-bits transferred to my note-books for future use!

Alec Motyer

Dr Ralph Davis' exposition of 2 Samuel has been eagerly awaited and does not disappoint. As with his earlier work this volume stands out first for its excellent Biblical Theology, so that 2 Samuel is seen in the whole sweep of salvation history leading to Christ. Secondly, although the focus is firmly on Jesus, Dr Davis' careful scholarship and examination of the text means that each chapter produces its own fresh message. Thirdly, Dr Davis' lively style and homely illustrations make it a delight to read and a mine for preachers. I cannot recommend it too highly.

Jonathan Fletcher

This is no ordinary commentary but an exposure of the very heart and soul of a Biblical book. You will be taken by the hand and sometimes by the scruff of the neck into the Israelite world of three millenia ago, but at the same time you will see Second Samuel's witness to Christ and be made to face real issues of Christian discipleship in today's world. All this is done with such scholarship, such insight, such verve and with such a unique style (he even adds a few new words to the English language!) that the book is compelling reading.

Geoffrey Grogan

Focus on the Bible Commentaries

Genesis – John Currid*
Exodus – John L. Mackay*
Deuteronomy – Alan Harman
Judges and Ruth – Stephen Dray
1 Samuel – Dale Ralph Davis*
2 Samuel – Dale Ralph Davis
1 and 2 Kings – Robert Fyall*
Ezra, Nehemiah, Esther – Robin Dowling*
Proverbs – Eric Lane
Isaiah – Paul House*
Jeremiah – George Martin*
Ezekiel – Anthony Billington*
Daniel – Robert Fyall
Hosea – Michael Eaton
Amos – O Palmer Robertson*
Jonah–Zephaniah – John L. Mackay
Haggai–Malachi – John L. Mackay
Matthew – Charles Price
Mark – Geoffrey Grogan
John – Robert Peterson*
1 Corinthians – Paul Barnett*
2 Corinthians – Geoffrey Grogan
Galatians – Joseph Pipa*
Ephesians – R. C. Sproul
Philippians – Hywel Jones
1 and 2 Thessalonians – Richard Mayhue
The Pastoral Epistles – Douglas Milne
Hebrews – Walter Riggans
James – Derek Prime
1 Peter – Derek Cleave
2 Peter/Jude – Paul Gardner
Letters of John – Michael Eaton
Revelation – Paul Gardner

Journey Through the Old Testament – Bill Cotton
How To Interpret the Bible – Richard Mayhue

Those marked with an * are currently being written.

Expositions of the book of

2 Samuel

Out of Every Adversity

Dale Ralph Davis

Christian Focus

Christian Focus Publications publishes biblically-accurate books for adults and children. The books in the adult range are published in three imprints.

Christian Heritage contains classic writings from the past.

Christian Focus contains popular works including biographies, commentaries, doctrine, and Christian living.

Mentor focuses on books written at a level suitable for Bible College and seminary students, pastors, and others; the imprint includes commentaries, doctrinal studies, examination of current issues, and church history.

For a free catalogue of all our titles, please write to
Christian Focus Publications,
Geanies House, Fearn,
Ross-shire, IV20 1TW, Great Britain

For details of our titles visit us on our web site
http://www.christianfocus.com

ISBN 1 85792 335 9

First published in 1999
by
Christian Focus Publications
Geanies House, Fearn,
Ross-shire, IV20 1TW, Great Britain

Cover design by Owen Daily

Printed and bound in Great Britain by
The Guernsey Press Co. Ltd., Guernsey, Channel Islands

Contents

Part 3: A Kingdom in God's Hands (chs. 21–24)

Preface

Writing expositional commentaries is a good bit like going to graduate school or repairing a lawnmower or constructing bookshelves (I could go on and on): if one knew what was involved at the beginning one would never have begun. But, having begun, one has no better sense than to keep going. Perhaps it's our passion for completion. I have previously treated Joshua, Judges, and First Samuel. Now the Second Samuel volume is finished and I am delighted that Christian Focus is publishing it.

I send it forth with thanks for the encouragement received from readers of the previous volumes in the series, whether lay people, pastors, or students. It is always heartening, for example, to hear when a commentary, of all things, has encouraged someone to preach through an Old Testament book, of all things!

Let me include a word about the format of this volume. The full biblical text is not printed in the commentary. This is a deliberate failure. To do so would increase cost. But that is not my reason for the omission. I want the commentary to drive you to your Bible and not to become a substitute for it. If you find yourself always having to refer back to your Bible for details, then you have fallen into my trap. The omission of a full printed translation is a conspiracy to keep you dependent on your Bible.

I dedicate this volume to the memory of my father and mother, J. Daryl Davis and Mary Wilson Davis. I have always been grateful for them but even more so as the years wear on. I confess God's grace named my name before the foundation of the world (Eph. 1:3-6); but when he poured out that grace in time he made most of it flow through my parents.

Ascension Day 1997

Abbreviations

ABD	*Anchor Bible Dictionary*
ANET	*Ancient Near Eastern Texts,* 3rd ed
BDB	Brown, Driver, and Briggs, *Hebrew and English Lexicon*
IDB	*Interpreter's Dictionary of the Bible*
IDB/S	*Interpreter's Dictionary of the Bible / Supplementary Volume*
ISBE	*International Standard Bible Encyclopedia*
JB	Jerusalem Bible
JSOT	*Journal for the Study of the Old Testament*
LXX	The Septuagint
NASB	New American Standard Bible
NBD	*New Bible Dictionary*
NEB	New English Bible
NIV	New International Version
NJB	New Jerusalem Bible
NJPS	Tanakh: A New Translation of the Holy Scriptures According to the Traditional Hebrew Text (1985)
NKJV	New King James Version
NRSV	New Revised Standard Version
REB	Revised English Bible
RSV	Revised Standard Version
TDOT	*Theological Dictionary of the Old Testament*
TEV	Today's English Version
TWOT	*Theological Wordbook of the Old Testament*
ZPEB	*Zondervan Pictorial Encyclopedia of the Bible*

Introduction: From Theft to Lie

I have stolen the title of this exposition from the RSV rendering of David's words in 2 Samuel 4:9. There David uses an oath formula and calls on Yahweh 'who has redeemed my life out of every adversity'. This was no flippant remark. Anyone who reads 1 Samuel 18–31 understands it. This formula, however, does not describe a mere stage or segment of David's life but his whole life. His statement in 2 Samuel 4:9 comes during his early reign in Hebron, but he uses the *very same words* at the end of his reign (1 Kings 1:29). David and distress walked together his whole life.[1] Since David is the premier human character of 2 Samuel, it seems fitting to steal his life-description for the title of this commentary.

However, let me hasten to add that 2 Samuel is not about David. If you think it is, you will not understand it. I get worried when someone says to me (e.g., after a 2 Samuel exposition), 'Oh, I just love anything about David.' I understand and yet I cringe. The church seemingly cannot divorce herself from this *People* magazine approach to biblical narrative. Again and again as we read 2 Samuel we have to shake ourselves and say, 'This is not about David; it is not even about covenant kings; it is about a covenant God who makes covenant promises to a covenant king through whom he will preserve his covenant people.' That must be our perspective.

Before jumping into the text, I want to say a word about the major divisions of 2 Samuel. In *Looking on the Heart* (Vol 1, pp. 11-12), I argued that First and Second Samuel are to be considered one work with clearly indicated divisions, the first four of which terminate with a summary section. Hence 1–2 Samuel breaks down like this:

---

1. Joab instinctively linked David's life with hardship. Note his rebuke of David in 19:7 (Heb., v.8): 'And this disaster will be worse than all the disaster that has come upon you from your youth until now.' Clyde Francisco draws attention to the graphic expression the Chronicler uses to describe David's days: 'the circumstances [lit., times] that came over him' (1 Chron. 29:30), i.e., as waves run to the shore, perhaps suggesting wave upon wave of difficulty ('1-2 Chronicles,' *The Broadman Bible Commentary,* 12 vols. [Nashville: Broadman, 1970], 3:360).

Textual Block	Primary Focus	Summary Section
1 Samuel 1-7	Samuel	1 Sam. 7:15-17
1 Samuel 8-14	Saul	1 Sam. 14:47-52
1 Samuel 15-2 Samuel 8	David / I	2 Sam. 8: 15-18
2 Samuel 9-20	David / II	2 Sam. 20: 23-26
2 Samuel 21-24	Kingdom	

This means that 2 Samuel begins in the middle of the third block of material and that the major divisions come at the end of chapters 8 and 20. On this basis I propose the following overall outline for 2 Samuel:

> A Man After God's Heart, chs. 1–8
> A Servant under God's Rod, chs. 9–20
> A Kingdom in God's Hands, chs. 21–24

I want you to read on. But it's a sad thing about 2 Samuel – the book begins with a lie.[2]

---

2. Regarding date and authorship I simply repeat what I wrote in my volume on 1 Samuel: We know neither the date nor author(s) of 1 and 2 Samuel. Some scholars hold to a very complex compositional history that places anything like the present form of the text into the Babylonian exile or beyond (see Georg Fohrer, *Introduction to the Old Testament* [Nashville: Abingdon, 1968], 217-26). Others would hold that, excepting minor alterations (like the note of 1 Sam. 27:6b?), 'the books seem to date close to the end of David's reign' (William Sanford Lasor, David Allan Hubbard, and Frederic William Bush, *Old Testament Survey: The Message, Form, and Background of the Old Testament* [Grand Rapids: Eerdmans, 1982], 229). See also H. Wolf, 'Samuel, 1 and 2,' ZPEB, 5:261.

Part 1

A Man after God's Heart

2 Samuel 1–8

1. Kingdom Principles
2 Samuel 1:1-16

Jean-Jacques Rousseau was not bashful about putting his views on child-rearing into print (e.g., his *Émile*), and he alleged that no one enjoyed playing with children more than himself. Why then did he abandon the five babies he had by his mistress Thérèse?[1] In Rousseau appearance and reality, publication and practice did not mesh.

It was the same with the Amalekite who came panting and heaving into David's outpost at Ziklag. He wore all the signs of genuine grief – clothes torn, dirt on his head (v. 2). He had come from the Philistine-Israelite conflict on Mt. Gilboa, located about eighteen miles southwest of the southern tip of the Sea of Galilee (Chinnereth in the Old Testament). The Philistines had carried the day and had trounced Israel. King Saul had been severely wounded and, not wanting the Philistines to have the delight of slowly torturing him to his end, had fallen on his own sword (1 Sam. 31:3-5). It was a dark, dark day for Israel. Jonathan, Saul's son and David's friend, was killed. Life was bleak and dark and bloody and grey in the kingdom of God.

And everything about this Amalekite seemed to reflect Israel's disaster. After all, no one will traipse over eighty miles unless one is in earnest about something.[2] The trip would have taken him several days. But it doesn't take David long to conclude he is a murderer, and it doesn't take the reader long to find out that he is, more accurately, a liar. Not that he wasn't sincere. He was – about getting a government job.

This passage raises the question David faced in 1 Samuel 24–26: How is the kingdom to come into David's hands? Will he wait for it to come as Yahweh's gift or seize it by his own initiative? Apparently the Amalekite held that there were times when Yahweh's promises (if he knew of them) required a slight push (v.10). Neither David nor the narrator agrees with this position. The story as we have it seems to say that kingdom principles must govern kingdom life, and we see several of those principles operating in this text. We begin with the exposure of falsehood.

---

1. Paul Johnson, *Intellectuals* (New York: Harper & Row, 1988), 21.
2. The fact that the precise location of Ziklag is disputed does not affect this point. Clearly it was in southwest Judah (cf. Josh. 19:1-9) and an outpost of Philistine Gath (cf. 1 Sam. 27).

The Exposure of Falsehood (esp. 1:6-10)

A casual reader who comes fresh from 1 Samuel 31 into this chapter and now hears the Amalekite's story may say, 'But I thought Saul finished himself off at Gilboa, and here's this Amalekite who claims his friendly act of euthanasia did the honours.' Do we have two accounts? Not really. We have this narrator's description of what happened (1 Sam. 31) and we have the Amalekite's story of what happened (vv.3-10). The solution is simple: the Amalekite lied. If you ever have a choice between the narrator and an Amalekite, always believe the narrator. Have you ever met an Amalekite you could trust?

Some will object that I am too quick to condemn this Amalekite. If so, perhaps it helps to point out that there's a suspicious hole in the Amakelite's story (and I should think David would have seen it at once). As C.F. Keil pointed out, it is not likely that Saul would have been so isolated in the thick of battle, with no armor-bearer or royal contingent at his side, that he had to depend on an Amalekite who accidentally came by to administer the *coup de grace*.[3] Yet if this Amalekite wanted a reward from David, he almost had to 'story' a little. How could he say he slithered around like a coward, waiting for Saul to fall so that, when the way was clear, he could pounce on the royal insignia? Certainly he had to explain how he obtained the crown and armband, but how much more gallant it sounded if in the thick of battle he kindly and coolly assisted Saul in death with dignity.[4] A far more rewardable scenario.

The Amalekite received justice (vv.15-16), but it is justice mixed with irony. He is punished for what he said he did even though (in our view) he didn't do it! He received what he should have received even though it was not based on fact. The judgment of God found

---

3. C.F. Keil, *Biblical Commentary on the Books of Samuel* (1875; reprint ed., Grand Rapids: Eerdmans, 1950), 286.

4. The Amalekite graphically describes Saul's predicament in v. 6: 'Why, the chariots and cavalry had zeroed in on him.' There is something almost heroic in the fact that the Amalekite was there in the thick of it (according to his story). However, if he had had genuine interest in Saul, he would have dragged Saul's body from the battlefield to deny it to the Philistine trophy collectors who would soon comb the area (1 Sam. 31:8-10); instead he only swiped Saul's symbols of office (so J.P. Fokkelman, *Narrative Art and Poetry in the Books of Samuel*, vol. 2, *The Crossing Fates (I Sam. 13-31 & II Sam. 1)* [Assen/Maastricht: Van Gorcum, 1986], 686).

him, found him in his lie and repaid him in line with his intent if not his deed.

So on the first page of another biblical book we run straight into the God who exposes us, who delights in truth in the inward parts (Ps. 51:6), who sets our secret sins in the light of his presence (Ps. 90:8). Nor will this be the last episode – there will be 'Amalekites' in the church. Ananias and Sapphira will feel the need to boost their self-esteem within the Jerusalem Church (Acts 5:1-11 in light of 4:32-37) and end up in twin graves for it. Even if we could fool kings and churches Jesus has taught us that no one will escape D-Day (for Disclosure): 'There is nothing concealed that will not be disclosed, or hidden that will not be made known. What you have said in the dark will be heard in the daylight, and what you have whispered in the ear in the inner rooms will be proclaimed from the roofs' (Luke 12:2-3, NIV). Yet strangely we find ourselves often cuddling this absurd notion that if we have duped man's eye we have eluded heaven's gaze as well.

There was once a Scottish lad who thought this way. An unresolved misdemeanor had occurred in Dingwall: a boy had entered a garden and stripped the plum trees. Several months had gone by yet the culprit was unknown. Then came a Sabbath when there was a children's service at the church, and the pastor, Dr. John Kennedy, was preaching. He spoke from Psalm 11:4 of the One 'whose eyes behold and eyelids try the children of men'. Then he came to his dramatic conclusion: 'The boy is with us this evening who stole the plums! I shall not look in the direction of his seat lest I betray him. But I know him. I saw him from my study-window – saw the wall leaped, the pockets filled – the breathless race home. He thought no one saw, but I saw the whole, and God saw.'[5]

The same principle holds for simple Scottish lads and for conniving Amalekites: in Yahweh's kingdom we have to do with a God who sees, exposes, and judges. We must not think that an episode at Ziklag (or Dingwall) is an unconnected fragment in the accidents of history. Rather, what you see in 2 Samuel 1 in the Amalekite's case is a preview of what will be true for all at the last day. 'There is *nothing* concealed that will not be disclosed.' Jesus should know – he's the one God has authorized to judge the secrets of men (Rom. 2:16).

---

5. Donald Beaton, *Some Noted Ministers of the Northern Highlands* (Glasgow: Free Presbyterian, 1985), 276-77.

The urgency of grief (1:11-12)

> Then David grabbed hold of his clothes and tore them – likewise all
> the men who were with him. And they wailed, wept, and fasted until
> evening over Saul, over Jonathan his son, over the people of Yahweh,
> and over the house of Israel, because they had fallen by the sword.

It sounds strange to suggest that the urgency of grief should mark
life in God's kingdom, but the text insists that this should be the
case. We can better appreciate this point – and verses 11-12 – if we
step back and see the way the whole story is told.

It may be set forth like this:

> Arrival of Amalekite, vv. 1-2
>> Conversation, vv. 3-10 (3 questions)
>>> Reaction, vv. 11-12
>> Conversation, vv. 13-14 (2 questions)
> Elimination of Amalekite, vv. 15-16

Note that verses 11-12 are at the structural center of the story. Note
also that you would not have told the story in this way. You would
prefer, I should think, to continue with verse 13 immediately after
verse 10, because (in the story as it is) you get nervous about that
Amalekite just standing there while all this grief goes up. You want
to clean up the immediate situation with this informer; then you
would tell of the reaction of David & Co. But, for our writer, the
Amalekite can wait. He thinks the most important item in his story
is the grief and wailing of David and his men over Israel – her
fallen leaders and troops. The 'people of Yahweh' have been
crushed. Grief cannot wait.

Now I do not know if our writer has altered the strict
chronological sequence of events in the text. Biblical writers are
not bound by chronology. But I do think he has stood our literary
tendencies on their heads by letting loose this hubbub of wailing
immediately after the Amalekite's report. Nothing else matters,
except giving vent to this anguish. Even executions can wait. The
writer's use of structure and sequence is his way of underscoring
the importance of this grief over God's people.

The literary pattern of our text might be akin to a third grade
girl who, with her schoolmates, saw a giraffe come striding across

the school yard during afternoon play time. When she goes home, she bursts into the kitchen with her giraffe story even though her spelling test and pizza-for-lunch may temporally have preceded the giraffe's debut. In such cases chronology is thrown to the winds because of something far more impressive.

The grief of David and his men is impressive. The condition of the people of God disturbed them. And the same principle should control our life in the kingdom. Do we not have an obligation to mourn over the unbelief, apostasy and coldness in the visible church? It is not difficult for us (who are sometimes evangelicals) to observe, analyze, or critique the apathy over faithful doctrine, the flirtations with paganism, and the infatuation with a politically correct moral-social agenda which infect bodies of the institutional church. The peril in all this, of course, is that it is so easy to take on a conservative haughtiness, a sort of humble version of Luke 18:11, a kind of evangelical arrogance (which is itself a contradiction of the gospel). Rather such unbelief or error in the church should drive us to mourning and grief and prayer and sorrow. It calls for intercession more than for pronouncements.

Scripture is so subtle: it begins with the literary technique of the writer and then brings us to our knees.

The safety of fear (1:13-16)
The Amalekite assumes that David is driven by the same passion for power as he is. So he tells his story and shows his trinkets. David can only take him at his word – he has no way of independently confirming it (though, as noted above, there are holes in his tale). David makes sure the Amalekite is no recent import but has been living in Israel for some time (v.13). He, therefore, should have known better. Hence David's question: 'Why were you not afraid to stretch out your hand to destroy Yahweh's anointed?' (v. 14)

The sanctity of Yahweh's anointed king had the status of dogma for David. This sacred respect for Saul in his official capacity was the principle that controlled David in 1 Samuel 24 and 26 (see esp. 26:10-11) and kept him from regarding temptation as opportunity.[6] The Amalekite had assumed that no scruples would stop David from seizing the kingship; David assumed that one fear should have

---

6. On the sanctity of Yahweh's anointed, see *Looking on the Heart: Expositions of the Book of 1 Samuel,* 2 vols. (Grand Rapids: Baker, 1994), 2:105.

stopped the Amalekite from destroying the king. 'Why were you not afraid?'

David's question expresses a principle that should direct all kingdom ethics and behavior. There is in kingdom living such a thing as healthy, saving fear; a fear that preserves, a godly fear that should control us. There was once a Polish prince who always carried a picture of his father next to his heart. At certain times he used to take it out, look at it, and say, 'Let me do nothing unbecoming so excellent a father.'[7] That is the way all kingdom servants should live – controlled by fear grounded in love. Only Amalekites would call that pathological.

Time for confession. I admit that this text does not furnish us with the most positive uplifting points: falsehood, grief, and fear. But don't blame me. It's not my fault. It's this lying, conniving Amalekite who puts God's word into the minor key. But even he may help me if he forces me to question myself. Is there truth in the inner person? Do I ever earnestly grieve over the desperate condition of the church? Do I live life fearing only to displease my King?

2. Good Grief
2 Samuel 1:17-27

There is a poignant entry in the diary of Andrew Bonar, the nineteenth-century Scottish pastor. He notes the death of Isabella, his wife of seventeen years, on October 14-15, 1864.[1] Subsequent entries reveal his state of mind and sorrow. But what caught my attention (and yet did not surprise me) was how Bonar inevitably refers to his loss every year on the anniversary of Isabella's death. Grief remains; sorrow is not merely a sad event but a continuing process. Grief not only irrupts (as in 1:11-12); it abides. And because it abides there must be some mechanism, some procedures, by which God's people can express that grief. That is what David does in this passage; in his lament over Israel, Saul, and Jonathan, he provides a vehicle by which Israel can continue her mourning.

---

7. John Whitecross, *The Shorter Catechism Illustrated from Christian Biography and History* (reprint ed., London: Banner of Truth, 1968), 58.
1. Marjory Bonar, ed., *Andrew A. Bonar: Diary and Life* (Edinburgh: Banner of Truth, 1960), 226-27.

Yet we must come cautiously to this text. We are so tempted to jump at this text and psychologize it, as if David meant to lead a seminar on how to cope with grief. We must not turn David into another Christian guru turning out 'how to' books. Though he may give us some help in facing grief, we must not start there. We must sit with David at Ziklag (1:1) and let our minds replay the disaster at Gilboa (1 Sam. 31). We must not pull David into our time; we must go back, sit with him, hear him, understand him – in his time. Since the text is difficult and many variations appear in English versions, I will provide a working translation for reference here.

V. 17   Then David uttered this lament
           over Saul and over Jonathan his son.

V. 18   And he ordered (them) to teach the sons of Judah
                 'The Bow';[2]
           Note – it is written in the Book of Jashar.[3]

V. 19:   The glory, O Israel – slain upon your high places![4]
           How the mighty (warriors)[5] have fallen!

---

2. 'The Bow' is the title of David's lament, named appropriately, in memory of Jonathan's weapon (v.22) and gift (1 Sam. 18:4). See Morris S. Seale, *The Desert Bible* (New York: St. Martin's, 1974), 19.

3. Joshua 10:13 contains the only other certain reference to the Book of Jashar (the upright). It may have been a collection of Israel's heroic or war songs. At any rate, it is both out of print and lost! Cf. J. Orr and R.K. Harrison, 'Jashar, Book of,' ISBE, 2:969-70.

4. I have retained a traditional translation for v. 19a. The line is an enigma. The first word *ṣĕbî* (as a Hebrew proper name it is Zvi), may mean (1) beauty, honor, glory, or (2) gazelle (BDB, 840). If the gazelle is in view, the image does not likely reflect gracefulness or swiftness so much as fragility and helplessness; see Edwin Firmage, 'Zoology (Animal Profiles),' ABD, 6:1141-2. Further, who is the glory/gazelle? The parallel language of v.25 suggests that ultimately it is Jonathan. In v.19a, however, it could refer to Saul and Jonathan (cf.vv.22-23) or to Israel or her warriors (the 'mighty' of v.19b). Seale construes the text interrogatively, which is possible, and renders, 'Is Israel a gazelle?' That Israel lies slain 'upon [her] high places' points to complete disaster, for the good defensive position is the higher ground (the Gilboa range) and if the attackers have overrun that turf they have decimated their enemy. See further, Seale, *The Desert Bible*, 43-44; and J.P. Fokkelman, *Narrative Art and Poetry in the Books of Samuel*, vol. 2, *The Crossing Fates (I Sam. 13–31 & II Sam. 1)*, (Assen/Maastricht: Van Gorcum, 1986), 651-53.

V. 20:   Don't tell it in Gath;
          don't spread the news in the streets of Ashkelon;
          lest the daughters of the Philistines rejoice;
          lest the daughters of the uncircumcised go bragging.

V. 21   Hills of Gilboa,
          Let there be no dew or rain upon you
          – nor fields that produce offerings;
          for there the shield of the mighty ones was thrown away,
          the shield of Saul not anointed with oil.[6]

V. 22   From the blood of the slain,
          from the fat of the mighty ones,
          the bow of Jonathan did not retreat,
          and the sword of Saul never returns empty.

V. 23   Saul and Jonathan – loved and lovely,
          in their life and in their death they were not parted;[7]
          they were swifter than vultures,[8]
          They were stronger than lions.

V. 24   Daughters of Israel, weep for Saul!
          The one who clothed you in scarlet and finery;
          The one who put gold jewelry on your clothes.

---

5. I have kept the traditional 'mighty' or 'mighty ones' for *gibborîm* throughout (vv. 19, 21, 22, 25, 27); the reference is to warriors.

6. Leather shields were rubbed with oil in readiness for battle. See P. Kyle McCarter, Jr., *II Samuel,* The Anchor Bible (New York: Doubleday, 1984), 76, drawing on Alan Millard's study. Far from being prepared for combat Saul's shield lies, like the others on Gilboa, discarded and covered with the dirt and muck of battle.

7. Here I follow S.R. Driver (*Notes on the Hebrew Text and the Topography of the Books of Samuel,* 2nd ed. [1913; reprint ed., Winona Lake, Ind.: Alpha, 1984], 238) and A. A. Anderson (*2 Samuel,* Word Biblical Commentary [Dallas: Word, 1989], 11,19) in the division of the clauses. So too NRSV, NJPS, and REB.

8. The *nešer* (eagle, vulture) is a bird of prey (Hab. 1:8; Job 39: 27-30); hence the line in this context celebrates the prowess of Saul and Jonathan in war – swooping down to devour a hapless enemy. Cf. John W. Klotz, 'Animals of the Bible,' *Wycliffe Bible Encyclopedia* (Chicago: Moody, 1975), 1:92; or H. van Broekgoven, Jr., 'Eagle,' ISBE, 2:1-2.

V. 25   How the mighty have fallen in the thick of the battle!
         Jonathan – slain upon your high places!

V. 26   How distressed I am over you,
         my brother Jonathan!
         You have been very pleasant to me;
         your love toward me has been marvellous –
         more so than the love of women.

V. 27   How the mighty have fallen!
         So the weapons of war[9] perished.

Now we may go on to sketch the teaching and import of David's
lament. Here we can observe...

Grief and discipline (1:17)

When David 'lamented this lament' (lit., v. 17a) over Saul and
Jonathan he produced a self-conscious, reflective expression of grief
that could be reduced to written form (v. 18b). A lament is a formal
expression of grief or distress, one that can be written, read, learned,
practiced, repeated. A lament differs from the informal,
spontaneous, immediate outbursts of grief like those of 1:11-12.[10]
A lament is no less sorrowful or sincere; but it is a vehicle for the
mind as well as for the emotions. A lament is an expression of
thoughtful grief.

In a written lament then words cannot simply be dumped or
gushed or mushed as in initial grief. Here one cannot simply vomit
out feelings but must choose words. Not that the lament is cold,
objective, and detached. Rather the intensity of one's emotions unite
with the discipline of one's mind to produce structured sorrow, a
sort of authorized version of distress, a kind of coherent agony. In
a lament, therefore, words are carefully selected, crafted, honed, to
express loss as closely yet fully as possible.

I wonder if there is a principle here for all Yahweh's people

---

9. The 'weapons of war' is likely a figure for the warriors themselves (Seale,
The Desert Bible, 42-43), analogous to the way a baseball fan might exclaim
'Some glove!,' when referring to a superb fielding shortstop.

10. See David L. Zapf, 'How Are the Mighty Fallen! A Study of 2 Samuel
1:17-27,' *Grace Theological Journal* 5 (1984): 116 (drawing on Eileen F.
DeWard).

when they lose, especially, Christian friends or loved ones. Along
with our emotional grief should we not also express our reflective
grief? Why not write down our grief in careful, thoughtful lament
form and offer it up to God as such?[11]And do so again and again?

The sorrows and wounds God's people receive from their losses
are not miraculously healed after a short time of emotional catharsis.
And sometimes in the church there is such an impatience with grief.
Why isn't Allan 'over' Carol's death or Connie over Tom's since
it's been eighteen months – why can't that mother get beyond the
death of her ten-year-old?[12] But the lament-form of the Bible
assumes that our grief is deep and ongoing, and it invites us to
enter the discipline of expressing that grief in words that convey
our anguish, in images that picture our despair, in written prayers
that verbalize despondency. Why should God's people be shoddy
in their sorrow?

Grief and disgrace (1:20-21)
Shame aggravates grief. And the shame David feels is associated
with two places: Philistia (v.20) and Gilboa (v.21). David would
curse Gilboa with barrenness because it is the place where Israelite
shields litter the corpses they did not protect (v. 21). Gilboa is a
national disgrace. But the shame in Philistia is likely more galling.
David knows his command is futile; there is no way he can censor
Philistine press releases (v.20a). They most certainly *will* broadcast
it in Gath, and it will be on big screen TVs in every bar in Ashkelon.
But what really riles David is the way the Philistine women will be
leading cheers and trash-talking Israel (v. 20b) – and, as David and
every Israelite knows, not only Israel but Israel's God. For implicit
in verse 20 is the recognition that Israel's shame is religious, not
merely military. All over Philistia the foolish faithful were gathering

---

11. Of course there are prayers of lament in the Psalms, and many believers
take over the psalmists' words and pray them back to God.

12. I do not deny that believers may deal with loss in grotesque and twisted
ways. However, the persistence of grief is normal not pathological. With
passage of time the acuteness of sorrow may lessen but its ache remains. I
recall a Christian woman in her seventies telling me that her husband had
been dead thirteen years and still she felt the loneliness and missed his
companionship. She was/is a well-balanced, mature, joyful Christian woman.
But she lost the husband she loved and, in one way, had never gotten over it.
Nor should she. Great love has the greater pain.

to sing 'Glo-ry be to Da-gon,' the sorry excuse for a god the Philistines thought had given them this recent victory.

Yet such disgrace is useful. At least David intends to use it. Remember the preface to David's lament: 'And he ordered (them) to teach the sons of Judah "The Bow!" ' (v. 18a). 'The Bow' is the title for David's dirge of verses 19-27. David wanted the fighting men of his own tribe to know this sad song, to know it by heart, to have it crammed into their pores. But why? Why should troops learn poetry? Why should the army of Judah always have the lyrics of defeat ringing in their ears? Because David intends it as part of their motivational military training. Gilboa was not the last time Israel would fight Philistines – and David wanted his men to remember Gilboa, remember the tragedy, remember the pagan arrogance. He wanted them deeply stirred and moved – for the next time.

The same principle is at work in the state of Israel today. The Israel Armored Corps swear their oath of allegiance on top of the old fortress of Masada. Masada was a fortress west of the Dead Sea, where, in AD 72-73, some 960 Jews held out against Flavius Silva's Roman army. After seven months of siege the Romans breached the fortress but were denied the pleasure of Jewish blood since the defenders had committed suicide in the night. Masada then stands as a symbol of courage, and Israeli troops today stand on its summit to swear their oath of allegiance: 'Masada shall not fall again.'[13]

We are far removed from Gilboa; we are not biding our time until we strike the Philistines. But David's charge to remember Gilboa still places its claim upon us. David knew that sadness packs a punch that frivolity can never muster (cf. Ecc. 7:2-4). And so a principle remains even after the Philistines have disappeared: somehow brooding over the tragic state of the covenant people stirs us to seek their restoration. Is this not what drives Christians to intercessory prayer? When we carry with us the afflictions of the people of God we are moved to cry out to the Father on their behalf. No, we cannot usually pretend to enter into their distress directly. But what is it that moves us to plead sustaining grace for the wife and children who've lost a forty-two-year-old husband

---

13. Y. Yadin, 'Masada,' *Encyclopaedia Judaica* (Jerusalem: Macmillan, 1971), 11:1091. Cf. also the way 'Remember the Alamo!' functioned for Sam Houston's army of Texans in 1836.

and father, for the friend who has cancer and whose wife has left him, for unknown believers in another country who are caught in the butchery of warring political factions? Is it not that to some small degree we enter into their sadness and disgrace and allow it to drive us to seek heaven's help for them? Don't hesitate to carry on your mind the sufferings of God's people.

Grief and gratitude (1:22-23)

These verses stand at the center of David's poem; a general structural outline can help us see this.[14]

> Lead-in, v.19
>> Negation, vv. 20-21
>>> 'Don't tell it...,' 20
>>> No dew/rain, 21
>
>> Commendation, vv. 22-23
>>> Jonathan & Saul – prowess in battle, 22
>>> Saul & Jonathan – Character in life, 23
>
>> Separation, vv.24-26
>>> Women to weep for Saul, 24
>>> David himself bewails Jonathan, 25-26
>
>> Closure, v.27

Note that verses 22-23 are also distinct because they are descriptive (i.e., they say something *about* Saul and Jonathan), whereas what precedes and follows verses 22-23 is in the form of address rather than description. In verse 20 David addresses anyone in general who may be prone to spread the news of Israel's defeat, while in verse 21 he speaks to the hills of Gilboa; in verse 24 he calls on the 'daughters of Israel' to mourn for Saul, while he addresses Jonathan in verses 25-26. In the middle stand verses 22-23, which contain

---

14. I offer only a simplified structure here. Some have worked out highly detailed structural analyses but reproducing those here would mean not seeing the forest for the twigs. I have found J. P. Fokkelman's comment on the poem's composition useful (*The Crossing Fates*, 655-56). The term 'separation' in my outline refers to the division of labor David proposes: the women are to weep for Saul (v. 24), and David will focus on Jonathan (vv. 25-26; this in contrast to the remembrance of them together in vv. 22-23).

no address but only description. Here David expresses his gratitude and appreciation for Saul and Jonathan, and the fact that he does this in verses that are distinctive in nature and central in position signals that the sentiments must be rather important to him.

Let us look at verses 22-23 by themselves. I am wary of over-analysis, but there may also be an intended focal point within these two verses. Note how verse 23a (general characterization) is surrounded by references to Saul and Jonathan's abilities as warriors.[15]

> Warriors – success with weapons, v.22
> Character – never parted, v.23a
> Warriors – comparisons with animals, v.23b

Hence David's deepest appreciation goes beyond their military skill and rests on their personal character:

> Saul and Jonathan – loved and lovely;
> in their life and in their death they were not parted.

No one should be surprised that David is so magnanimous in speaking of Saul.[16] In any case, I think David graciously allowed Jonathan's character to color Saul's at this point. His appreciation seems to center on their not being parted, even in death. Friend of friends that Jonathan was to David – that never swayed Jonathan from loyalty to his father or from standing beside him at the last. David's gratitude highlights Jonathan's faithfulness to his calling, even when that calling was unrewarded and, in this world's terms, hopeless.[17] Such a consideration ought to haunt (in a positive way) the hearts of Christ's disciples.

---

15. Some think that in verse 22 David is describing Jonathan and Saul's usual prowess in battle; however, he may be including Gilboa as well. David likely assumed that Jonathan's bow and Saul's sword must have taken their share of Philistine flesh on that day.

16. See John Calvin, *Sermons on 2 Samuel*, trans. by Douglas Kelly (Edinburgh: Banner of Truth, 1992), p. 38.

17. I refrain from expanding on the theme of Jonathan's 'tragic' fidelity because I have done so in previous volumes; see *Looking on the Heart: Expositions of the Book of 1 Samuel*, 2 vols. (Grand Rapids: Baker, 1994), 1:139-42, and 2:182.

Grief and love (1:25-26)

If verses 22-23 hold the central position in David's dirge, verses
25-26 hold the climactic position. David assigns the women of Israel
the task of weeping for Saul (v.24), but he turns away to mourn
alone over Jonathan (vv. 25-26). Saul may have decked Israel's
women in crimson (v. 24); but Saul's son had extended a love to
David that surpassed the love of women (v. 26b).

It is utterly wrong-headed to read the idea of homosexuality
into this text.[18] The comparison between Jonathan's love and a
wife's love is not at the point of sexuality but at the point of fidelity.
Matthew Henry saw this long ago:

> He had reason to say that Jonathan's love to him was wonderful; surely
> never was the like, for a man to love one who he knew was to take the
> crown over his head, and to be so faithful to his rival: this far surpassed
> the highest degree of conjugal affection and constancy.[19]

Jonathan was totally devoted to David's becoming king of Israel.
Nowhere can one find a better summary of Jonathan's attitude than
when he encouraged David in Horesh: '*You* will be king over Israel,
and *I* will be second to you' (1 Sam. 23:17; emphasis in Heb.).
That statement – 'I will be second' – epitomizes Jonathan's whole
approach to life in the kingdom. David knows he has lost the friend
par excellence.

Therefore, the intensity of David's grief is no mystery: ('How
distressed I am over you, my brother Jonathan!', v. 26a). 'The more
we love the more we grieve' (Matthew Henry). Sorrow will be
hardest where love is deepest. This is hardly a 1010 BC phenomenon.
How often God's people are called upon to learn this in experience.
I often cringe when I think of married couples I know who have
shared thirty or forty or more years together. I refer to couples that
are not only together but like and enjoy one another! What will it
be like when one is taken? What would it be like if *my* wife were
taken from me? My concern is not to become grave before the
time. Rather I want seriously to consider the principle behind
David's distress: greater love, greater grief. Shouldn't we soberly

---

18. In opposition to such a suggestion, see A. A. Anderson, *2 Samuel*, 19.
19. Matthew Henry, *Commentary on the Whole Bible*, 6 vols. (New York:
Revell, n.d.), 2:451. See also my *Looking on the Heart*, 2:66-67.

prepare ourselves? How can we endure such sorrow unless we are convinced that underneath it all stands a love from which we can never be separated (Rom. 8:35-39)?

3. A Tale of Two Kingdoms
2 Samuel 2:1-11

At first glance this passage seems to detail one more Near Eastern political power struggle. First glances are notoriously superficial. What we actually see is a kingdom established under divine guidance (vv. 1-4a) opposed by another kingdom inaugurated by human ambition (vv. 8-11).[1] And so this text proclaims its dominant truth: people are hardly eager to receive the kingdom of God.

The three references to David's being king over the house of Judah (vv. 4a, 7b, 11) help us break the passage into its proper divisions.[2] Each of these sections portrays something of the kingdom struggle; we will look at these pictures in turn as a way of getting at the teaching of the passage.

Inaugurating the kingdom under divine guidance (2:1-4a)
David makes no move before he seeks direction from Yahweh – probably through Abiathar the priest (cf. 1 Sam. 23:6-14).[3] Though the mechanics of guidance are unclear, Yahweh authorizes David to leave Ziklag for Judah and for Hebron in particular. By this David burns his Philistine bridges behind him. That is why the writer mentions David's two wives (v.2) and the fact that David

---

1. Robert P. Gordon, *I & II Samuel: A Commentary* (Grand Rapids: Zondervan, 1986), 212.

2. J.P. Fokkelman, *Narrative Art and Poetry in the Books of Samuel*, vol. 3, *Throne and City (II Sam. 2-8 & 21-24)*, (Assen/Maastricht: Van Gorcum, 1990), 16, 25-26.

3. Calvin puts it nicely *(Sermons on 2 Samuel*, trans. Douglas Kelly [Edinburgh: Banner of Truth, 1992], 53): 'Even though David clearly knew that God had constituted him as king and that Saul had trespassed, even though the time was ripe for him to enjoy the crown, nevertheless he asked God to tell him what he should do. Why? Because although he was on the way, he still knew that he could err seriously if God did not guide him. Let us learn through all of life to go to the Lord, especially when we are facing an important decision. Let us find out what is to be done, and let us not be so self-assured that we fail to pray God to show us what is useful and expedient.'

brought his men – each one with his household (v. 3a) – with him, so that they 'settled in the towns around Hebron' (v. 3b). David has broken completely with Philistia and has made a new beginning in Judah.[4] At Hebron, a town rich in covenant memories, since Abraham and Sarah, Isaac and Rebekah, Jacob and Leah were all buried there (Gen. 23:17-19; 25:9-10; 49: 29-32; 50: 13). Hebron stood nineteen miles south/southwest of Jerusalem at some 3,000 feet elevation and was the most important town in Judah. Here the men of Judah 'anointed David king over the house of Judah' (v.4).[5] Here the kingdom of God becomes visible in the world – for those who have eyes to see.

David had long since been promised the kingship, a fact which many seemed to know (cf. 1 Sam. 16:1-13; 20: 14-16; 23:17; 25:30-31), but he is a far cry from being king over all Israel (2 Sam. 5:1-5) and he will not receive the charter of the kingdom until 2 Samuel 7 (i.e., that Yahweh's kingship in the world will express itself through the Davidic dynasty). But all of this should not blind us to the massive significance of 2 Samuel 2:1-4a. The passage should have a 'historical marker' sign in the margin of your Bible. No, we have not yet heard of extensive Davidic victories (cf. 2 Sam. 8); it will be long before we are dazzled by Solomon's lavish splendor (cf. 1 Kings 4 and 10) and longer still before we enjoy the just rule of the Shoot and Root of Jesse (Isa. 11:1-10). But here, for the first time, Yahweh's chosen king visibly rules on earth. At Hebron, in the provincial backwater. Over only one tribe. This was no bump-along piece of maybe-stance; it was under Yahweh's guidance at every point (v. 1). It is a small beginning, but it is the kingdom of God – concrete, visible, earthy. The kingdom of God has for the

---

4. Hans Wilhelm Hertzberg, *I & II Samuel*, Old Testament Library (Philadelphia: Westminster, 1964), 248. The Philistines are probably not very concerned about David's desertion so long as his activity continues to divide and fragment Israel.

5. Calvin *(Sermons on 2 Samuel,* 56) rightly says: 'So when the people anointed David they were not implying that what Samuel did [1Sam. 16:13] was ineffective, or that it was not powerful enough to accomplish anything. Rather, it is as though they were replying "Amen", and ratifying what had been done. We should understand, therefore, that David is not elected king here by the desire of men, but that he received approbation because God authorized it, and thus men agree with it.'

moment tucked itself away in the hills of Judah. The kingdom of God *is* like a mustard seed.[6]

Alexander Whyte, the Scottish pastor, wrote his friend James Stewart from near Grenoble, France. Whyte was vacationing there; he was impressed with the hopeless-looking vineyards: 'For all the vines at present are so many roots in a dry ground. Black, dry, twisted, gnarled, hacked at their roots with axes, and all hacked up their stems and branches with the frosts of winter: there is no tree, or plant, or bush in all the land so unpromising, so almost forbidding to look at, as just the vine. No language could describe to one who had not seen it with his own astonished eyes, the picture of death that all the vineyards are at present.' By contrast, he said, the apple, plum and cherry trees are flaunting their life in lavish blossoms; nevertheless, he dogmatized, 'Be sure that in spite of all appearances at present this land will in a few months be covered with grapes.'[7]

That is what we must say about David's kingship in Hebron: Do not allow the unpromising form of the kingdom to blind you to the real presence of the kingdom. It is no trifle when Yahweh's chosen king begins to reign! By the Spirit's chemistry this truth is what keeps many of God's servants on their feet. Scores of Jesus' disciples find most of their labor is done in a 'Hebron stage' in which they see little of the power and the glory. But as long as they know he already reigns (Eph. 1:19b-21), they are content.

Extending the kingdom with winsome appeal (2:4b-7)

Now David is mixing politics and faith, he is being both sharp and sincere. In fact, in this vignette one could say David is sincerely complimentary, blatantly political, and earnestly evangelistic – all at once.

Someone tells David about the last kindness the men of Jabesh-

---

6. The emphasis in that parable (Matt. 13:31-32 and parallels) is not the growth of the kingdom but its obscurity and hiddenness in its present form. There doesn't *seem* to be anything regal in the life and work of Jesus and his disciples, but that should not obscure the fact that, where Jesus is, the kingdom (kingship) of God is already present (cf. Luke 17:20-21). On the mustard seed parable, see George Eldon Ladd, *The Gospel of the Kingdom* (Grand Rapids: Eerdmans, 1959), 58-59, and D.A. Carson, 'Matthew,' *The Expositor's Bible Commentary,* 12 vols. (Grand Rapids: Zondervan, 1984), 8:317-319.

7. G.F. Barbour, *The Life of Alexander Whyte, D.D.* (London: Hodder and Stoughton, 1923), 460.

gilead had shown to Saul's memory (v. 4b). They had made a forced
night march of over twenty miles (round trip), at great risk had
stolen the bodies of Saul and his sons off the walls of Beth-shan
where the Philistines had nailed them for display, and – back at
Jabesh-gilead – had properly cared for the remains (1 Sam. 31:11-
13). They had never forgotten how Saul, in the early days and in
the power of the Spirit, had rescued their city from Nahash, the
Ammonite hatchet man (1 Sam. 11). So Jabesh-gilead had always
been pro-Saul to a man.

But now Saul is dead and people cannot live merely on the fumes
of memory. So David sends an appeal to the men of Jabesh-gilead.
His message is both candid and complimentary. We might break it
down like this:

1. Gratitude, v. 5b
May you be blessed by Yahweh because you have
done this kindness with your master, with Saul,
so that you buried him.

2. Proposal, v. 6
And now – may Yahweh deal kindly and faithfully
with you, and even I, I too, want to deal well[8]
with you because you have done this thing.

3. Invitation, v. 7
And now, let your hands be strong and be
courageous men, for Saul your master has died,
and – what's more – the house of Judah has
anointed *me* as king over them.

David thanks Jabesh-gilead and asks blessing on them – then
makes a bid for their allegiance to his kingship. No reason why one
cannot mix condolences and campaigning.[9] In his bold politics
David asks for a bold response. The men of Jabesh were used to

---

8. The idiom in v.6 is lit., 'to do goodness with you,' apparently equivalent to
an Akkadian expression meaning to establish a treaty of friendship. See T.N.D.
Mettinger, *King and Messiah,* Coniectanea Biblica (Lund: CWK Gleerup,
1976), 147, and P. Kyle McCarter, Jr., *II Samuel,* The Anchor Bible (New
York: Doubleday, 1984), 85, citing Hillers.
9. No one, however, should doubt that David's appeal to Jabesh is genuine
and sincere, for he commends them for having 'kept faith' (REB) with Saul,
and it was for lack of that he had had the Amalekite disposed of in chapter 1.

taking risks, now let them take another one. They had shown how gutsy they were in that night raid at Beth-shan (1 Sam. 31:11-13); let their courage appear in living color again – let them be the first in the north to acknowledge the kingship of David.[10]

So David calls Jabesh-gilead to submit to the nascent kingdom of God in Hebron. But his call, his appeal, is extended with such winsomeness. Is this not what is so striking about the call of David's Descendant into his kingdom as well? 'Take my yoke upon you and learn from me, for I am gentle and lowly in heart, and you will find rest for your souls' (Matt. 11:29). Oh, we know what the yoke means. There is no getting around that absolute submission. But Jesus' appeal – demand? – is so winsome. He attracts us by his character ('for I am gentle and lowly in heart') and by his promise ('and you will find rest'). This reminds me of the New York lady who explained how the Holy Spirit had captured her heart for God under the ministry of George Whitefield: 'Mr. Whitefield was *so cheerful* that it tempted me to become a Christian.'[11] Tempted?! To become a Christian? That is often Jesus' way. He does not hide the yoke; he does not hide the fact that we may be lonely in that yoke (Matt. 10:34-39); but he lures us by his person and promise.

A right response, however, to Christ's – or David's – appeal can be costly. Most of us reading this text probably detach ourselves from Jabesh-gilead. That is a town, we think, long ago and far away. On the contrary, we must reckon ourselves citizens of Jabesh-gilead. That is where I live, for the text clearly shows that Jabesh-gilead (2:4b-7) is sandwiched between David and Abner, between the true kingdom in its mustard seed form (2:1-4a) and a bastard kingdom that expects its allegiance (2:8-11). To defy this latter kingdom takes guts, and such guts only come from grace.

Opposing the kingdom by stubborn defiance (2:8-11)
No one knows how Jabesh-gilead responded to David's appeal, or if they did at all.

---

10. Thus 'the first recorded act of the new king of Judah was to offer friendship and comfort to a group of Israelites, with the implication that David may be a Judean but his heart belongs to all Israel' (A.A. Anderson, *2 Samuel,* Word Biblical Commentary [Dallas: Word, 1989], 29).

11. J.C. Ryle, *Christian Leaders of the 18th Century* (1885; reprint ed., Edinburgh: Banner of Truth, 1978), 58-59 (emphasis in Ryle's quotation).

But Abner son of Ner, captain of Saul's army, took Ishbosheth, Saul's
son, brought him over to Mahanaim, and made him king over Gilead,
Ashuri, Jezreel, and over Ephraim, Benjamin – even over all Israel
(vv. 8-9).

We do not need to solve the riddles of chronology, names, or
claims[12] in order to assess verses 8-11, but we must grasp the
significance of Abner's action in the larger context. Keil has stated
that clearly:

The promotion of Ishbosheth as king was not only a continuation of
the hostility of Saul towards David, but also an open act of rebellion
against Jehovah, who had rejected Saul and chosen David prince over
Israel, and who had given such distinct proofs of this election in the
eyes of the whole nation, that even Saul had been convinced of the
appointment of David to be his successor upon the throne.[13]

Abner's move then is not merely the beginning of a predictable
civil conflict as opposing parties vie for power. No. Abner knew
Yahweh had promised the kingship to David and could play that
fact as a trump card when he had no viable alternative (3:9-10, 18).
In opposing Yahweh's chosen king Abner was opposing Yahweh's
kingship and will. He knew that will but chose to fly in the face of
it. So here Abner joins his colleagues in Psalm 2:2-3 and Herod

---

12. About chronology: We don't know precisely how Ishbosheth's two-years
reign in the north (v.10) fits with David's seven years-six months reign in
Judah (v.11). Some argue that Ishbosheth's two years coincided with the last
two years of David's rule in Judah, assuming it took Abner about five years
after Saul's death to garner support for his new nominee (so Schedl,
Youngblood). But we simply don't know. We do know, based on the years of
each reign, that David outreigned Ishbosheth. On the name Ishbosheth: his
original name may have been Eshbaal/Ishbaal (1 Chron. 8:33; 9:39). It may
be that later scribes changed the –baal element (associating it with the
Canaanite god) to –bosheth (shame) as a dig at Baal worship. Since the world
does not depend on it we will use Ishbosheth here. (Some think Ishvi in 1
Sam. 14:49 may refer to Ishbosheth.) On the extent of the Abner-Ishbosheth
dominion (v.9; 'Ashuri' is an anomaly): I think it is a paper claim (following
John Bright, *A History of Israel,* 3rd ed. [Philadelphia: Westminster, 1981],
196). If Ishbosheth effectively controlled Jezreel, Ephraim, Benjamin, even
all Israel, why did Abner find it necessary to set up headquarters at Mahanaim
east of the Jordan.

13. C.F. Keil, *Biblical Commentary on the Books of Samuel* (1875; reprint
ed., Grand Rapids: Eerdmans 1950), 292.

and Pontius Pilate *et al* (Acts 4: 27-28) in their press release: 'We do not want this man to reign over us' (Luke 19:14).

In 2 Samuel 2 the regime of the chosen king has met with rebellion and opposition. And this kingdom conflict will continue, in one form or another, until Jesus comes in power and great glory (cf. Matt. 13:40-41). If we are among Yahweh's remnant, we must not allow the defiance of the latest Abners to deter or depress us. It can certainly do so. Witness the dejection of John Knox, the Scottish reformer, when in 1566 he poured out his despair: 'Lord Jesus, receive my spirit, and put an end at thy good pleasure to this my miserable life, for justice and truth are not to be found among the children of men.'[14] 'Only the house of Judah was following David' (v. 10b) – that is our place and our calling. Even in low times; even in a day of small things (cf. Zech. 4:10 in context).

But there is no reason in the world to be discouraged even if you only see the mustard seed form of the kingdom. For we have it on good authority that Hebron and its hamlets will become a great mountain and fill the whole earth (Dan. 2:35)!

4. Promise Rules
2 Samuel 2:12–3:39

There are reasons for swallowing such a large mass of text in one gulp. First, we can keep all the Abner-materials together; and, second, we are not overtly given the lens through which we are to view these episodes until 3:9-10, 18. Since the passage is so extensive it may be useful to set forth its overall structure at this point. However, I prefer to do this by setting it within the larger structural outline of 2:1–5:5, a section that seems to have been carefully crafted together.

```
Hebron – kingship, 2:1-7
          Ishbosheth – installed, 2:8-11
                    Abner's militarism & its failure, 2:12-32
                              (death of Asahel)
                    Abner's power move & its failure, 3:1-11
                    Abner's negotiation & its failure, 3:12-39
                              (death of Abner)
          Ishbosheth – eliminated, 4:1-12
Hebron – kingship, 5:1-5
```

14. A.M. Renwick, *The Story of the Scottish Reformation* (Eerdmans, 1960), 148.

Note that the three middle episodes seem to carry the literary theme: the failure of Abner. Abner attacks and fails (2:12-32); Abner plots and fails (3:1-11); Abner negotiates and fails (with help from Joab, 3:12-39). Here is the triple failure of the strong man. Abner was right – only promise will rule (3:9-10, 18). We develop the teaching of the text by typifying these three failure sections.

Resisting the kingdom by force (2:12-32)

These verses constitute a fascinating narrative. Note that verses 17 and 30-31 give the result of the conflict. Had the writer merely wanted to provide a just-the-facts report he could have given us something like verses 12-13a, 17, and 30-31. But he does not do that. He tells most of his story as a series of gripping scenes: (1) the twelve-on-twelve match-up in hand-to-hand combat at what came to be known as Knife Commons (vv.12-16); (2) the thrilling and tragic track race of Asahel pursuing Abner (vv. 18-23); and (3) Abner's whining to Joab about how terribly vicious it is of him not to call off his Judeans (vv. 26-27). So instead of a mere battle box score our writer has given us a full and interesting story. It breaks down into four main scenes:

> Gibeon – around the pool, vv. 12-16
> Battle – on the run, vv. 17-23
> Ammah – at the hill, vv. 24-28
> Return – to the towns, vv. 29-32
> > To Mahanaim, v.29
> > To Hebron via Bethlehem, vv. 30-32

It is essential to understand that Abner is the aggressor in this whole affair. Geography does not lie, and verse 12 clearly states that Abner & Co 'went forth.... from Mahanaim to Gibeon'. The precise location of Mahanaim is debatable, but we know it was some distance east of the Jordan River and probably on the north bank of the Jabbok.[1] To leave headquarters east of the Jordan, cross the river, and come within five miles of Jerusalem shows that Abner is taking the offensive. The Hebron regime doubtless got wind of Abner's move; the advance of Joab and his force to Gibeon was simply a sane defensive move. What takes place then in verses 12-32 is not a civil conflict erupting from a chance encounter between

---

1. See K.A. Kitchen, 'Mahanaim,' NBD, 3rd ed., 718.

northern and southern militia. It is Abner's deliberate attempt to impose northern might on David's Judean kingdom. Abner is on the attack.[2]

We readers may be blinded to this fact because our sympathies are aroused for Abner by the vignette of Asahel's relentless pursuit of Abner (2:18-23). Asahel apparently coveted the premier glory of taking the top man (cf. Judg. 4:9). In spite of Abner's warnings (Were these given at breathing intervals in the pursuit?), Asahel kept pursuing. Asahel had the speed, but Abner had the spear, and the spear won when Abner, having no choice, gored Asahel with either the butt end of the spear, or, if the NEB is right, a 'back' thrust of his spear (v.23). It was Asahel's last race. As readers we need to know this story-segment in order to understand 3:26-27; and we understand that Abner only acted in reluctant self-defense. But this consideration must not mesmerize us from seeing Abner's fault: he came on the offensive (v.12); his casual remark instigated the twelve-on-twelve fiasco (vv. 14-16); and his bleeding-heart speech about brotherhood and the tragedy of war (v. 26) was exposed for the baloney it was by Joab, who retorted that none of this would have happened had Abner never opened his mouth in the first place (v. 27).[3] As it was, Abner lost – badly, as the tallies show (vv. 30-31).

Since Abner clearly knew that Yahweh had promised David the kingship (3:9-10, 17-18), his armed resistance seems baffling. But for anyone who looks at humanity and history through the doctrine of original sin, it is not baffling at all. Only perverse.

Abner's resistance reminds me of an anecdote about Hermann Goering, head of German's Luftwaffe in World War II. Sometime in 1942-43 Goering was upset with General Galland, commander of his fighter planes, for reporting to Hitler that several American

---

2. A fact which Calvin saw clearly; see John Calvin, *Sermons on 2 Samuel*, trans. Douglas Kelly (Edinburgh: Banner of Truth, 1992), 64,70,78.

3. I follow Keil and Fokkelman on the translation of Joab's oath in v.27. The sense is, as Fokkelman notes, 'if you had not proposed a tournament this morning, then as far as I am concerned there would have been no need for a fight.' See his *Narrative Art and Poetry in the Books of Samuel*, vol. 3, *Throne and City (II Sam. 2-8 & 21-24)*, (Assen/Maastricht: Van Gorcum, 1990), 59-60, for explanation. The NIV rendering ('If you had not spoken, the men would have continued the pursuit of their brothers until morning') understands Joab to speak of the following rather than previous morning.

fighter planes had been shot down over Aachen. Galland told
Goering it was a true report. Goering was obstinate: That is simply
not true. It's impossible. Galland challenged Goering to go to
Aachen and see for himself – the downed planes were there. Goering
then tried a more diplomatic approach, urging Galland to admit he
had made a mistake. But Galland wouldn't budge, so Goering ended
the debate: 'I officially assert that the American fighter planes did
not reach Aachen.' Galland entered one last eye-witness objection:
'But, sir, they were there!' Goering lost all self control as he
pontificated, 'I herewith give you an official order that they weren't
there! Do you understand? The American fighters were not there!'
Off he stalked.[4] Never mind evidence. Never mind facts. Never
mind testimony. Goering will believe what he wants to believe.
Never mind Yahweh's promise to David. Never mind that Abner
himself can quote the promise! Never mind that Yahweh has already
established David as king in Judah. Abner will try to impose his
own authority. It is absurd; it is, in a word, sin.

Abner is not far from any one of us. We share an Abner-nature
that harbors sin's stupidity, perversity, and twistedness. Let Abner
preach to you. Let him tell you that it is possible to know the truth
but not embrace the truth, to quote the truth but not submit to the
truth, to hold the truth and yet assault the truth. And so Abner joins
all the other anti-christs who strut around and say, 'I will be king'
(1 Kings 1:5).

Seeking the kingdom by necessity (3:1-11)
These verses highlight a contrast. Both verses 1 and 6 note the
ongoing 'war' between the house of David and the house of Saul.
Verse 1 indicates that David 'kept getting stronger' and verses 2-5
give a sample of this strength in the number of David's wives taken
and sons born during the Hebron days.[5] Abner too was 'making

4. Albert Speer, *Inside the Third Reich* (New York: Avon Books, 1970), 377-
78.
5. In the Ancient Near East, the 'king's reputation and power could be measured
in terms of the number and beauty and importance of his wives, as well as by
the number of his sons' (Claus Schedl, *History of the Old Testament,* 5 vols.
[Staten Island, N.Y.: Alba House, 1972], 3: 190). David's taking multiple
wives agrees with Near Eastern culture but violates biblical demands (Deut.
17:14-20, esp. v.17). Kings took wives more to cement alliances than to satisfy
lust; e.g., David's marriage to Maacah made Geshur (a small Aramaean kingdom

himself strong' (v. 6) in the house of Saul, claiming one of Saul's harem (Rizpah) as his own (v. 7). In the Near East 'the man who took over the harem of the deceased king thereby asserted his claim to succession to the throne'.[6] We simply do not know how far Abner intended to go in vying for the kingdom. Ishbosheth may have been a puppet and a weakling, but he was not stupid; he raised such a fuss over Abner's ploy (v.7) that Abner's 'strength' turned to frustration (v. 8), so that Abner out of both spite and logic decided to pull the north into the arms of David. In Abner's own words (vv. 9-10):

> May God act against Abner, and terribly so, if I do not do for him as Yahweh has sworn to David, namely, to transfer the kingdom from the house of Saul and to raise up the throne of David over Israel and over Judah from Dan as far as Beersheba.

And there was nothing Ishbosheth could do about it (v.11).

Abner was not driven to this expedient by theology but by politics. He did not seek to expand David's kingship because he felt the authority of Yahweh's promise but because he sought his own advantage. If Ishbosheth was not going to roll over and play dead, then the next best option for Abner was to swing his support to David and use his influence over the northern tribes as a bargaining chip with David, thereby assuring himself of a powerful spot in David's regime. Abner only quotes Scripture when it supports a pro-Abner move. Abner seeks the kingdom not because it is a matter of divine promise but because it is now a piece of sharp policy. Not love for Yahweh's designs but concern over Abner's position is all that matters to him.[7]

---

northeast of the Sea of Galilee) his ally (3:3), strategically in Ishbosheth's rear. Since I hold to a Mosaic date for Deuteronomy, I think David violated the provision of Deuteronomy 17:17; however the writer of 2 Samuel is only concerned to highlight David's growing strength not his incipient error. So he doesn't moralize on the point. However, readers should not be blind to the matter. Too often, I think, readers adopt such a pro-David emotional attachment that they refuse to see any failure in him except in the racy Bathsheba incident.

6. Schedl, 3:169. See 2 Samuel 16:21-22 and 1 Kings 2: 13-25 for samples of this thinking.

7. Calvin has a pungent exposition of Abner's duplicity (*Sermons on 2 Samuel*, 118-19, 121); cf. also Fokkelman, *Throne and City*, 74,89.

Abner reminds me of a story Donald Grey Barnhouse told about little Willie, who had crawled out on the ice and rescued a playmate who had fallen through. Praise and admiration were being heaped on him. Then a lady asked him, 'Tell us, my boy, how you were brave enough to risk your life to save your friend.' In between breaths Willie shot back, 'I had to – he had my skates on.'

Abners don't disappear. We meet more of them in Scripture. Not bearing Abner's name – only his disposition. For example, Simon the magician in Acts 8 was the premier convert in Samaria under Philip's ministry. Went the whole nine yards – profession of faith and baptism. Then, when Peter and John came, he flew his flag, offering to pay them well if they would give him the power to bestow the gift of the Holy Spirit when he would lay his hands on someone (Acts 8:18-19). True, the coming of the gospel under Philip had eclipsed Simon's popularity (8:9-12), but here was a chance for Simon to work within the gospel establishment and win his reputation back.

Whether 2 Samuel 3 or Acts 8, Christian workers must be alert to their own Abner-mentality. Our orthodox line about supporting Christ's kingdom may only be a cover for using it. As we sing 'Onward, Christian Soldiers', we realize there are many mercenaries in the ranks. And even faithful preachers, for example, who desire to proclaim and make plain God's truth, know there are times when they seem more concerned with whether God's people will be impressed with *them,* like *them,* congratulate and dote over *them.* Abner is not far away from any one of us.

Subverting the kingdom by revenge (3:12-39)

We can get a mental handle on this long stretch of narrative if we break it up into scenes:

> Abner's offer and David's demand, vv. 12-16
> Abner's conferences and David's peace, vv. 17-22
> Abner's departure and Joab's anger, vv. 23-25
> Abner's return and David's ignorance, vv. 26-30
> Abner's funeral and David's defense, vv. 31-39

With this summary before us I want to comment on some details before underscoring the primary burden of the passage.

First, David's demand for the return of Michal, Saul's daughter and David's very first wife, was at least as much political as romantic. He doubtless hoped that a male offspring via Michal would unite the claims of his house and Saul's (an empty hope as 2 Sam. 6 shows).[8] That would have gone a long way toward luring and keeping the loyalty of the northern tribes. Note that David not only keeps the upper hand by making the return of Michal the absolute condition of any negotiations with Abner (v. 13), but he also undercuts Abner's power by making his demand directly to Ishbosheth (v. 14), thus reducing Abner to a mere middleman in the episode.[9] Abner can talk tough (v. 16) but he is not the power broker he would have preferred to be. The scene reeks with sadness as we watch Paltiel (vv. 15-16), heart-broken and helpless, turn back for home. First prize for blame can be awarded Saul, who first made Michal a pawn (1 Sam. 25:44).[10]

Secondly, we are told three times that David dismissed Abner and that Abner 'went off in peace' (vv. 21,22,23). This likely means that he had been granted safe conduct; 'in peace' means 'in security'. All of which explains why Abner returned so unsuspectingly to Hebron, why he was so naïve about the little chat with Joab (vv. 26-27).[11] He had been promised immunity. Why should he be suspicious? He never saw Joab's dagger until it was too late – it had been concealed behind David's promise. Hence Joab committed the most sinister form of treachery.

Thirdly, David bent over backward to show that he repudiated Joab's deed and that he himself had no part in it. David publicly asserted his innocence (v. 28), called down a scathing curse upon

---

8. John Bright, *A History of Israel,* 3rd ed. Philadelphia: Westminster, 1981), 198.

9. Karl Gutbrod, *Das Buch vom Reich,* Die Botschaft des Alten Testaments, 2nd ed. (Stuttgart: Calwer, 1973), 48. Robert Gordon, on the other hand, sees the appeal to Ishbosheth as simply the expected protocol and assumes that he complied because he was taking orders from Abner *(I & II Samuel: A Commentary* [Grand Rapids: Zondervan, 1986], 218).

10. As Gordon points out, David did not violate Deuteronomy 24:1-4 here, since his separation from Michal was not voluntary. 'The right of a husband to reclaim his wife after enforced separation – if, for example, he has been taken prisoner and removed from his homeland – is well entrenched in Mesopotamian law, and may be assumed to have operated in Israel' (*I & II Samuel,* 219).

11. Joab's men caught up with Abner at the well of Sirah (v.26), which may possibly be identified with a site two and a half miles north of Hebron (Ronald F. Youngblood, '1,2 Samuel,' *The Expositor's Bible Commentary,* 12 vols. [Grand Rapids: Zondervan, 1992], 3: 838).

Joab and his father's house (v. 29), and ordered Joab and the troops
to participate in the public mourning rites (v. 31), while he himself
walked behind the corpse and wept openly and audibly and
unabashedly at the grave (v. 32). He also produced a lament
commemorating the tragedy (vv. 33-34) and, on oath, insisted on
fasting until sundown (v. 35). All this convinced most folks that
David was guiltless of complicity in Abner's death (v. 37). As John
Bright has written:

> Even when Abner was murdered by Joab (vs. 22-39), the landslide to
> David was not halted. The people understood that this was a blood
> feud and apparently believed David when he protested his innocence
> – after all, he had nothing to gain by it.[12]

Now let us return to Joab. What was it that moved him to
eliminate Abner and potentially to sabotage David's winning the
allegiance of the northern tribes? The immediate reason is given in
verses 27 and 30: he (and Abishai) were avenging Asahel's death.
Abner had killed Asahel; now Joab kills Abner. But Asahel's death
should not have been avenged since Abner killed Asahel 'in battle'
(v.30) – and only after gracious warning (2:20-23). Had it been
murder or even manslaughter Joab would have had grounds for
vengeance (cf. Num. 35:9-34). But it was neither. Joab settled public
battles with private vendettas.

I am more suspicious than Abner, however. And I think Joab
was concerned about Joab as much as about Asahel. It is likely,
though admittedly the text does not crassly say so, that Joab smelled
a rival in Abner and that he feared Abner might replace him as
commander of the army. That could well have been in the works as
part of David's deal with Abner (vv. 12-13a).[13] Hence envy of
position may have been Joab's actual motive, with vengeance over
Asahel providing a partial and useful justification. Joab seemed to

---

12. *A History of Israel,* 197. Not everyone, however, was so believing. Shimei
(16:5-8) apparently thought he smelled a rat (or wanted to). Even some modern
scholars cannot swallow David's innocence; cf. James C. Vanderkam, 'Davidic
Complicity in the Deaths of Abner and Eshbaal,' *Journal of Biblical Literature*
99 (1980): 521-39, and Diana V. Edelman, 'Abner,' ABD, 1:28. In their view
our narrative has been 'doctored' in David's favor.
13. At a later time David had determined to give Joab's position to Amasa
(19:13), who was soon eliminated in vintage Joab style (20:4-10).

subvert the kingdom by revenge; more likely it was out of fear that he would lose that place he coveted for himself.

If Abner is not far from any one of us, neither is Joab. And Joab is not so different from Abner. But we are far more subtle than Joab – even than the disciples who crassly displayed their Joab-attitude at the Last Supper, debating about which of them was to be thought the greatest in the same breaths as they debated who could possibly betray Jesus (Luke 22:24). And though I profess to care only about Jesus' kingship, I fear I am far more concerned about my place in his regime than with the honor of his name. I want to be first in my area of the Christian Ghetto, recognised, appreciated, well-received; under the guise of service in the kingdom I crave all the strokes I can – even at Jesus' expense. Joab is not dead, only transmuted. Some of us know him all too well.

Expecting the kingdom in confidence

We do not yet see David as king over all Israel according to 3:9-10,18. But we have read the rest of the story and know what is coming in 2 Samuel 5. Therefore, we should pause to look at chapters 2 and 3 in the light of the whole for our own encouragment.

Chapters 2 and 3 cause us to marvel that Yahweh's promise regarding David's kingship does eventually come to pass, for all we see here are people who resist the kingdom promise by force (Abner & Co. in 2:12-32) or who seek it for the wrong reasons (Abner in 3:1-11) or who are only concerned for their own 'kingdom' (Joab in 3:23-39). Some would even charge David with contributing to the mess because he did not take retributive action against Joab (3:38-39).[14] Yet for all the opposition, scheming, and folly, Yahweh's promise comes to pass *anyway*. As Karl Gutbrod has written (especially in reference to Abner's proposed assistance), what came about for David was 'according to God's decree and sworn promise; but not because Abner lent God his arm, but because God, against and without Abner, makes the deed to follow his word.'[15]

---

14. The jury remains out on David's reaction in v.39. Some think he was prudent in not punishing Joab since, on this view, David could not yet afford to sacrifice Joab and the army's support (cf. Youngblood); others see David's severe words but absent action as a moral failure on David's part (cf. Fokkelman).

15. *Das Buch vom Reich,* 47. Cf. also Walter Brueggemann *(First and Second Samuel,* Interpretation [Louisville: John Knox, 1990], 232): 'David's "new

Yahweh's people must remember these earlier kingdom episodes, for sometimes nothing looks so unlikely and remote to us as the day when the kingdom of the world will become the kingdom of our Lord and of his Christ (Rev. 11:15). But come it will, for God has decreed it to Jesus (Ps. 2:8-9), and no Abner or Joab or greater conspirator will be able to stop it.

5. The Gore of Man Does Not Work the Righteousness of God
2 Samuel 4:1-12

It was no longer business as usual in Mahanaim. When news came of Abner's treacherous death in Hebron Ishbosheth 'lost heart' (lit., 'his hands dropped') and 'all Israel was terrified' (v.1). Was Abner only the beginning? Would David's henchmen work their way north in a program of systematic butchery? The Plan for Reconciliation and Reunion has dissolved in Abner's blood. Who knew what to do now?

Baanah and Rechab thought they did. These two fraternal thugs who led Ishbosheth's raiders decided they must seize the hour, and chapter 4 is the account of their attempt. The movement of the chapter can be reduced to four segments:

Situation, vv. 1-4
Action, vv. 5-7
Interpretation, vv. 8-11
Retribution, v. 12

However, I do not want to rehearse the content but to expound the significance of the narrative. Let us move to exposition then and get at the teaching of the text.

Sarcasm provides an excellent vehicle for truth (4:1-7)

Our writer seems to give Baanah and Rechab a rather hum-drum introduction (vv. 2-3); they belonged to Saul and Ishbosheth's tribe

---

age" wells up in the midst of conventional people, who may ignore the promise but who wind up serving that promise. The narrator lets us see the operation of Yahweh's determined promise through these unwitting characters, their devious words, and their self-serving actions. Through the sordid narrative, the kingdom has advanced a step toward Jerusalem.'

(Benjamin) and came from Beeroth.[1] However, even in this situation section (vv. 1-4) the writer implies a negative estimate of Baanah and Rechab for he wraps his non-committal, bare-facts introduction of them (vv. 2-3) in pictures of a powerless puppet (Ishbosheth, v. 1) and a helpless cripple (Mephibosheth, v. 4). Apparently, the writer wants to impress us with the total weakness of Saul's house – Saul's son lacks the courage to continue resistance (v. 1) and the only (?) other heir, Jonathan's son, lacks the ability, since he is a totally dependent cripple (v. 4).[2] Whatever Baanah and Rechab do then will hardly be heroic but in the class of a junior-high ruffian who beats up five-year-olds. Some subtle sarcasm is already seeping out of the text.

I would suggest the writer levels another dig at Rechab and Baanah in the action section (vv. 5-7). These verses[3] read:

5. Now the sons of Rimmon the Beerothite, Rechab and Baanah, went off and came at the heat of the day to the house of Ishbosheth, who was taking his noon-day nap.

6. And indeed they came to the middle of the house (as?) ones getting wheat, and they struck him in the stomach; but Rechab and Baanah his brother escaped.

7. So they came into the house, and he was lying on his bed in his bed-room; and they struck him and killed him and took off his head. Then they took his head and went by way of the Arabah road all night.

Some think there are two confused accounts here since verse 7 seems repetitious beside verses 5-6. After all, they share the three elements of Rechab and Baahah's coming to/into Ishbosheth's house, Ishbosheth's being asleep, and their striking him down. But this is normal Hebrew narrative: it will often give a fact or depict a

---

1. Possibly Khirbet el-Burj about two miles south of Gibeon (cf. Anson J. Rainey, Beeroth, IDB/S, 93), but still in doubt. I take verse 3 to mean that Benjaminites drove out the native population of Beeroth; hence it was now counted as Benjamin's town (v. 2b).

2. Cf. C.F. Keil, *Biblical Commentary on the Books of Samuel* (1875; reprint ed., Grand Rapids: Eerdmans, 1950), 309.

3. My translation follows the traditional Hebrew text except for repointing the first word in verse 6. I am not convinced that LXX (with its lady doorkeeper dozing off – see RSV or REB, which follow LXX here) is to be preferred to the Hebrew text. Note that NRSV has returned to the Hebrew text.

situation and then repeat the same but with an added detail that expands on the previous statement. In the next chapter we are told flatly that David captured fortress Zion (2 Sam. 5:7), yet in the next verses (8-9) are flashed back and told *how* he captured it. Same ground, more detail. In the present case (4:7), not only does our writer *add* the detail about slicing off Ishbosheth's head but *repeats* the item from verse 5 that he was resting in his bedroom. I think the repetition deliberate. One can almost hear the writer's sneer: Rechab and Baanah are so macho they can kill a man in his sleep. Tough hombres indeed! They came; he slept; they stabbed. The writer will report David's judgment of their deed (vv. 9-11), but he has already given us his own. He tells us about Rechab and Baanah and mocks them at the same time.[4]

One could use this technique in numerous instances. Suppose you were reporting Nazi Germany's 1939 blitzkrieg against Poland. You might tell how the Germans had more than a three-to-one advantage in air power and how their tanks cut to ribbons charging Polish cavalry. You would be highlighting German power, even German audacity. But would you be tooting German courage? Hardly. What courage does it take to fire from tanks and reduce the enemy to piles of screaming human and horse flesh? Panzers against ponies – does that take guts? Hence in the way you told the story you could hold up 'courage' for ridicule rather than for respect.

Biblical writers are quite adept at using sarcasm to shock (mildly or severely) God's people into having a true perspective on things. Sometimes the sarcasm is overt and blatant (e.g., Isa. 41:5-7; 44: 9 -20; 46:5-7), sometimes subtle. I think Daniel 3 is a good example of the latter. That narrative tells of Shadrach, Meshach, and Abednego's refusal to bow down and worship Nebuchadnezzar's humongous golden image (90 feet high by 9 feet wide). There is a fascinating undertone in the story: nine times the story refers to the image as what Nebuchadnezzar had 'set up' (RSV; see vv. 1,2,3 [twice], 5,7,12,14,18). The term is used by the narrator himself or found in the mouths of the characters. Maybe it's too subtle but even subtlety ought to sink in after nine times! It's as if the writer

---

4. There would have been nothing reprehensible if Baanah and Rechab simply wanted to throw their support to David – many did (1 Chron. 12). But they wanted premier positions in David's regime and wanted to use Ishbosheth's head for leverage.

is saying: Don't be cajoled into worshiping Nebuchadnezzar's massive monster. See what it is! He 'set it up'. There is nothing real or divine about it; it is only a colossal chunk of liturgical hardware taking up space in the Plain of Dura.

Back to 2 Samuel 4. I am arguing that the writer laces his story with sarcastic innuendo. Oh yes, he implies, Rechab and Baanah may appear bold and daring. But take another look. They are not strong but weak, not courageous but cowardly, not manly but mercenary. The whole matter underscores something about ourselves: how urgently we need discernment and how prone we are to lack it; how we must see the real beneath the veneer of the apparent.

Theology provides an excellent cloak for evil (4:8)

I recall hearing an episode from our family lore about an older brother in his very early years, who, though warned to stay away from a certain pond, had ventured too near, and became immersed. He had, however, his explanation ready: 'I stood beside the pond, and I said, "Get thee behind me, Satan" – and he pushed me in!' Or, in college days, a fellow student was giving a testimony. He alluded to his driving habits in his hometown – as one is prone to do in a testimony. There was an intersection where he seldom stopped, though either prudence counseled or law required that he do so. However, in all his non-stopping days God never allowed him to have a wreck. It's wonderful indeed to have God! Both dripping boys and ignorant collegians find theology useful; it can explain most anything by devilish impulse or divine blessing.

Rechab and Baanah were given to theologizing as well. Their trek from Mahanaim to Hebron must have taken at least two days,[5] but, upon arrival, they display their trophy to David with commentary:

> Here is the head of Ish-Bosheth son of Saul, your enemy, who tried to take your life. This day the LORD has avenged my lord the king against Saul and his offspring (v. 8b, NIV).

There is no disputing the fact. I presume David knows whose head it is. The fact is one thing, the interpretation another. Was this Yahweh's vengeance upon Saul and his seed? Were Rechab and Baanah then (as they were implying) the servants of the Lord in

---

5. The distance was approximately 80 miles (not 30, as Youngblood has it – surely a misprint).

executing his justice by eliminating David's rival and solidifying David's position? They were not claiming to be (as the hymn title suggests) 'channels only' but channels surely, and therefore ones to whom David owed the debt of posh government jobs. They come with blood on their hands but theology on their lips, expecting that the latter will magically bleach the former. Murder always seems more pleasant when wrapped in religious considerations.

Baanahs and Rechabs are still extant; some are in our churches. Their methodology is unchanged: use theology to cover sin and folly. For them theology is not truth that lures us to worship God but technique that enables us to justify ourselves. We may recognize them in the self-appointed defender of doctrinal precision, who is eager to explain, correct and inform with all harshness and severity. If accosted about his stringent style (even on matters of lesser moment or debatable clarity), he argues theologically: he is only concerned that we hold to the 'whole counsel' of God; the slightest indifference on doctrinal matters may begin the plunge to unbelief. Or suppose the church elders begin informal or formal discipline against an erring and recalcitrant church member. What will they hear? Theology. About how *all* of us are sinners, but God is compassionate – certainly more so than church elders; and who gave you the right to assess my life anyway? We must beware; when we explain things theologically we may simply be using God, using him as an argument, manipulating him for our convenience to keep from submitting to his grace or to his law.

Gratitude provides an excellent antidote for idolatry (4:9)

Idolatry? What does idolatry have to do with verse 9, especially when this verse only constitutes the oath formula that introduces David's assessment of Rechab's and Baanah's deed? All I am claiming, however, is that David here faces a temptation to think in an idolatrous way.

Back to the text. Some (e.g., Gordon and Fokkelman) have called attention to the similarity of language and contrast in meaning between Rechab's and Baanah's claim in verse 8 and David's confession in verse 9:

'...Saul, your enemy, who tried to take your life' (v. 8, NIV)
' .... Yahweh, who has redeemed my life out of every adversity' (v.9, mostly RSV)

As Fokkelman says: 'The correspondence is a subtle hint that the gentlemen do not need excite themselves about the enemies of David out for his blood, because he is already under the protection of the Lord and does not need any henchmen.'[6]

Certainly Rechab and Baanah are not claiming to be Yahweh; they are only saying that by their deed they have decisively eliminated the whole threat against David from Saul's house. They dare not claim too much; but they want to put a certain spin on their treachery to suggest that David is indebted to them for this finishing touch that makes his person and kingdom secure. And therein lurks the temptation. Are they not, however subtly, pretending to be David's redeemers to whom he owes something for coming to the kingdom? But as these pseudo-redeemers show up out of nowhere on some Thursday morning David is able to recognize them for what they are and repudiate their claim because he remembers his true and only Redeemer. 'Yahweh, who has redeemed my life out of every adversity.' What gratitude breathes in those words! What memory (cf. Jer. 2:6)! What itemizing of benefits received and favors granted (cf. Ps. 103:2-5)! And because he remembers how Yahweh rescued him from every one of his troubles he is not suckered into crediting evil men with the deliverance of a gracious God.

Kings have no corner on this principle (that gratitude nurtures fidelity); it has always proven the safeguard for all Christ's flock. About AD 155 Polycarp of Smyrna was arraigned before the authorities and required to call Caesar 'Lord' and burn the requisite pinch of incense. Polycarp refused. The consul assured him that he had wild beasts and would feed Polycarp to them if he refused. 'Send for them,' Polycarp replied. 'If you despise the wild beasts,' threatened the consul, 'I will send you to the fire; swear and I will release you: curse the Christ.' This stirred Polycarp's stellar response: 'Eighty and six years have I served Christ, and he has done me no wrong; how then can I blaspheme my King who has saved me?'[7] The words are different; the principle is the same; the result is the same. Gratitude provides an excellent antidote for idolatry.

---

6. J.P. Fokkelman, *Narrative Art and Poetry in the Books of Samuel*, vol. 3, *Throne and City (II Sam. 2-8 & 21-24)* (Assen/Maastricht: Van Gorcum, 1990), 132.

7. S.M. Houghton, *Sketches from Church History* (Edinburgh: Banner of Truth, 1980), 18.

Justice provides an excellent encouragement for saints (4:9-12)
David's oath (v.9) introduces his judicial decision (vv. 10-11). He
alludes to the Amalekite in 1:1-16, who was sure David would
relish his good news about Saul's death. 'I executed him,' David
says. Baanah and Rechab begin a cold sweat and understand why
when David continues his argument: 'How much more when wicked
men have killed an innocent man in his house upon his bed!' (v.11a).
David could not have known this last item unless Rechab and
Baanah had told him; they must have rehearsed the whole scheme
in detail. They likely thought of it as a slick move; David called it
dirty pool. He gives the order and they are killed, their extremities
hacked off, and their handless, feetless forms hung for public
contemplation by Hebron's pool (cf. Deut. 21:22-23). There was
no government statement issued bemoaning how 'morally outraged'
the king was. These fellows would never sneak nor stab again;
Hebron was a kingdom with dissection and justice for all.

I would imagine David felt compelled to give the corpses of
Baanah and Rechab brief billboard status. He must show that he
repudiated the deed for, as with Abner's death, there would be those
in the northern tribes, especially Saul's Benjamin, who would say
the whole thing smelled to high heaven, that it was too 'convenient'
for David, and that he was obviously the mastermind behind it.
Even the execution wouldn't quiet the skeptics. They would only
respond that that is the way politicians work – they hire hit-men
with promise of reward, then knock off their hirelings to make
themselves look clean. The fact that David had no need of Baanah's
and Rechab's deed since Saul's regime was already at its last gasp
would carry no weight at all, for such people do not stop to reason
when their blood is boiling.

But for us this sample of justice in Hebron should be
encouraging, for Yahweh's chosen king justly redressed wrong.
Admittedly, it is only a single instance; it has only occurred within
the postage-stamp kingdom of Judah; and some will think it is only
a publicity gimmick. But, like the new growth of Samson's hair,
(see Judg. 16:22ff.), it is the sign of something greater. Every bit of
micro-justice enacted under David's regime should be taken as a
foregleam of the macro-justice that David's promised Descendant
will enforce throughout the earth in his own time (Isa. 9:6-7; 11:1-
5, Ps. 72).[8] God's people desperately need to hold on to this hope

for the Bible knows what pressure and temptation the prevalence of *injustice* brings on the church (Isa. 59:14-15). If Christ's flock are continually wronged and crushed they may be tempted to join the other ranks (Ps. 125:3). It may be the South Sudanese believer who has been forcibly banished from his land and separated from his family; it may be the Christian wife whose husband has gone after a newer model and worked the legal process to leave her with nothing. Whatever the particulars, God's people must be assured that the time will come when the Davidic King will institute Hebron justice throughout the earth.

David will soon assume the kingdom Yahweh promised him (2 Sam. 5), but what an array of hindrances and frustrations there have been on the way to it. Yet one finds immense encouragement looking back over 2 Samuel 2–4, for this section clearly teaches:

No power can overcome the kingdom (Abner, Chap. 2)
No folly can thwart the kingdom (Joab, Chap. 3)
No injustice can establish the kingdom (Baanah and Rechab, Chap. 4)

6. Kingdom Collage
2 Samuel 5:1-25

I have just now noticed the dust jacket on a book about the geography of Israel. One graphic scene does not monopolize the cover; rather there are four photographs – a landmark, an individual, a landscape, a town. All suggest the kind of sights you would see should you find yourself in Jerusalem or Hebron or Galilee or Bethlehem. The cover is a collage; in this case, of the land of Israel.

2 Samuel 5 is a collage. It is not a single flowing narrative but a collection of 'chunks,' episodes or pieces of information placed side-by-side, all of which, however, relate to the establishing of David's kingdom. We are sure about the collage-condition of the text because the various sections (vv. 1-5, 6-10, 11-12, 13-16, 17-25) do not follow a strict chronological order. Hiram sent masons and materials to build David a palace (v. 11), but this did not happen

---

8. See *Looking on the Heart: Expositions of the Book of 1 Samuel*, 2 vols. (Grand Rapids: Baker, 1994), 1:22-26, where I develop a similar argument from Hannah's prayer.

immediately after David's conquest of Jerusalem (vv. 6-9) since Hiram's reign seems to have overlapped only with the last ten years of David's (Hiram, 980-947 BC; David, approx. 1010-970 BC); hence verse 11 reports something from relatively late in David's reign.[1] The report of concubines, wives, and births in verses 13-16 obviously summarizes some years of David's reign in Jerusalem, yet verse 17 pulls us back to the time immediately after David's anointing in verses 1-3. Moreover, chronology enthusiasts may be delighted to note that the defeats of the Philistines in verses 17-25 may have *preceded* David's capture of Jerusalem in verses 6-8, for if the Philistines reacted immediately to Israel's new unity (v. 17), David would not have had the time (or freedom) to press immediate offensive operations against Jerusalem until he had dispensed with the Philistine threat.[2]

Most of us, however, do not live and breathe chronology. I only included the preceding paragraph to convince the skeptical. My point is that biblical writers are not chained to chronological order – and in 2 Samuel 5 the chains have certainly fallen off. The chapter is orderly but not sequential. It is a collage; it is a collection of fragments intending to give us a proper view of the kingdom. On to the teaching.

The Promises that Secure the Kingdom (5:1-10)

The Promise to David
The northern tribes (v. 1), probably via the elders representing them (v.3), came to Hebron, accepted David's covenant commitments to them, and anointed him king over Israel. These northerners have their speech prepared and state their pro-David case in three arguments:

(1) Relationship: We are your bone and your flesh (v.1b)
(2) Leadership: Previously, while Saul was king over us, you were the one who was leading us out to and in from battle (v. 2a);
(3) Promise: 'Yahweh said to you, "*You* will shepherd my people Israel, and *you* will be leader over Israel" ' (v. 2b. emphasis in Heb.).

---

1. On the chronology, see Eugene H. Merrill, *Kingdom of Priests* (Grand Rapids: Baker, 1987), 238-40, and Claus Schedl, *History of the Old Testament*, 5 vols. (Staten Island: Alba House, 1972), 3: 218-19.

2. See further C.F. Keil, *Biblical Commentary on the Books of Samuel* (1875; reprint ed., Grand Rapids: Eerdmans, 1950), 323.

The last argument is the climactic one, and, in the view of the biblical writer, I am sure it is the crucial one. Yahweh's promise of the kingdom to David begins in a threat (1 Sam. 13:14), becomes visible – at least to Samuel – in the anointing among Jesse's family (1 Sam. 16:1-13), hangs as a suspicion over a tormented Saul (1 Sam. 18:8) or as a foregone conclusion over an almost resigned Saul (1 Sam. 24:20-21; 26:25), and is assumed by both David's friends (1 Sam. 23:16-17; 25:30-31) and his opponents (2 Sam. 3:9-10, 18). Hence, when the northern tribes cite Yahweh's promise at the Hebron negotiations, the writer wants us to highlight it in our text, as if to say, 'See there? See how Yahweh's promise to David has come to pass? See how it has weathered the venom of Saul (1 Sam. 18–26), the follies of David (1 Sam. 25,27,29), the rebellion of the north (2 Sam. 2:8-32), and the self-seeking of "friends" (2 Sam. 1:1-16; 3:22-30; 4:1-12)? See how Yahweh's promise has proved firm in the face of *intense opposition,* chapters and chapters of it since 1 Samuel 18?' He implies that all Yahweh's promises are certain no matter how much resistance they may meet.

The Promise to Abraham

I think Robert Gordon hits the mark when he links the defeat of the Jebusites in verses 6-10 with the promise of Abraham in Genesis 15:18-21.[3] Most readers, however, do not see 'Jebusite' and think 'Genesis 15'. We hear the Jebusites' cocky wisecrack (v. 6); and read the teasingly concise report of David's victory (vv. 7-8) – and find that few details mean more questions. Our curiosity becomes hopeless when some suggest David's success may have been connected with the Jebusite water system. Let us touch on these historical matters and then return to the promise-connection.

The main difficulties arise in verses 6-8, which may be broken down as follows:

> Jebusite defiance, v.6
> Davidic success, v.7
> Additional information, v.8a
> Resulting proverb, v.8b

---

3. Robert P. Gordon, *I & II Samuel: A Commentary* (Grand Rapids: Zondervan, 1986), 226; also John Calvin, *Sermons on 2 Samuel,* trans. Douglas Kelly (Edinburgh: Banner of Truth, 1992) 188-89.

In verse 6 we hear a bit of local Jebusite chutzpah. The defenders think their citadel impregnable (v. 6c) and so defy David: 'You will never come in here, but the blind and the lame shall turn you away' (v. 6b). It is simply an arrogant put-down: sightless eyes and helpless legs are enough to repel any attack of yours.[4] It's a good line; memorable words – unless one has to eat them.

Verse 7 attests that they did. The real puzzle, however, comes with the further explanation in verse 8 that seems to hint at how the Jebusites were taken. David said, 'Whoever strikes down the Jebusite, let him reach the ṣinnôr [watershaft?]; and as for the lame and the blind, they are hated by David's soul' (I take 'the lame and the blind' as referring to the jeering Jebusites themselves). The text is tough. The ṣinnôr is the teaser.[5] What exactly is it? Can we make any sense of this?

Archaeology has suggested an attractive possibility that keeps tantalizing translators. Old Jerusalem's water system (on the eastern hill, Ophel) could be entered inside the city by means of a stepped tunnel, which in turn opens into a gradual sloping tunnel that continues about 90 feet until it comes to the top of a vertical shaft; this shaft drops some 37 feet where it meets a lower horizontal tunnel bringing water from the Gihon Spring outside the city wall. The following schematic depicts a simplified lay-out of the system.[6]

---

4. Yigael Yadin *(The Art of Warfare in Biblical Lands,* 2 vols. [New York: McGraw-Hill, 1963], 2:267-70) has proposed that the Jebusites put the lame and blind on the city wall and used them as a dire magical curse. Citing Hittite analogues, Yadin argues that the curse threatened that whoever attacked these lame and blind would themselves become maimed and sightless. The pagan hoky-poky, however, failed to scare David off. I remain unconvinced; for one thing, the biblical text never says the blind and the lame were placed on the walls. That is a bit of local color from Josephus *(Antiquities,* 7.3).

5. The *(ṣinnôr)* is probably not an instrument (cf. NEB, 'Let him use his grappling-iron,' or NIV mg., 'Use scaling hooks') but a destination, because the verb and following preposition here *(nāgaʿ + bĕ)* almost without exception allude to reaching, touching, or striking an object/objective. *ṣinnôr* occurs only here and in Psalm 42:7 (v.8, Heb.); there it seems to refer to some kind of channel for flowing water.

6. For an overview, see Dan Gill, 'Jerusalem's Underground Water Systems: How They Met,' *Biblical Archaeology Review* 20/4 (July-August 1994): 20-35. Contrary to some, Warren's Shaft system (named after its British discoverer) was probably already in use prior to David's attack. On the dating, cf. further Zvi Abells and Asher Arbit, 'Some New Thoughts on Jerusalem's

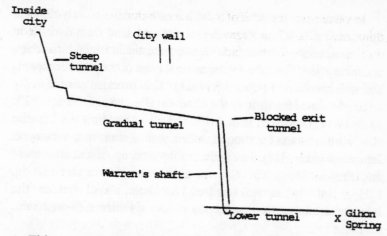

This system is a life-saver. Though under siege, a city has access to water even when the water source is outside the wall (which source they would camouflage). Some suggest that David urged his troops to seize and negotiate their way one-by-one up the water system and so gain entrance for a surprise attack inside the city.[7] But they could have saved the effort. If David's men discovered (or already knew) the source of the city's water, they could simply sit at the bottom of brother Warren's shaft and cut the rope on every Jebusite bucket lowered for water, and so dry the town into submission.

All of this to say we know the fact but not the method of David's victory. It could have been via the water system but we cannot be sure. In any case, he had selected a superb capital for the united kingdom.[8] We now return to the promise connection of the text.[9]

Ancient Water Systems,' *Palestine Exploration Quarterly* 127 (1995): 2-4.

7. Note how NRSV reflects this: 'Whoever would strike down the Jebusites, let him get up the water shaft to attack the lame and the blind, those whom David hates.'

8. Cf. John Bright, *A History of Israel,* 3rd ed. (Philadelphia: Westminster, 1981), 200: 'By this move David both eliminated a Canaanite enclave from the center of the land and gained a capital from which he could rule a national state. Hebron, located far to the south and on Judahite soil, could not have been permanently acceptable as a capital to the northern tribes. But a capital in the north would have been doubly unacceptable to Judah. Jerusalem, centrally located between the two sections and within the territory of none of the tribes, offered an excellent compromise.'

9. On the proverb in 8b ('Therefore they say, "The blind and lame will never

We have met the Jebusites before (2 Samuel 5 is only the first time they talk). When Yahweh promised the land from the Nile to the Euphrates to Abraham's descendants he meant land which others occupied at that time; the Jebusites are the last of the other occupants Yahweh mentioned (Gen. 15:18-21). This promise is repeatedly referred to until the time of the conquest (Ex. 3:8, 17; 13:5; 23:23; 33:2; 34:11; Deut. 7:1; Josh. 3:10; 12:8).[10] At that time the Jebusite clause hit a snag, for though Judah won a smashing victory at Jerusalem (Judg. 1:8), they were unable to occupy it and dispossess the Jebusites (Josh. 15:63) – nor did Benjamin ever do so (Judg. 1:21).[11] But now, several hundred years later, David overruns the Jebusite stronghold and takes possession of Fortress Zion (2 Sam. 5:7).[12]

Yahweh's promise to Abraham (Gen. 15:18-21) has proven true. If verses 1-5 taught us that Yahweh's promises are certain in spite of intense opposition, verses 6-10 teach us that his promises are certain in spite of *chronological distance.* Eight hundred years (Abraham-to-David, plus or minus) does not erode the reliability of Yahweh's word. His promises are not stamped with an expiration date in small print. All of which should make a difference in the way waiting Christians read their Bibles and look to their future

---

come into the house" ') I prefer to say nothing because I don't know what it means. I could tell you there are three views and explain each, but to little profit. On some possible connections with Matthew 21, see Gordon, *I & II Samuel,* 50-52.

10. Note how often the Jebusites appear last in lists of the various people groups.

11. On the problems between Joshua 15:63 and Judges 1:8, 21, see my comments in previous volumes, *No Falling Words* (Joshua), 88-90, and *Such a Great Salvation* (Judges), 19; see also Marten H. Woudstra, *The Book of Joshua,* The New International Commentary on the Old Testament (Grand Rapids: Eerdmans, 1981), 254-56.

12. Verse 7 contains the first mention of Zion in the Bible. Originally it referred to this conquered Jebusite town, this 'city of David,' on the (southeast) Hill Ophel (1 Kings 8:1) but also came to designate the temple mount (Ps. 74:2-3; 84:7), the city of Jerusalem (Ps.87:2-3; 147:12), the people of God (Isa. 49:14; 51:16), and, significantly, the center of Yahweh's kingdom in the age to come (Isa. 2:3; 4:3-5; Mic. 4:7; Zech.8:1-3). The day will come when 'Yahweh of hosts will reign on Mount Zion and in Jerusalem' (Isa. 24:23), but that reign first became visible in old Jebusburg on a mere eleven acres of real estate.

(cf. 2 Peter 3). Hence 'Let us be grateful for receiving a kingdom that cannot be shaken' (Heb. 12:28, RSV) – not because we are unshakeable but because Yahweh's promises are firm, so firm that time cannot dissolve them (the case of Abraham) nor enemies sabotage them (the case of David). Yahweh's promises may be old or opposed but never false.

The Vision that Prospers the Kingdom (5: 11-12)

The next fragment reports a bit of foreign recognition, coming from Tyre, a commercial and maritime center twenty-five miles south of Sidon on the Phoenician coast.

> King Hiram of Tyre sent envoys to David with cedar logs, carpenters, and stonemasons; and they built a palace for David. Thus David knew that the LORD had established him as king over Israel and had exalted his kingship for the sake of His people Israel (vv. 11-12, NJPS).

As already noted, Hiram's building operations did not occur until relatively late in David's reign; yet the notice about them is placed here, immediately after David's conquest of Jerusalem early in his reign. The writer is not writing a consecutive narrative but giving a collection of vignettes to stress the nature of the kingdom.

One could almost look at verse 11 (Hiram's supplies, workmen, and building operations) and see a foregleam of the nations' future homage to Yahweh's restored people (cf. Isa. 60:3, 10-14). But that is not the emphasis. Instead the text underscores David's inferring that his new permanent residence is a sign of how Yahweh had established or confirmed his kingship over Israel (v. 12). Even more significant is the rationale for Yahweh's stabilizing work: David realized Yahweh 'had exalted his kingship for the sake of His people Israel'. That is, Yahweh did not anchor David's throne so he could act like a king but so that he could function as a servant toward his people.[13] David's kingship was not for David's aggrandizement but for Israel's welfare. Kingship was not an end in itself but a means to an end – the benefit of Yahweh's people. David is *over* Israel *for* Israel.

---

13. Cf. the reason why Israel's king was to devote himself to reading Yahweh's law; 'so that he will not think himself superior to his brothers' (Deut. 17;20, NJB).

This whole mentality runs cross-grained to sinful human nature, whether royal or common. We crave homage; we do not chase service. Paul Johnson writes a revealing assessment of Leo Tolstoy in this vein: 'He was willing to make a sacrifice, of comfort, pleasure, even life, provided it could be done as a grand, theatrical gesture, and everyone noticed.' He notes that in the army Tolstoy was willing to perform but not to serve. Though he later renounced his gambling he felt no need to pay off gambling-connected debts, some of them owed to poor men. As Johnson notes: 'There was nothing dramatic about paying an old debt.'[14] It would not serve him, only others; and that was too servile.

Yahweh does not confine his call to serve his people to Israel's premier king; Christ insists that all his disciples must hold this vision, especially those placed in leadership capacities (see Mark 10: 35-45, esp. vv. 42-45). It is all too easy to see when a biblical king inflates himself and neglects the welfare of God's people; but what pastors and teachers cannot always see is that, for all their ministerial propaganda, their ego shapes their vision in a constant concern for recognition, acceptance, even adulation, from their people. It is a hard discipline to keep to the true kingdom vision – serving Christ's needy and frequently obnoxious sheep.

The Compromise that Mars the Kingdom (5:13-16)

This brief segment, a companion-piece to 3:2-5, reports the new tally of (more) concubines and wives David took and of (more) sons and daughters David fathered during the Jerusalem years. It is a plus-and-minus section. On the one hand the number of David's sons (vv. 14-16) indicates his strength; on the other hand, the number of his concubines and wives reveals his folly, for this practice was in direct violation of Yahweh's prescriptions for the covenant king (Deut. 17:17).[15] I think we must hear both notes in verses 13-16. Granted, chapter 5 as a whole is positive toward David; it is only in

---

14. Paul Johnson, *Intellectuals* (New York: Harper & Row, 1988), 111,115.
15. Ronald F. Youngblood, '1,2 Samuel, *The Expositor's Bible Commentary*, 12 vols. (Grand Rapids: Zondervan, 1992), 3:859; and Calvin, *Sermons on 2 Samuel*, 206-7. (Calvin suggests David could have had numerous offspring without a harem since one wife 'could have had twelve – indeed, even up to twenty-five' children!) Cf. also Walter Brueggemann, *First and Second Samuel*, Interpretation (Louisville: John Knox, 1990), 246: 'David acts like a king.

verses 13-16 that we meet with a yes and a no.[16] We must not mute the 'no'. Here is both David's strength and his stupidity.

Sometimes one blemish can taint an otherwise excellent record or achievement. Luther once praised his colleague Justus Jonas for having all the qualities of a good preacher but added that 'people cannot forgive the good man for hawking and spitting so often'.[17] Hence preaching may be excellent, but if it's too wet it tends to dampen one's estimate of it. In the same way we may admit that on the whole David's kingship was admirable and his fidelity to Yahweh consistent. Yet we must not doctor the data. We must not sweep away evidence that shows his faithfulness less than complete or his practices controlled by human culture rather than by God's law.

Such observations should be deeply instructive. They should check our tendency to Christian hero worship, our passion for becoming so enamored with certain kingdom servants that we fail to remember that they too are sinful people who will inevitably disappoint in some way or another. Even David compromises and mars the kingdom over which he rules; ultimately, the kingdom is only safe in the hands of David's Descendant who *always* does what pleases the Father (John 8:29).

The Defender Who Protects His Kingdom (5:17-25)

The Philistines hear the news and don't like the news. The last thing they want is Israel united under one king. (v. 17) – so they

---

He has concubines. He already had many wives (3:2-4), but in Hebron the word 'concubine' was not used. Now in the royal city there is a new vocabulary for a new practice. The new language and the new practice appear without apology. David is well into the process of sexual politics.' See above, sect. 4, fn.5. On the case for a Mosaic date for Deuteronomy, see Gleason L. Archer, Jr., *A Survey of Old Testament Introduction,* updated and rev. ed. (Chicago: Moody, 1994), 108-12, 274-83.

16. Someone could point out that verse 13 only records David's action and does not overtly reject it. That is true, but narrative sometimes expects the reader to infer a point of view even if it is not explicit. For example, 2 Samuel 6 does not explicitly say that David was wrong to transport the ark on a cart Philistine style, but the change in mode of transport on the second attempt (vv. 12-13) leads a reader correctly to infer as much.

17. Preserved Smith and Herbert Percival Gallinger, eds., *Conversations with Luther* (New Canaan, CT: Keats, 1979), 189-90.

come up to track down their slippery vassal (David) and occupy the Valley of Rephaim southwest of Jerusalem. Philistines hear and go up (v. 17a); David hears and goes down (v. 17b) – to the stronghold, wherever that is.[18] In any case, what follows reports two victories over the Philistines. That is significant – it shows that Yahweh's promise in 3:18 ('By the hand of David my servant I shall save my people Israel from the hand of the Philistines') is already coming to pass.[19]

These episodes not only depict Yahweh as the defender of his kingdom but show *how* he protects it.

First, he protects it *by his guidance*. At the very start of both episodes David asks direction from Yahweh (vv. 19,23; see also 2:1), probably through the priest (1 Sam. 23:6-14). (Here David stands in marked contrast to Saul [1 Sam. 28:6,15]; David receives direction from Yahweh while Saul had been cut off from it.) And he discovers an interesting twist in Yahweh's direction, for, although David faces two almost identical situations (vv. 18,22), Yahweh *varies* his guidance in the second episode. The first time Yahweh answered, 'Go up, for I will certainly give the Philistines into your hand' (v. 19b), but on the second occasion he cautioned, 'You must not go up – go around behind them and come on them opposite the balsam trees' (v. 23b).

The text, however, does not stress the diversity but the fact of Yahweh's guidance, primarily in its protective capacity. Nor is its vigilance limited to new kings and nascent kingdoms, for legions of kingdom servants remember being placed behind this protective shield. About 1545 in Montrose, Scotland, George Wishart, the mentor of John Knox, received a letter alleging to come from an intimate friend who had become suddenly ill and earnestly desired Wishart's presence at his death-bed. Wishart set out with a few friends but had scarcely gone a quarter of a mile before he stopped and abruptly announced, 'I am forbidden of God to go on this journey; will some of you be pleased to ride to yonder place [he

---

18. Some think the stronghold may have been Adullam (cf. 1 Sam. 22:1, 4-5; 2 Sam. 23:13-14), but we can't be sure. I don't think the stronghold/fortress Zion (vv. 7,9) is meant, for if David was in Jerusalem he would not 'go down' (v.17) to it.

19. Matthew Henry, *Commentary on the Whole Bible,* 6 vols. (New York: Revell, n.d.), 2:470; P. Kyle McCarter, Jr., *II Samuel,* The Anchor Bible (New York: Doubleday, 1984), 159.

pointed to a little hill], and see what you find, for I apprehend there is a plot laid against my life.' His scouts checked the hill and discovered some sixty horsemen concealed behind it, ready to seize Wishart. The 'friend's' letter had been a forgery of his eminence, the most bloody, treacherous Cardinal Beaton.[20] In multiple ways Yahweh's guidance never ceases to secure his cause and his people.

Secondly, these Philistine vignettes teach that Yahweh protects his kingdom *by his power*. In the first episode David describes the victory Yahweh gave by using the root *prṣ* (in fact, it is used four times in 5:20):

> So David came to Baal-*perazim*, and David struck them down there and said, 'Yahweh has *broken through* my enemies before me like an *outbursting* of waters.' Therefore he called the name of that place Baal-*perazim*.

'Baal-perazim' means 'lord of burstings out', commemorating the way Yahweh had broken down the Philistines. David compared Yahweh's activity to the way a massive torrent of water breaks down everything in its path. Just so Yahweh levels the opposition, and David names the site Smasherton.[21]

The second episode also highlights Yahweh's power as he describes himself as a warrior leading his troops into the fray:

> When you hear the sound of marching in the tops of the balsam trees, then you must spring into action, for then Yahweh shall have gone out before you to strike down the Philistine army (v. 24).

The verb 'to go out/forth' (*yāṣā'*) is a very common one but frequently refers to going into or leading into battle (see v. 2 in this very chapter).[22] For example, when Deborah ordered Barak into battle against Sisera's hordes she exclaimed, 'Has not Yahweh gone out (*yāṣā'*) before you?' (Judg. 4:14). That is, the divine captain had entered combat and his people had only to follow. So here in

---

20. Thomas McCrie, *The Story of the Scottish Church from the Reformation to the Disruption* (1875; reprint ed., Glasgow: Free Presbyterian, 1988), 19-20.

21. Micah 2:13 refers to 'the Breaker' (*happōrēṣ*) who will lead his remnant in breaking out of confinement into deliverance/freedom. I think the term refers to the Messiah.

22. H.D. Preuss, TDOT, 6:229, claims it is used more than 120 times in this sense.

verse 24 Yahweh styles himself as the Warrior who plunges into battle and knocks off the Philistines.

Note what vigorous images the text gives us of Yahweh's power: the Leveler and the Warrior. Contemporary Christians must not tone these down, for the text means to impress us with the fact that we do *not* have a namby-pamby godlet who is house-broken in line with our canon of conceivability. (People abandon gods like that, and they're carried off to the landfill, v. 21). No, Yahweh's people have a God who is a smasher and a fighter, a God 'mighty in battle' (Ps. 24:8), who can *therefore* defend his sheep and restrain and conquer all his and our enemies.[23] Hence 2 Samuel 5 leads us straight into eschatology, that is, last things, for if this is our God who protects his kingdom under David, then his people never need fear, for this God is more than able to always lead us in triumph (cf. 2 Cor. 2:14) and to impose his kingdom at the last in all its power and glory. There can be no doubt. After all, he is the Leveler and Warrior.

7. The Terror and Ecstasy of God
2 Samuel 6:1-23

A picture hangs on my wall – two-by-two inch snapshots of twelve men arranged in an x-configuration with a date (1926) stamped in the middle. I can easily imagine folks happening on to this picture amid the clutter and rubble of an antique shop. It would mean nothing to them, unless they had an inordinate interest in studying collars and ties of the 1920s. But it is no mere relic to me since it is my father's seminary class and his shot is third from the top on the right side. I prize it because I know its significance.

In the same way you may not find yourself immensely excited over an ancient box 3¾ x 2¼ x 2¼ feet made of acacia wood, plated with gold, and called the ark of the covenant. Your apathy might be shaken, however, once you realized that this piece of sacred furniture represents the very presence of Yahweh among his people. So this narrative about the ark should matter to you, for 2 Samuel 6 is not a travelogue of the ark of the covenant but a revelation of the God of Israel.

Before I discuss the teaching of the chapter I want to lay out a

23. Westminster Shorter Catechism, No. 26.

proposed structure for the narrative, which, if analyzed with the text, should highlight the rhythm and contrasts of the story for the reader.

Structure of 2 Samuel 6

Bringing up the Ark, vv. 2-4
    Joy, v.5
        Tragedy vv. 6-7
            David's reaction: anger and fear, vv. 8-9
                In the house of Obed-edom – Blessing, vv.10-11

Bringing up the Ark, vv. 12-13
    Joy, vv. 14-15
        Tragedy, v.16
            David's reaction: worship and generosity, vv. 17-19
                In the house of David – Contempt, vv. 20-23

Now let us go on to the teaching emphases of the chapter.

The Centrality of Yahweh's Presence (6:1-2)

Baale-judah (v. 2), or Kiriath-jearim as it was also known (cf. Josh. 15:9-10; 1 Sam. 7:1), was bursting its seams, for here, eight to nine miles west/northwest of Jerusalem, the military (v. 1) and the king and crowd (v.2) had assembled for the order of the day: to bring up the ark of God to Jerusalem.

Before we allow the ark to leave for Jerusalem, let us take a careful look at what it represents. We find the specifications for its construction in Exodus 25:10-22 but can best catch its significance in Moses' wilderness prayer in Numbers 10:35-36:

> When the Ark was to set out, Moses would say:
>   Advance, O LORD!
>   May your enemies be scattered,
>   And may your foes flee before you!
> And when it halted, he would say:
>   Return, O LORD,
>   You who are Israel's myriads of thousands! (NJPS)[1]

---

1. The NJPS translation is correct. Yahweh does not return 'to' Israel's myriads of thousands (as in RSV and NIV); rather Yahweh *is* Israel's myriads of thousands, i.e., he himself is worth divisions. He himself is all the protection Israel needs. There is no 'to' in the Hebrew text.

So closely was the ark identified with Yahweh's presence that when the ark set out to lead Israel Moses would say, 'Advance, O LORD!' and when the ark was put down in the next camping spot, he would exclaim, 'Return, O LORD!' This close identification between the ark and Yahweh does not mean the ark was an image of Yahweh but that it was a sacrament of his presence. If the ark signifies God's presence, what sort of God (does it imply) is present?

First, the ark underscores Yahweh's *rulership*. David makes this clear in 1 Chronicles 28:2 when he calls the ark of the covenant 'the footstool of our God'. Kings sit on thrones and use footstools; if the ark is Yahweh's footstool then surely Yahweh is king.[2] Secondly, the ark speaks of Yahweh's *reconciliation*, for on the annual Day of Atonement the high priest would sprinkle the blood of the sin-offering on the lid of the ark and in front of the ark (Lev. 16:14-15). And, third, the ark emphasizes Yahweh's *revelation*, for the stone tablets containing the covenant commandments were placed inside the ark (Ex. 25:16,21; Deut. 10:1-5). Moreover, the ark was the trysting place where Yahweh would meet with Moses to communicate additional instruction for Israel (Ex. 25:22). The ark was the place of Yahweh's directing word.

All the hubbub in Kiriath-jearim really matters then. By bringing the ark to Zion David is saying that Yahweh's presence can no longer remain, so to speak, on a side rail (cf. 1 Chron. 13:3) but must be the central focus and reality of the Davidic kingdom.[3] The worship of Yahweh, this ruling, reconciling, revealing God, must be at the heart of Israel's life. The ark in Jerusalem proclaims that the majestic, pardoning, speaking God is in the midst of his people.

A footnote or two. Do you see what 2 Samuel 6 is saying to God's people in the wake of 2 Samuel 5? It is not saying that whipping Jebusites and Philistines doesn't matter; but it does imply

2. Some think verse 2 of our present chapter carries this idea when it speaks of Yahweh of hosts, who, as NASB has it, 'is enthroned above the cherubim [figures of celestial beings attached to the lid of the ark].' However, 'who dwells between the cherubim' may be a preferable translation. See especially Marten H. Woudstra, *The Ark of the Covenant from Conquest to Kingship* (Philadelphia: Presbyterian and Reformed, 1965), 68-73. On the ark as royal footstool, see C.L. Seow, 'Ark of the Covenant,' ABD, 1:388-89.

3. This point holds even if this event is dated relatively late in David's reign, as, e.g., Eugene H. Merrill, (*Kingdom of Priests* [Grand Rapids: Baker, 1987], 238-48) argues.

that God's people are not sustained merely by crises. They do not thrive by knocking off Philistines but by seeking God's face. The evangelical church easily loses sight of this. We can always dredge up more adrenaline because of the latest moral or ethical or social or cultural or political emergency. Crises may stimulate us to action but they do not sustain life. The church must never look to the latest cause for her life. We cannot ignore the enemies outside the city of God, but we must not be absorbed by them. War must not efface worship. The real question is not 'Who is against us?' but 'Who is among us?'

The second footnote: observe how Jesus Christ fulfills all that the ark signifies. In my communion we often say that as our Redeemer Christ carries out the offices of prophet, priest, and king (see Westminster Shorter Catechism, nos. 23-26). Does the ark signify Yahweh's revelation? So Christ is our prophet who reveals to us, by his word and Spirit, the will of God for our salvation. Does the ark speak of Yahweh's reconciliation? So Christ is our priest who brought his own blood into the sanctuary (Heb. 9:12). Does the ark as Yahweh's foot-stool proclaim his rulership? So Christ is our king 'in subduing us to himself, in ruling and defending us, and in restraining and conquering all his and our enemies'. It shouldn't surprise us that this Old Testament furniture that so fully speaks of Yahweh should as fully point to Christ 'for in Christ all the fullness of the Deity lives in bodily form' (Col. 2:9, NIV). How can I keep Yahweh's presence central in my life, in my church? Answer: Turn your eyes upon Jesus.

The Danger of Yahweh's Holiness (6:3-11)

It was fun. It was loud. It was religious. Dancing and singing and the likes of lyres, tambourines, cymbals, and so on (v.5). Kiriath-jearim was rocking. The ark was traveling on a new cart pulled by oxen with Ahio and Uzzah serving as attendants. A strange thing happened near the threshing floor of Nacon. It took a moment for everyone to realize it. The dancing stopped; the music stopped. All eyes turned to Uzzah, on the ground, writhing, twitching. Then still. Someone called 911. The party was over.

'Then Yahweh's anger burned against Uzzah, and God struck him down there for his error; so he died there beside the ark of God' (v.7).[4]

Doesn't this offend you? After all, Uzzah was only trying to help – was he to allow the oxen to bounce the ark right off the cart (v. 6)? Why didn't Yahweh cut him some slack? Why so severe? So arbitrary? We should be angry, shouldn't we (v. 8)? Or, should we fear (v. 9)?

For me, passages like this are evidence of the supernatural origin and trustworthiness of the Bible. This Uzzah story goes so against the grain of human preferences. We would never have 'invented' a God like this – not if we want to win converts and influence people. This God is not very marketable. Anyone who says the God of the Bible is merely a projection of our wish fulfillment has not read the Bible.

Back to the text. What was the problem, the error, here? We must recall that Yahweh had long ago given specific instructions to Moses and the priesthood about how the ark, among other items, was to be transported (see Num. 4:4-6, 15, 17-20; and 7:9). The rules were: no touch, no look, no cart. The priests were to cover the sacred furniture after which they would assign Levites of the Kohathite clan to carry such items (hence, implicitly, no carts). The Kohathites were not to touch or look upon the sacred items 'lest they die' (Num. 4:15, 20). Clearly, Yahweh did not want them to die; his *kindness* was written all over that warning. So it was not as though David and Uzzah and company had had no warning. Yahweh's blow was scarcely arbitrary.[5]

In addition to this background, we must note how Yahweh's deed is described in verse 8:

> Now David became angry because Yahweh had broken out with an outbreak against Uzzah; so that place is called Outbreak-of-Uzzah to this day.

---

4. Perhaps a distinction would be helpful for some readers: Uzzah's ultimate salvation is not at stake here. It is a temporal judgment he suffers. That, however, does not mean we should stop shaking.

5. One meets a conspiracy of silence about Numbers 4 among most commentators on 2 Samuel 6; they refuse to use Numbers 4 to help explain the text. They cling to their critical orthodoxy which holds that most of Numbers comes from the P (=Priestly) materials of the post-exilic era. In their view most of Numbers is much later than David and, in any case, not accurate historically (see R.C. Denton, 'Numbers, Book of,' IDB, 3:571). However, such orthodoxy is a fading fashion; see Jacob Milgrom, 'Numbers, Book of,' ABD, 4:1148-50, on the antiquity of the priestly materials.

I have translated literally so that the three uses of the root *prṣ* (to break out) can be noted. Anyone reading through 2 Samuel cannot help remembering how the same root was used four times in 5:20:

> And David came to Lord-of-outbreakings, and David struck them down there; then he said, 'Yahweh has broken through my enemies before me like an outbreaking of waters'; therefore he called the name of that place Lord-of-outbreakings.

In 5:20 Yahweh 'breaks out' against David's enemies; in 6:8 against David's friend. Yahweh may break out against the Philistines – or Israel. God's lethal holiness levels both pagans and churchmen. 'Once again the deity has broken loose, with a numinous power and unexpectedness which petrifies a mortal, and this time not in favour of David's undertaking, but to its detriment.'[6]

Of course, as readers we can continue to object if we like. But the application of the text is clear: you dare not trifle with a God who is both real and holy. Yahweh is not your neat, warm, fuzzy friend in the sky.

I recall reading a story about two men making their way to a reception on a drippy Washington D.C. evening. The one had offered to share the shelter of his umbrella with the stranger on his way to the same affair. As they sloshed along and conversed the stranger declared his opinion that General Grant was highly overrated. Naturally, he wouldn't have said that had he known Grant was holding the umbrella over him. He acted foolishly because he did not know with whom he was dealing. And Yahweh's people tend to forget what sort of God they face. We forget that there is heat in his holiness. No, we do not need to be terrified, but being scared wouldn't hurt.[7]

The Celebration of Yahweh's Joy (6:12-23)
God soon made it plain that his severe deed was not his last word about the ark. True, when Uzzah grabbed the ark (v.6) he was cut

---

6. J.P. Fokkelman, *Narrative Art and Poetry in the Books of Samuel,* vol. 3, *Throne and City (II Sam. 2-8 & 21-24)* (Assen/Maastricht: Van Gorcum, 1990,), 189.

7. I should not have to repeat that the God of 2 Samuel 6 is the same God you meet in the New Testament (See Acts 5:1-11; 1 Cor. 11:30-31; Heb. 10:26-31).

down; but the ark was not automatically deadly – witness the blessing Obed-edom experienced while it sat three months in his house (v. 11).[8] And this news gladly leaks to David: 'So King David was told, "Yahweh has blessed the house of Obed-edom and all he has on account of the ark of God" '(v.12a). Verse 12a is actually the hinge of the chapter, the bridge between verses 2-11 and 12b-23. In the structure I set out earlier in this chapter, I included verse 12a with the second half of the structure, but it might more accurately stand by itself between verses 2-11, and 12b-23. In any case, David gets the point: Yahweh's true intent is to bless not destroy his people via the ark. And, although the writer doesn't ring any bells or write *nota benes* all over the margin, he does clearly indicate in verse 13 that the ark is now being carried as ordered (Num. 4:15).

You cannot miss the accent on joy: they bring the ark into the city of David 'with gladness' (v. 12b); and there is David dancing and cavorting with all his gusto (vv.14,16); the people are shouting and the ram's horn blasting away (v. 15). Here is a holy delirium over the presence of God.

Now I want you to combine this point (from vv. 12-23) with my previous main point (from vv. 3-11) in order to see the full truth. Here you are to cheer with Yahweh's joy; there you are to tremble before Yahweh's holiness. So you see how the Bible balances truth? How you have *both* these emphases within *one* chapter? Fearfulness and gladness are held together. In Yahweh's presence you should both shudder *and* dance! Whether you can comprehend it or not, 2 Samuel 6 teaches you that a fearful sense of God's holiness does not suppress joy but stimulates it. Psalm 2 pulls it all together in three words: 'Rejoice with trembling!' (v. 11b). You have to be one of Zion's children to know how true this paradox is.

---

8. Yahweh's 'blessing' (v.11b) likely took the form of fertility in field, flocks, and family. The fact that Obed-edom was called 'the Gittite' does not, contrary to some, mean he was a Philistine (from Gath). See for details, Ronald F. Youngblood, '1,2 Samuel,' *The Expositor's Bible Commentary,* 12 vols. (Grand Rapids: Zondervan, 1992), 3:872, and Terence Kleven, 'Hebrew Style in 2 Samuel 6,' *Journal of the Evangelical Theological Society* 35 (1992): 306. Obed-edom the Gittite may well be the Levite Obed-edom of 1 Chron. 15:18, 21,24; 16:5, 38, though the evidence is not air-tight (see H.L. Ellison, 'Obed-edom,' ZPEB, 4:482).

The Humility of Yahweh's Servant (6:20-23)

The second half of our chapter is a success story – the ark does arrive in the city of David. However, if you will flip back to our chart depicting the structure of 2 Samuel 6, you will note that even the 'successful' half of the story contains a tragedy corresponding to the death of Uzzah in verses 6-7. It is in verse 16. When the ark had arrived in the city of David, 'Michal, the daughter of Saul, looked down through the window, saw King David leaping and dancing before Yahweh, and despised him in her heart.' In contrast to the house of Obed-edom in verses 10-11, David's house (vv. 20-23) exudes contempt instead of blessing. Michal's sarcasm has almost liquified as she goes out and meets David with

> Didn't the king of Israel do himself honor today – exposing himself today in the sight of the slave girls of his subjects, as one of the riffraff might expose himself! (v. 20, NJPS).[9]

It is revealing that the writer refers to Michal three times as 'the daughter of Saul' (vv. 16, 20, 23). He wants you to understand that hers is the voice of the 'old age,' of the former regime.[10]

Michal is concerned with royal dignity, proper decorum, outward appearances. A king has a certain image to maintain and he shouldn't put himself on a level with the, well, riffraff. David had

---

9. David's gyrating in that skimpy ephod was simply indecent in Michal's view. I remember seeing a drunk urinate in the street outside our town's Bakery Thrift Store during afternoon business hours. Michal is saying David's behaviour was on that level – disgusting.

10. John Hercus catches the flavor of Michal's demeanor in his graphic retelling: 'When David came home at last, tired and flushed, still delirious with the truth he had been singing and dancing all that day, Michal rose from the chaise longue [American = lounge] on which she had been reclining. Her makeup was just right, not a wisp of untidied hair was out of place, not a crease in her beautifully fitted gown.' He continues: 'Her long lashes hung disdainfully over eyes that looked him up and down with a quick contemptuous glance of scorn. "Well!" she said slowly, deliberately averting her eyes as if from some distinctly repugnant sight. "What a spectacle! What a scene the king of Israel made of himself today! It was simply disgusting. Dancing about like that with all the people watching, kicking your legs up in the air in that shameless way. You should have seen the gaping of all the servant girls! It was positively vulgar!" And she turned her back' (*Out of the Miry Clay*, [Downers Grove: InterVarsity, 1968], 87).

an answer. He did not think the slave girls were the audience. 'It was before Yahweh' (v. 21a). He was the audience. It was not performance for people but worship for Yahweh, 'who chose me in place of your father and all his house to appoint me as leader over Yahweh's people, over Israel, and I shall celebrate before Yahweh' (v. 21b). Not only does David have a different view of the audience but a different view of dignity: 'And I shall become even more despicable than this, and I shall be low in my own eyes, but, among the servant girls you spoke about – may I be honored' (v. 22). David does not see himself so much as Israel's king but as Yahweh's servant; and humility is appropriate for servants. For David humility *is* dignity. To him there is nothing servile about groveling before God![11]

Michal and David then represent two kingdoms. The old regime craves propriety, the new celebrates joy. Michal is like someone putting new wine into old wineskins – it simply doesn't work (Mark 2:18-22).

I think this Michal-David altercation holds a telling application to the sphere of our worship and devotion. In our churches there are any number of folks who are very concerned with services and externals and procedures and mechanics and meetings and decency and order but who really can't understand anything of the joy of the Lord. There are some who can muster enthusiasm and gusto over professional sports but who somehow cannot fathom anything but professional detachment over Jesus Christ. Exuberant praise and tears of repentance are strangers to them. W.G. Blaikie has carefully drawn the bottom line:

> There are, doubtless, times to be calm, and times to be enthusiastic; but can it be right to give all our coldness to Christ and all our enthusiasm to the world?[12]

Does the presence of God ever move us?[13]

---

11. I commend a prayerful reading of Calvin's exposition, entitled 'Before the Lord,' in John Calvin, *Sermons on 2 Samuel,* trans. Douglas Kelly (Edinburgh: Banner of Truth, 1992), 279-94.

12. W.G. Blaikie, *The Second Book of Samuel,* The Expositor's Bible (Cincinnati: Jennings & Graham, n.d.), 96.

13. The last verse (23) baffles us: How to explain Michal's childlessness? Did David merely cease sexual relations with her? Or was this Yahweh's

Endnote

Observe how 2 Samuel 6 portrays David in a priestly as well as a kingly role.[14] He wears a linen ephod (v.14), which seems to be a priestly garment (1 Sam. 2:18; 22:18), and he utters a blessing on the people (v. 18), a priestly function (Num. 6:22-27). David is not arrogantly infringing on the priests' office; clearly, he views himself as 'the humble and serving priest of the true King' (Gutbrod). Nevertheless, we should not miss this glimpse of the king in a priestly role, for we will meet it again in prophecy (Ps. 110:1, 4, and Zech. 6:12-13), and yet again in person, in Jesus, David's Descendant, our reigning king and interceding priest.

8. Getting to Know the Covenant God (2 Samuel 7:1-17)

Any reader could drown in the ink that has been spilled over 2 Samuel 7. And the chapter richly deserves all that ink since it records Yahweh's promise of a dynasty to David, sometimes called the Davidic covenant. It is a major chapter in biblical revelation. All the ink, however, tempts the expositor. One feels the pull to interact with all that has been written to explore every critical nook and theological cranny, to justify one's own positions over against those one rejects, and, in the process, to leave readers destitute of much benefit from this text as God's word. So let us resist the temptation, and let us not focus on the covenant but (where Scripture always places the emphasis) on the covenant God, not on the promise but on the Promiser. We need to know the covenant God. What can we observe about him here?

Yahweh's Wisdom (7:1-5)

One can almost see David and Nathan sporting mugs of decaffeinated coffee, enjoying an after-dinner conversation on the roof of David's house. The military situation is stable (v. 1), but

---

chastening stroke? Probably the latter; cf. Hans Wilhelm Hertzberg, *I & II Samuel,* The Old Testament Library (Philadelphia: Westminster, 1964), 281.

14. I am indebted here to Terence Kleven, 'Hebrew Style in 2 Samuel 6,' 307-9, and Karl Gutbrod, *Das Buch vom Reich,* Die Botschaft des Alten Testaments, 2nd ed. (Stuttgart: Calwer, 1973), 94-95.

there's something bothering David: he now lives in a house of cedar (cf. 5:11) but the ark of God sits in a mere tent (v.2). It's not enough to have the ark in the city of David (2 Sam. 6); it must have suitable quarters. There is something wrong when the Lord's servant lives among cedar while the sign of the Lord's presence sits among curtains. David need say no more; Nathan *knew* what he was thinking. It was noble, rational, and right. One didn't need to think twice about it. Nathan urged David to 'just do it' (v.3).

Later that night revelation rejected reason. It was strange – it all seemed as obvious as serving pancakes at a pancake supper. But Yahweh's word was clear: 'Go, and you shall say to my servant David, "Here's what Yahweh says: Are *you* the one who is to build me a house to dwell in?" '(v. 5). The answer was not 'No,' but 'Not yet.' In any case, David was not the one to build a temple for Yahweh. Yahweh will explain further; at this point we have his answer. David's (and Nathan's) plan is to be put on hold.

This passage signals the re-appearance of a possible theme of the Samuel materials: the limitation of Yahweh's servants. One can think of other instances. There is Eli eyeing the strange-acting woman at the tabernacle (1 Sam. 1:12-18). He is sure she's drunk – but he was wrong. Or there is Samuel looking over the fine physique of Eliab, Jesse's oldest son (1 Sam. 16:6-7) He's sure he has detected Yahweh's choice for king – but he was wrong. And David is convinced that dealing with Nabal renders patience passé; he is sure the time has come to squash Nabal and all his household (1 Sam. 25). Yet he discovered he was wrong. Here (2 Sam. 7) we happen on to David and Nathan conspiring a good and godly plan for Yahweh's honor and Yahweh will not have it. We will meet Zadok and Abiathar ready to tote the ark with David into exile (2 Sam. 15:24-29); their motives are fine but their theology fallacious (vv. 25-26). God's servants often mean well but lack the wisdom of God. In the present case a human plan (vv. 1-3) must be corrected by a divine revelation (vv. 4-17).

Our text testifies that the kingdom of God is never safe in human hands, no matter how godly those hands may be. Yahweh's finest servants are often deficient in properly discerning his will. This observation should keep us from deifying any of our Christian heroes and should expose our own need, leading us to cry out for the wisdom we lack (cf. Jas. 1:5), pleading to see beyond the way that seems right to lay hold of 'what is good, well-pleasing, and perfect' (Rom.12:2).

Yahweh's Humility (7:6-7)
The Lord begins to explain why David's house/temple plan must be tabled:

> For I have not dwelt [*yāšab*] in a house from the day I brought up the sons of Israel from Egypt to this day, but I have been travelling around in a tent and tabernacle. In all the places where I travelled around with all the sons of Israel, did I speak a word with one of the leaders of Israel whom I commanded to shepherd my people Israel – did I say, 'Why have you not built a house of cedar for me?' (vv. 6-7)

I cannot help sensing a certain playfulness in Yahweh's words here. In any case, he says that he had never lobbied Israel's previous leaders about building him a proper temple. He is contented as things stand (v.7). Yahweh's answer paints a vivid contrast: he has not 'dwelt' (*yāšab*, to sit, remain, dwell) in a house but has been 'travelling around' (Hithpa'el participle of *hālak*, here – walk around, back and forth) in a tent (the tent-shrine or 'tabernacle'). He means he has not 'settled' in a house because he has been 'on the go,' as we say. And why is that? Because, to date, his people Israel have been on the move (wandering in the wilderness and enduring the unsettled conditions of the judges' period; see vv. 10b-11a) and he has 'travelled' or 'wandered' with all the sons of Israel (v. 7). How can he settle down when they are unsettled?

Do you see what Yahweh is saying about himself? He is the God who travels with his people in all their topsy-turvy, here-and-there journeys and wanderings. Do his people live in tents? So does he. Are they a pilgrim people on their way to the land of promise? So he is the pilgrim God, sharing the rigors of the journey with them.

Perhaps we glimpse now why Yahweh wants no cedar temple yet. He must make a secure place for Israel first (v.10). He will not rest till he gives rest to his people (cf. Deut. 12:9-11)! Can you not see the astounding condescension of our God here? How can this revelation fail to overwhelm us and move us to adoring tears? 'I have been travelling around in a tent...with all the sons of Israel.'

Paul Boller has passed on a story about Sam Rayburn during

his tenure as Speaker of the House. The teenage daughter of a reporter Rayburn knew died suddenly. The next morning the reporter heard a rapping on his apartment door, opened it, and found Rayburn standing there. 'I just came by to see what I could do to help.' The reporter, stuttering and trying to recover from his surprise, indicated that he didn't think there was anything the Speaker could do – they were making all the arrangements. 'Well, have you all had your coffee this morning?' The reporter confessed they hadn't had time to do that yet. 'Well, I can at least make the coffee this morning.' Rayburn went in and made his way to the kitchen in search of coffee. While Rayburn was busy with coffee-making, the reporter remembered that Rayburn usually had a stated weekly appointment on this particular morning. So he half-inquired, 'Mr. Speaker, I thought you were supposed to be having breakfast at the White House this morning.' 'Well, I was,' Rayburn admitted, 'but I called the President and told him I had a friend who was in trouble, and I couldn't come.'[1]

That is only a pale glimpse of the condescension of the covenant God, the God who will not enjoy rest until he gives his people rest, the God who stoops down to share the hardships of his people, the God who is not ashamed to say he has been 'travelling around in a tent' with them. See how *close* he is to you! You may be forced to revise your theology if you think deity and humility are mutually exclusive categories. But if you've really paid attention to 2 Samuel 7:6-7 you are not surprised at Philippians 2:5-8. Indeed, you may almost have suspected as much.

Yahweh's Grace (7:8-11)

The first words of Nathan's revised-version counsel to David are introductory and explanatory (vv. 5-7). Now, however, Nathan is to declare the main substance of Yahweh's word to David, the very word Yahweh of hosts has spoken (v. 8a), and that word is grace (vv. 8b-11). In this section Yahweh rehearses his goodness to David in the past and promises his goodness to David and Israel in the future – and all apart from any temple-building on the king's part.

I will schematize the text so that we can follow its development and use it for reference in the following discussion.

---

1. Paul F. Boller, Jr., *Congressional Anecdotes* (New York: Oxford University, 1991), 261.

2 Samuel 7: 8-11

Experienced Grace, vv. 8-9b

Yahweh's choice, 8b	'I took you from the pasture, from following the flock, to be the leader over my people, over Israel'
Yahweh's presence, 9a	'And I was with you wherever you went'
Yahweh's power, 9b	'And I cut off all your enemies from before you'

Promised Grace, vv. 9c-11

To David, 9c	'And I shall make for you a great name, like the name of the great ones who are in the earth'
To Israel, 10-11a	'And I shall appoint a place for my people, for Israel, and I shall plant them, and they (he) shall dwell in his place, and they will no longer tremble with fear, and the sons of wickedness will not afflict them any more as before (that is, from the day that I appointed judges over my people Israel)'
To David, 11b[2]	'And I shall give you rest from all your enemies'
Climax, 11c	'And Yahweh declares to you that Yahweh will make a house for you'

Let us now develop what the text teaches about Yahweh's grace.

---

2. On the relation of the 'already' rest of verse 1 to the 'not yet' rest of verse 11, see Robert Polzin, *David and the Deuteronomist* (Bloomington: Indiana University, 1993), 78.

The Insistence on Grace

Yahweh, true to form (John 1:16), promises grace (vv. 9c-11) on top of grace (vv. 8-9b). This future grace, however, is not in response to David's building a house/temple for Yahweh, for Yahweh has rejected that plan for now. In fact, verse 11c is Yahweh's counter-punch to his question in 5b:

> Are *you* to build me a house for me to dwell in? (5b)
> And Yahweh declares to *you* that Yahweh will make a house for *you* (11c)[3]

David is not to be an active initiator but a passive recipient. And Yahweh obviously puts a spin on the term 'house' (Heb., *bayit*), which can mean a place with walls and a roof (in the case of a deity = temple) or a collection of people as a family or household (in the case of a king = dynasty). Yahweh graciously insists: Yahweh will be the Builder and the house will be David's, not *vice versa*.

However, there is some evidence that the *vice versa* was common in the Near East; that is, a king would build or restore a god's temple and *then* receive a promise regarding his reign or victories. Let me trot out some examples of this pattern.

The god Enlil chose Ur-Nammu (ca. 2100 B.C.) to be king of Sumer and kept Ur-Nammu's enemies under control so that the king could rebuild Enlil's temple. Ur-Nammu not only did this but also refurbished the palace of Mrs. Enlil (a k a Ninlil) for all of which Enlil 'decreed a great fate for Ur-Nammu, into distant days.'[4] The pattern is similar in the case of Yahdun-Lim, a 19th century B.C. king in Mari. His god Shamash had granted him substantial victories, after which Yahdun-Lim had erected a magnificent temple for Shamash. For this he wanted Shamash to give him ability to 'defeat the enemies, a long and happy rule and everlasting years of abundance and happiness.'[5]

---

3. See Walter C. Kaiser, Jr., *Toward an Old Testament Theology* (Grand Rapids: Zondervan, 1978), 150-51. Note the shift to third person at v. 11c. The preceding text has Yahweh speaking in the first person (I...I...) but at 11c Nathan abruptly shifts to the third person (he [Yahweh] declares). The grammatical change sets verse 11c somewhat off by itself.

4. James B. Pritchard, ed., *Ancient Near Eastern Texts,* 3rd ed. with Supplement (Princeton: Princeton University, 1969), 583-84 (translated by S. N. Kramer). Hereafter = ANET.

5. ANET, 556.

In Egypt the victory hymn of Thut-mose III (ca. 1490-1436 B.C.) records the words of Amon-Re, who rehearses all the victories he has granted Thut-mose, acknowledges that Thut-mose has 'erected my dwellingplace' and out-stripped other kings in building his monuments, and then declares: 'I have established thee upon the throne of Horus for millions of years, that thou mightest lead the living for eternity.'[6] Amen-hotep III (ca. 1413-1377 B.C.) details his lavish building enterprises on behalf of Amon-Re. Amon-Re responds with a hymn of gratitude to Amen-hotep in which he promises the subjugation of the king's enemies on every side.[7]

In the first millennium B.C. Esarhaddon of Assyria (680-669 B.C.) rebuilt the temple of Asshur which had fallen into decay. He did this 'for length of days, for the stability of my reign, for the welfare of my posterity, for the safety of my priestly throne, for the overthrow of my enemies, for the success of the harvest(s) of Assyria, for the welfare of Assyria.'[8] No doubt about what he expected from Asshur in return for this big favour.

These examples from pagan materials come from various dates and locales and I do not want to impute something to them which they do not contain. Yet it seems to me that the mind-set they reflect is light years removed from that of 2 Samuel 7. One might summarize as follows:

Pagan Materials	2 Samuel 7
Previous favor from god	Previous favor from Yahweh
Temple-building by king	Future favor from Yahweh
Future favors from god	Temple-building by king
(in response to temple-building)	(delayed to later time)

In 2 Samuel 7 Yahweh will not permit David to build a temple-house for him (v.5) but insists on building a dynasty-house for David (v.11). Not that the temple doesn't matter; but it can wait a

---

6. ANET, 373-75

7. ANET, 375-76

8. Henri Frankfort, *Kingship and the Gods* (Chicago: University of Chicago, 1948/1978), 267. Frankfort is citing Luckenbill's translation. Nabonidus (556-539 B.C.), the neo-Babylonian maverick, claimed that the moon god Sin called him to kingship and appeared to him in a dream with a command and a promise: 'Rebuild speedily Ehulhul, the temple of Sin in Harran, and I will hand over to you all the countries' (ANET, 562).

few years down the time-line (v.13). Is it Yahweh's agenda here to underscore grace in order to show he is nothing like the pagan gods? Yahweh's king does not place a claim on Yahweh's favor by building him a lavish temple. Instead Yahweh, the giving God, reviews past grace, lavishes more grace – and puts a temple on the back burner. You would never catch Shamash, Sin, or Asshur doing that. But then they are not the God of all grace.[9]

The Preoccupation of Grace

I want to refer you again to the layout of verses 8-11 given above. Note that in the section labeled 'promised grace' there are two brief promises 'to David' (vv. 9c,11b), and note that the grace promised to Israel (vv. 10-11a) is sandwiched between those promises to David. That structure is revealing; it tells us that Israel's security is at the center of Yahweh's concern. Yahweh will make David secure (vv. 9c, 11b) because he wants to make Israel secure (vv. 10-11a); *he establishes the Davidic dynasty for the sake of his people.* David will not be exalted for his own sake but for the good of Israel. David's kingship is to be the instrument by which Yahweh's exodus redemption reaches its goal, that is, to 'plant' (v. 10a; see Exod. 15:17) Israel safely in the land he gave them. Yahweh intends David's kingship to inaugurate a new era; he means to end the terror, trembling, and turmoil of the judges' years (vv. 10b-11a). Yahweh wants his people to have a home and to enjoy it in safety.[10]

Living in post-David time we know that the Davidic kings by and large miserably failed to promote a secure place for Israel and/ or Judah. The people were, in time, carted off to Babylon and exile. Yet Yahweh never cancels his program. He fills his promises of a future and a hope (Jer. 29:11) with assurances that his people will 'dwell securely' and that 'no one shall make them afraid' (Jer. 23:6; 32:37; 33:16; Ezek. 28:26; 34:25, 27, 28; Hos. 2:18; Mic. 4:4; Zeph. 3:13; Zech. 14:11). God seems possessed over the safety of his people.

---

9. This point is no academic trifle. I did not know the joy of the Lord until, as a high school sophomore, I came to see his 'grace-shuss' character.

10. My view assumes that 'place' in verse 10 means a secure home for Israel. McCarter (*II Samuel*, The Anchor Bible, 202-3) argues that it refers to a 'place of worship' or sanctuary. Against McCarter, see the fine argument by D.F. Murray, 'MQWM and the Future of Israel in 2 Samuel VII 10,' *Vetus Testamentum* 40 (1990): 298-320.

We have recently suffered an outbreak of (good clean) graffiti on the walls of one of our faculty rest-rooms. Not that we write on the walls but on paper, which we then tape to the walls. Several of us in the Biblical Division are the culprits. One of these colleagues, however, has confessed to me that when one of us posts a fresh piece of nonsense he cannot keep himself from thinking out and formulating a 'response' to it. His mind cannot rest until he has composed and crafted more humor for our cubicle.

Yahweh our God seems to have that kind of preoccupation for the security of his people. Both in 2 Samuel 7 (where he exalts the king especially as a shield for his people) and the rest of Scripture (cf. texts cited above) God never abandons his passion to establish a safe home for his people – at least not until he brings them into a city so safe that gates can be left wide open (Rev. 21:25).

Yahweh's Constancy (7:12-16)

Now we have come to the heart and soul of the Davidic covenant, Yahweh's promise to David. Reams have been written on these verses; we can only give them paragraphs. In one sense, I would prefer to do even less and underscore but one word. I wish I could bring a stamp from the print shop, one with bold, block letters, containing just that one word, press it on a pad saturated with bright red ink, take your Bible from you, and over the print of verses 12-16 stamp: INDEFECTIBLE. That is the primary mark of Yahweh's promise – it will endure any and all casualties that might threaten it. As Yahweh states the promise he seems to be staring down every adversary. Hence, Yahweh's promise to David is indefectible because:

> Death does not annul it, vv. 12-13
> Sin cannot destroy it, vv. 14-15
> Time will not exhaust it, v. 16

We consider each of these briefly.

First, the promise will not be negated by David's death.

> When your days reach their limit and you shall lie down with your fathers, I shall raise up your seed after you – that comes out of your body, and I shall establish his kingship. *He* will build a house for my name, and I shall establish the throne of his kingship forever (vv. 12-13).

David may 'lie down' in death but Yahweh will 'raise up' David's seed. As Yahweh promised Abraham's seed the land (Gen. 12:6-7), so he promises David's seed the kingship. David's seed refers both to any individual descendant (the 'he' who will build Yahweh's house, i.e., Solomon, as we discover) and to an ongoing line (dynasty) of kings who will rule.

Nor, secondly, can sin destroy this promise:

> I will be a father to him, and he will be a son to me, so that when he commits iniquity [or: does wrong] I shall punish him with the rod of men and with blows from the sons of men; but my covenant love I will never take away from him as I took it away from Saul, whom I took away from before you (vv. 14-15).

'When he commits iniquity....' Yahweh is a head-on realist. Whenever a reigning Davidic king commits iniquity, he will find that having Yahweh for his father is not all warmth and intimacy but discipline and punishment. However, Yahweh inserts a limit. Three times in verse 15 we find a form of the verb *sûr*, to remove, take away. With this verb Yahweh as it were builds a bottom in the bottomless pit, for if the promise depended on human fidelity it would be doomed from the start. He will certainly chasten and punish Davidic kings who go astray, but that judgment will never go so far as to involve a total removal of his *ḥesed*, his covenant love. Yahweh is going to be dealing with sinful kings but he will not allow sin to have dominion over his dominion! Iniquity will not dissolve *ḥesed*. David's line will never meet Saul's end. The idea seems to be that any individual Davidic king may meet disaster because of his infidelity, but that will not overthrow the promised endurance of the Davidic dynasty. To steal the 'house' analogy: sin can bring disaster on any current 'resident' but cannot demolish the 'house' (dynasty).[11]

Thirdly, the ravages of time will never wear out this promise:

> And our house and your kingship shall be made firm forever before me; your throne will remain established forever (v.16).

Three times (twice here in v. 16, once in v. 13) in this promise section we find the phrase (*'ad 'ôlām*), of which 'forever' is a fair

---

11. On this see Kaiser, *Toward an Old Testament Theology,* 156-57.

rendering.[12] James Oscar Boyd, though writing a polemic against negative biblical critics, nicely captured the thrill of this '*ôlām*/ forever note:

> Do critics who assert that ver. 13 contains nothing save what was in ver.12 realize that this is the first time that David's ear caught the music of those wonderful words which are repeated twice in ver. 16 as the climax of the whole oracle, and which are echoed and re-echoed in David's prayer, and thereafter in poets' psalms and prophets' visions down the centuries, until at last in the 'Hallelujah Chorus' of the Apocalypse they break in waves of glory, 'And he shall reign for ever and ever, for ever and ever, Hallelujah! Hallelujah!' Here – here in this wretchedly misunderstood and maltreated verse 13 of 2 Sam. vii – we hear for the first time the determination of Almighty God, that as long as He shall have a human people for His own possession (and that too is 'for ever', see ver. 24), so long shall the seed of David be the covenanted bearer of a divinely conferred and divinely maintained sovereignty over it.[13]

Yahweh's promise to David then would never simply play out, exhausted by passage of time.

Much more could be said, should be said; but I want you to hear the keynote, not every conceivable note. And the text says: let death, sin, and time do what they will, they will never frustrate Yahweh's kingdom plan through David's dynasty-house. I want you to sense the note of *inevitability* in the promise.

The tone of this text reminds me of a story about Aeneas Sage,

---

12. See further the brief but useful discussion in Merrill F. Unger and William White, Jr., eds., *Nelson's Expository Dictionary of the Old Testament* (Nashville: Thomas Nelson, 1980), 117-118; also TWOT, 2:672-73.

13. James Oscar Boyd, 'The Davidic Covenant: The Oracle,' *The Princeton Theological Review* 25 (1927): 430. Even the span of David's dynasty from David to the fall of Jerusalem (587 B.C.) was remarkable. Palmer Robertson has noted: 'From David's accession somewhere around 1000 B.C. to the fall of Jerusalem, over 400 years had transpired. The average dynasty in Egypt and Mesopotamia during their days of greatest stability was something less than 100 years. David's successors even outlasted the long-lived eighteenth dynasty of Egypt, which endured for about 250 years' (*The Christ of the Covenants* [Phillipsburg, NJ: Presbyterian and Reformed, 1980], 239). However, even though the Davidic kings no longer reign after the fall of Jerusalem, the Davidic line continued (Matt. 1:12-16) until it surfaced in 'Jesus who is called Messiah.' You can smash Jerusalem and cart exiles to Babylon but you can't break God's 'forever'.

an eighteenth-century minister in the Scottish Highlands. Mr Sage, a powerfully built man of the cloth, announced one Sabbath his intention to hold a meeting for catechizing the people in the house of a certain laird well-known for his evil living. When Mr. Sage arrived at the laird's door, the latter asked why he came. Sage replied, 'I come to discharge my duty to God, to your conscience and to my own'; which the laird met with, 'I care nothing for any of the three; out of my house, or I'll turn you out.' The minister simply responded, 'If you can.' There followed a sort of catechism preparatory meeting with the laird, said to be a very powerful man. Yet when the interchange was over the laird was lying on the floor with a rope around his hands and feet. Since the laird 'was now bound over to keep the peace', as Mr. Sage put it, the minister called in the people of the area and taught them the Shorter Catechism, no one – of course – refusing![14]

Now our text has that Aeneas Sage tone about it: I am going to hold a catechism meeting in your house and there is nothing you can do to stop it. Yahweh's kingdom plan through David's dynasty is simply unstoppable; he will overwhelm death, sin, and time if need be to bring it about. And he has. The years wore on; everything from foolish failures to blatant wickedness marked the reigns of the Davidic kings; Israel is swept into exile and remains in subjugation to foreign powers. But a child, a Davidic child, is born, a Son is given. In him is no sin. He trampled all over death and has begun his endless reign at the place of supreme power and authority in the universe (called in the Bible 'the right hand of God', Eph. 1:20-23). Nothing more remains to be done but display to the world what is already the case, as it were, behind the 'seens'. Yahweh's kingdom is unstoppable. And if the big Davidic promise is so sure, can't Yahweh's people trust all his smaller ones?

You may want to recap this chapter – Yahweh's wisdom, Yahweh's humility, Yahweh's grace, Yahweh's constancy. Do you get the picture? When you look at Scripture you look for how it reveals *God.* It is in getting to know the covenant God that we will find our needs most adequately met.

---

14. John Watson, *The Scot of the Eighteenth Century* (New York: A.C. Armstrong and Son, n.d.), 192. The laird, by the way, became a decided Christian – Who cares under what compulsion?

9. Sit Down and Stand on God's Promise
2 Samuel 7:18-29

Perhaps you occasionally find yourself sitting second in line at a traffic light. The light is red. It changes. The vehicle in front of you remains unmoved. This, however, causes you little concern since from long experience you have discovered many motorists are not as poised to go at the crack of green as you are. With some it takes a long three seconds for the sight of color to enter their cranial transmission center, dash over the prescribed circuits, and reach feet that release brakes and tramp accelerator. But should the lapse last six or seven seconds, you become worried – even agitated. You rue blowing your horn lest you be thought impatient but love for fellow motorists behind you compels you so to stir the slumbering. It is absurd to be unmoved by a green light.

Or by God's revelation. Our Lord does not declare his promises and plans to us, his agenda for the security of his people, so that we can allow it all to sit in cold print. Rather we must welcome his words, revel in his plans, delight in his promises, exulting in their Maker and pleading for their fulfillment. David knew this. There was no way he could remain unmoved by Yahweh's plans in verses 5-16. So he 'went in and sat before Yahweh' (v. 18), perhaps somewhere near the ark-shrine, in happy frustration groping for words to express his astonished praise (vv. 18b-24) and urgently pleading with Yahweh to fulfill his Nathan-sent word (vv. 25-29). Yahweh's declarations stirred David's devotions; his promises ignited David's praises and prayers. That's how it should be.

Our passage breaks down into two main sections:

Responding in praise: marveling at the grace of God, vv. 18-24
Responding in petition: praying for the word of God, vv. 25-29

However, since verses 23-24 in the first section are somewhat distinct, we will divide our exposition into three segments.

Marveling at Yahweh's Plan (7:18-22)
David's prayer does not begin with petition but with wonder, not with supplication but with surprise. He is breathless over Yahweh's grace and opens his prayer by staggering under it. No one can dissect ecstasy or rapture, but perhaps we can capture the keynotes of David's joy.

First, David marvels over *previous grace:* 'Who am I, Lord
Yahweh, and what is my house that you have brought me to this
point?' (v. 18b). Gratitude can never forget – nor explain – the
past. How can David fathom why Yahweh's plan ever centered
upon him? And there is no answer except: '*I* took you from the
pasture, from following the sheep' (v. 8). But David not only praises
the mystery of Yahweh's choice but the miracle of his preservation:
'Who am I... that *you have brought me to this point*?' Bethlehem
(1 Sam. 16:1-13) was only six miles from Jerusalem (2 Sam. 5:1-
10) but for David that distance meant twenty-one chapters (and
over ten years) of danger, escapes, treachery, folly, despair, and
slander. Yet here he was. Amazing: Yahweh had brought him 'to
this point' (cf. vv. 8-9a).

David goes on to marvel over *promised grace,* future grace:

> Yet, to you, Lord Yahweh, this seemed too little, and now you extend
> your promises for your servant's family into the distant future. Such
> is human destiny, Lord Yahweh (v. 19, NJB).

As if preserving David – as Calvin would say – from a thousand
deaths was altogether too trivial, Yahweh had committed himself
to a forever-promise regarding David's dynasty. But David seems
especially excited over the role his house will play in all human
history: 'Such is human destiny,' as the NJB renders it.

We need to spend some time with that last clause of verse 19b.
The reader can find a confusing cafeteria of renderings among
English versions. For example:

> And this is the custom of man (NASB)
> Is this your usual way of dealing with men? (NIV)
> Is this the manner of man? (NJKV)
> And hast shown me future generations (RSV, 'correcting' the text)
> May this be instruction for the people (NRSV)
> Such... is the lot of a man embarked on a high career (NEB,
> correcting in line with 1 Chron. 17:17)

A literal translation of the Hebrew text (*wĕzō't tôrat hā'ādām*)
would be: 'And this the torah of man.' Concise, abrupt, puzzling.
Several considerations. First, I question that this is a question as in
NIV and NKJV. Given David's wonder and awe the question form

would be appropriate. But there is no distinct grammatical sign that the clause is interrogative, so taking it as an interjection or exclamation is preferable. Secondly, 'torah' is the Hebrew word frequently translated 'law', but the legal connotation is often too restrictive. Torah means instruction, teaching, direction, almost always from God. Torah deals with content not manner, with the what not the how; hence the 'custom, way, manner' of NASB, NIV, and NKJV are not likely correct. When David says, 'This (is) the torah,' his 'this' refers back to Yahweh's promise about his dynasty in, say, verses 12-16. That word is the torah – the divine prescription or directive. Third, this is the 'torah of man'. If 'torah' here refers to God's directive about David's dynasty, then this phrase cannot mean that man is the source of this torah. It must therefore mean man is the beneficiary. Hence, it is the 'torah of man', and 'man' means, as often, 'mankind', or simply, humanity. NJB's 'Such is human destiny' comes pretty close.

We must forgive David his goosebumps. He seems to see that the kingship Yahweh guaranteed his dynasty would not only bring rest to Israel (vv. 10-11a) but would extend Yahweh's sway and benefits to all humanity – as if the Davidic dynasty were to be the mechanism for fulfilling the Abrahamic promise of blessing to 'all the families of the earth' (Gen. 12:3). Walter Kaiser, who translates (*tôrat hā'ādām*) 'the Charter for Humanity,' sums it up well:

> We call this *torah* a 'charter' because it is the plan and prescription for God's kingdom whereby the whole world shall be blessed.... It is a grant conferring powers, rights, and privileges to David and his seed for the benefit of all mankind.[1]

Finally, David marvels over *sovereign grace* (vv. 20-21). I do not think the verb 'know' (Heb., *yāda'*) in verse 20 should be

---

1. Walter C. Kaiser, Jr., 'The Blessing of David: The Charter for Humanity,' in *The Law and the Prophets: Old Testament Studies Prepared in Honor of Oswald Thompson Allis,* ed. John H. Skilton (n.p. : Presbyterian and Reformed, 1974), 314. My discussion relies heavily on Kaiser's article, especially pp. 310-315. For a similar view, see Karl Gutbrod, *Das Buch vom Reich,* Die Botschaft des Alten Testaments, 2nd ed. (Stuttgart: Calwer, 1973), 97, 112-13. Cf. Claus Schedl (*History of the Old Testament,* 5 vols. [Staten Island: Alba House, 1972], 204), who, citing H. Cazelles, notes that *tôrat hā'ādām* is related to the Akkadian *terît niše,* the oracle by which human fate is determined.

construed as merely an appeal to Yahweh's omniscience ('You know your servant') but should be translated as an English past tense, 'Now *you* [emphatic] have known your servant, with 'know' understood in the sense of 'choose, select,' which it has in such contexts.[2] Anderson is on target with 'You yourself have singled your servant out, Lord Yahweh.'[3] David goes on to add, 'On account of your word and *according to your will* [lit., heart] you have done all this greatness' (v. 21, emphasis mine). Yahweh's kingdom plan arises solely out of Yahweh's choice and desire, not from any human ingenuity, least of all David's.[4]

So David begins his prayer by marveling at Yahweh's gracious plan. And my pile of words explaining David's wonder may snuff the wonder out of it. Go back to the text then: David is nearly incredulous that Yahweh preserved him 'to this point'; that he has made hard promises about his dynasty, that it will endure the treacheries of history and embrace the whole of humanity; and Yahweh has done it simply because he wanted to do it. Yahweh has taken his breath away. What can David say? Don't you hear the sense of helplessness in David's praise ('What more can David say to you?,' v. 20a), the happy frustration he feels? Yahweh's massive grace in deed (v. 18), word (v.19), and desire (vv. 20-21) has doomed David's worship to inadequacy. What can he do but begin with 'Who am I?' (v.18) and end with 'There is no God beside you!' (v. 22)? The perfect combination of frustration and fidelity. *God* has impressed him.

Walter Kaiser tells how Louis XIV requested that at his funeral in the cathedral of Notre Dame all would be darkened – except for

---

2. See, e.g., Gen. 18:19; Amos 3:2; and TDOT, 5:468.

3. A.A. Anderson, *2 Samuel,* Word Biblical Commentary (Dallas: Word, 1989). 124.

4. Though the root of Yahweh's plan rests in his will, verse 21a indicates that part of its rationale is to remain faithful to previous promises: 'For the sake of /on account of your word...you have done all this greatness.' Keil takes 'your word' as 'an allusion to the earlier promises of God, or the Messianic prophecies generally, particularly the one concerning Judah in Jacob's blessing' (Gen. xlix.10), and the one relating to the ruler out of Jacob in Balaam's sayings (Num. xxiv.17 sqq.), which contain the germs of the promise of the everlasting continuance of David's government' (C.F. Keil, *Biblical Commentary on the Books of Samuel* [1875; reprint ed., Grand Rapids: Eerdmans, 1950], 351).

one candle burning on his casket at the front. However, when the court preacher Masillon rose to give the funeral oration, he strode over to the casket, snuffed out the light, and began his message with 'Only God is great! Only God is great!'[5] But David didn't need a funeral to make the point. He simply reviewed Yahweh's grace and went away muttering, 'Only God is great' (cf. v. 22). Seeing grace always leads to that doxology.

Considering Yahweh's People (7:23-24)

David's praise takes a different focus (Israel) in these verses but not a different burden. He describes Israel as a nation without peer but for David this only reflects Israel's peerless God. David is still held in happy fetters of praise; however, since his praise meditates on Yahweh's people, we must hear how he describes them.

Note the text:[6]

23. And who is like your people, like Israel,
    a unique nation in the earth,
    whom God went to redeem for himself as a people,
    and to make a reputation for himself,
    and to do for them grand and fearful deeds,
    by your causing nations – and their gods – to flee from before your
       people,
    whom you have redeemed for yourself from Egypt?

24. So you established for yourself your people Israel
    as your very own people forever,
    and *you*, Yahweh, have proven to be their God.

David knows that Israel is unique because she is a *redeemed* people. This is the clear note amid the grammatical obscurities in verse 23. Israel is the people whom 'you have redeemed for yourself from Egypt'. This one clause contains both poles of redemption: redeemed from and redeemed for (or, to). When Yahweh redeemed

---

5. Walter C. Kaiser, Jr., *Micah-Malachi,* The Communicator's Commentary (Dallas: Word, 1992), 192.
6. Verse 23 is clear enough in most translations, but since it bristles with grammatical riddles and textual problems I have provided this working translation as reference for this exposition. Those wanting to track down the problems and check out sane solutions can see J.P. Fokkelman, *Narrative Art and Poetry in the Books of Samuel,* vol. 3, *Throne and City (II Sam. 2-8 & 21-24)* (Assen/Maastricht: Van Gorcum, 1990), 244-47, 382-83.

Israel he liberated them from bondage (Egypt) in order that they might belong to a new Master. Biblical redemption always involves both elements: liberation and possession. Yahweh revealed his power in smashing Egypt's chains but revealed his purpose in binding Israel to himself. If anything it is the latter aspect that our text stresses, for David's first words about Israel are 'whom God went to redeem for himself as a people'. We might say that Yahweh grants his people freedom but not independence; they are to belong to him. Changing testaments changes nothing, for if we have been ransomed out of our 'empty way of life' by Christ's costly blood (1 Pet. 1: 18-19) we are not our own, precisely because we have been bought with a price (1 Cor. 6:19b-20a).

Yet this redeemed people is also a *preserved* people: 'So you established for yourself your people Israel as your very own people forever' (v. 24a). There are two code words in this statement that blink in neon. One is the verb 'established' (a form of the Hebrew *kûn*), which is used three times in verses 12-16 when Yahweh promises he will 'establish' the kingdom/throne of David and his descendants. The second eye-catcher is the term 'forever' (*'ad 'ôlām*), which Yahweh also uses three times (vv. 13,16) to affirm the unlimited duration of David's dynasty.[7] So David recognizes that Israel is as permanent as his dynasty, not because they are so durable but because Yahweh intends to keep them. All this does not surprise us. We've read Leviticus 26:44-45 and Deuteronomy 30:1-6 before. Where did we ever get the idea that the Sinai Covenant was somehow defectible? Yahweh's people and David's dynasty are sure things, God's forever-entities.[8]

---

7. On the meaning of *'ad ôlam* and *lĕ 'ôlām* in 2 Sam. 7, see T.E. McComiskey, *The Covenants of Promise* (Grand Rapids: Baker, 1985), 23-24. These terms occur a total of eight times in 2 Sam. 7 (vv. 13,16 [twice], 24,25,26,29 [twice]).

8. In the previous chapter I linked David's dynasty to Yahweh's provision for Israel (vv. 10-11a), and in this chapter to Yahweh's program for Abraham – to bless all the families of the earth through him (see on v. 19b). The Davidic covenant then is to be the mechanism or means by which Yahweh fulfills both the Abrahamic and Sinaitic covenants. Readers should understand that the point just made about Israel as preserved in no way implies every Israelite would be or was a faithful disciple of Yahweh. Just as a king of David's line could by his iniquity forfeit the benefits of the Davidic covenant (2 Sam. 7:14), so any individual Israelite by unbelief placed him/herself outside the circle of covenant blessings. Yet Yahweh always insisted on preserving a faithful people, even if only a remnant (1 Kings 19:18).

We walk into the New Testament and breathe the same air. It is as if the Lord of the covenant knows his people live amid 'fightings and fears, within, without'. One easily thinks of Jesus' assurance to his flock/sheep in John 10. There is debate about the text of verse 29 in that chapter; I think the best rendering is: 'What my Father has given me is greater than all, and *no one* is able to snatch (them) out of the Father's hand.'[9] On this view Jesus is not saying here that the Father is greater than all but that 'the flock that the Father has given the Son is greater in his eyes than anything else on earth' and that since 'he thus attaches the highest value to it he will look after it to the end'.[10] It seems as though the covenant Lord never tires of reassuring his people, and we, with 'many a conflict, many a doubt', never tire of hearing the Shepherd's voice on that score – whether in 2 Samuel 7 or John 10.

Finally, David declares that this redeemed and preserved people is, above all, a *privileged* people (v. 24b). 'And you, Yahweh, have become their God' (or: proven to be their God). These familiar sounding words are part of the Old Testament covenant formula (see, e.g., Gen. 17:7, Exod. 6:7, Lev. 26:12), which seems to reflect a marriage contract formula.[11] Note, for example, Exodus 6:7, where Yahweh promises: 'And I shall take you for my own people and I shall be your God.' The verbs 'take' (*lāqah*, as in taking a wife) and to 'be someone's' (*hāyāh + lĕ*) are used of securing and belonging to a marriage partner.[12] Israel is the people who have Yahweh as their God! He redeems from bondage and keeps through history, but that is not enough for Yahweh. He gives *himself* to Israel, to belong to them, to be their God.

Here are Yahweh's people – redeemed, preserved, privileged. This is not out of place in the praise section of David's prayer but

---

9. Emphasis in Greek. For discussion on the text, see Bruce M Metzger, *A Textual Commentary on the Greek New Testament* (London: United Bible Societies, 1971), 232.

10. Leon Morris, *The Gospel According to John*, The New International Commentary on the New Testament, rev. ed. (Grand Rapids: Eerdmans, 1995), 464. Cf. Morris also on the textual variants. Note that Jesus' flock, according to John 10:16, consists of Jewish-Gentile sheep!

11. Moshe Weinfield, 'Berith – Covenant vs. Obligation,' *Biblica* 56 (1975): 125.

12. Nahum M. Sarna, *Exodus*, The JPS Torah Commentary (Philadelphia: Jewish Publication Society, 1991), 32, 242.

is part of the fuel that ignites praise. David cannot look at the flock without praising the Shepherd. That's as it should be.

John Stott tells of the retirement ceremony for the Rev. Paul Gibson as Principal of Ridley Hall, Cambridge. Someone had painted his portrait and the portrait was unveiled at this occasion. In his remarks Mr. Gibson expressed a gracious and well-deserved tribute to the artist. He said that in the future people looking at the portrait would not ask 'Who is that man?' but 'Who painted that portrait?'[13] So David leads us to ask not 'Who are these subjects?' but 'Who is their King?', not 'Who are these sheep?' but 'Who gathered them?' That's as it should be.

Praying Yahweh's Promises (7: 25-29)

Now David's prayer moves from praise to petition; he asks that astounding promises be converted into historical reality. But Yahweh's promise is the whole starting point and basis of David's petition. Note how he begins:

> And now, O Yahweh God,
> the word which you have spoken
> about your servant and about his house –
> cause it to stand forever (v. 25a).

The translation is woodenly literal in order to show what David puts right up front: 'the word which you have spoken.' David refers, of course, to the promise of verses 12-16. That is the foundation. On the basis of that he prays, 'And now… cause it to stand forever.'

Let us stick with the major lesson David teaches here: prayer pleads promises.[14] Or, in David's own words, 'Do as you have promised' (v. 25b). There is a whole theology of prayer in that statement. It is the heart of verses 25-29.

Observe how all David's petitions here are grounded in Yahweh's promise:

---

13. John R. W. Stott, *God's New Society: The Message of Ephesians*, The Bible Speaks Today (Downers Grove: InterVarsity, 1979), 82.

14. This is the way Alec Motyer puts it in his exposition of Psalm 89: 'The question which the Psalm poses is this: What is to be done when the promises of God are denied by the facts of experience? It answers: Turn the promises into prayers and plead them before God' ('The Psalms,' *The New Bible Commentary: Revised* [Grand Rapids: Eerdmans, 1970], 506).

(1) In v. 25a 'cause it to stand forever' refers back to 'the word which you have spoken'.

(2) In v. 27b David ventures to offer his petitions because (note the logic of the 'therefore' at mid-verse) Yahweh made this revelation to David about building David's dynasty.

(3) A careful reading of vv. 28-29 shows that the petition of 29a ('And now be pleased and bless the house of your servant to continue forever before you') is based both on v. 28 ('you have promised to your servant this goodness') and on v. 29b ('For *you*, Lord Yahweh, have spoken...').

Here then is still the major task for prayer today: to take God's promises and pray he will bring them to pass. We must, of course, be certain any promise is a promise that rightly applies to us. Certainly David's promise does. For this is the promise we ask God to fulfill every time we pray that God's name will be held sacred throughout the earth (see v. 26; cf. Ezek. 36:20-23), when we ask for God's kingdom to come and his will to be done on earth. The final King of David's dynasty has come, yet his kingship must yet be fully, publicly, and universally displayed. But since the promises are reliable (v. 28a: 'And now, Lord Yahweh, you are the One who is God, and your words will prove true') the petition is sure to be granted.

'Do as you have promised.' That is at the heart of our praying. Yahweh's promise gives prayer its passion, boldness, and confidence. David knew that. That's why he sat down (v. 18a) and stood on the promises of God.

10. The Coming of the Kingdom
2 Samuel 8

It seems terribly primitive. I have it at home. I don't use it; but it still works. It is my father's Remington Portable typewriter, circa 1920. I obviously prefer my current electric model with automatic correction – on which my colleagues and students (who have been computerized and word processorized for at least a decade) look with arrogant disdain, considering it and me hopelessly antiquarian. Nevertheless, even the untrained eye can see a clear resemblance, a certain continuity, between the old Remington Portable and the contemporary computer keyboard.

Now 2 Samuel 8 may be something like that old Remington Portable to us. We have more redemptive history and biblical revelation before us than the writer of 2 Samuel had. We are privileged to live in the wake of the crucifixion, resurrection, ascension, and enthronement of David's Descendant Jesus, who both brought (e.g., Luke 17:20-21, NRSV) and will bring (Luke 17:22-37) his kingly rule. We must, however, discipline ourselves not to despise older kingdom revelation, for there is a clear continuity between the kingdom teaching of, e.g., 2 Samuel 8 and later kingdom doctrine. All the essentials are the same. Second Samuel 8 asserts that God's kingdom did come on earth under David's kingship, that the promise in 2 Samuel 7 did receive a real (though not final) fulfillment even in David's own time. Hence 2 Samuel 8 is a historical record of how Yahweh's kingdom was established under David. But the kingdom teaching of 2 Samuel 8 transcends the immediate historical situation – it describes what will always be true when God's kingdom is present and when it comes in its final form. So 2 Samuel 8 is both report and preview, both history and prophecy.

The following summary will show the breakdown of the chapter at a glance:

vv. 1-6	Four victories + 'Yahweh saved' formula
vv. 7-12	Spoil/gifts for the Lord
vv. 13-14	Victory over Edom + 'Yahweh saved' formula
vv. 15-18	Summary

Note that the summary in verses 15-18 (David's government appointments) is the tailpiece for all of 1 Samuel 15–2 Samuel 8. See the Introduction for discussion. Now to the exposition.

The Conflict and Conquests of the Kingdom (8:1-6, 13-14)

Let us look at the two victory sections (vv. 1-6, 13-14) first as the conflict and conquests of the kingdom. The key word in these verses is (nākāh), to smite or strike down; it occurs five times (vv. 1, 2, 3, 5, 13; it also appears in vv. 9 and 10). We have then a rapid report of David's victories: he struck down the Philistines (v. 1), Moab (v. 2), Hadadezer of Zobah (vv. 3-4), Aram-Damascus (v. 5), and Edom (vv. 13-14). These verses harbor a small army of problems and questions for us, [1] but no army could withstand David. The text is clear about the main point. David's rule extended from the far north (vv. 3-4) to the deep south (vv. 13-14).[2] For approximate location of these enemies/opponents see the schematic.

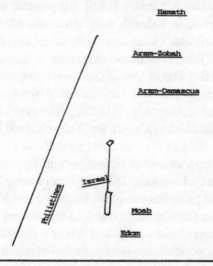

1. For example: (1) Is Metheg Ammah (v.1) a place name (NIV) or a descriptive phrase, 'bridle of the mother-city' i.e., 'control of the chief city' (NASB)? (2) Why is David so severe in his treatment of Moab (v.2) when Moab had previously given asylum to David's parents (1 Sam. 22:3-4)? No data; don't know. (3) It may be that the '1,700 horsemen/charioteers' of v.4 should read '1,000 chariots and 7,000 horsemen/charioteers' as LXX and the parallel in 1 Chron. 18:4. (4) Why do we read of Joab and David fighting the Syrians and Hadadezer in 2 Samuel 10 if they were subjugated here in chapter 8? Chronologically, the episodes in 2 Samuel 10 preceded these in chapter 8; cf. C.F. Keil, *Biblical Commentary on the Books of Samuel* (1875; reprint ed., Grand Rapids: Eerdmans, 1950), 358-59, and John Bright, *A History of Israel,* 3rd ed. (Philadelphia: Westminster, 1981), 202-203. (5) Did David defeat Aram (Syrians, NASB) or Edom in v. 13? Probably Edom. The received Hebrew text has 'Aram,' but a few Hebrew manuscripts and LXX have 'Edom,' which fits better geographically (the 'Valley of Salt' was south of the Dead Sea). Aram and Edom are very similar in Hebrew script and are easily confused.

2. J.P. Fokkelman, *Narrative Art and Poetry in the Books of Samuel,* vol. 3, *Throne and City (II Sam. 2-8 & 21-24)* (Assen/Maastricht: Van Gorcum, 1990), 259.

We are apt to regard these conflicts as mere episodes of 'trouble in the Middle East', as disputes of petty states fighting to control trade routes and wear the territorial pants. But the Bible view is different. David is not one more candidate for prima-donna-at-large. David and his seed have been granted kingship for the security and welfare of Israel (and, ultimately, of mankind); Yahweh has promised him rest from all his enemies (all this from 2 Sam. 7). Now in 2 Samuel 8 Yahweh fulfills his promise to David.[3] Since David, however, is Yahweh's chosen, authorised king, David's kingdom is Yahweh's kingdom in (we might say) its introductory, visible form. Wherever David reigns, there the kingdom of God holds sway. But David's neighbors were not men of good will longing for his jurisdiction; David must 'strike down' his enemies to establish his kingship. All this, however, is not David's achievement but Yahweh's gift, for 'Yahweh saved David wherever he went' (vv. 6,14).[4]

David's kingdom is not a perfect but a preliminary and principial form of Christ's kingdom. The kingdom pattern, however, is the same: conflict precedes conquest. Both Old and New Testaments testify that, on the whole, men and nations do not long to receive but live to resist Christ's reign and that he will establish his rule at the last not by popular demand but by armed might (see, e.g., Ps.2; Isa. 11:3b-5; Joel 3:9-17; Zech. 14: 1-5, 12-15; 2 Thess. 1: 7b-8, 2:8-10). The church tends to mute this virile biblical note and thereby emasculates the doctrine of the kingdom. Sometimes this bland sentimentality has become canonized in our hymns, e.g.,

> For not with swords' loud clashing,
>   Nor roll of stirring drums,
> With deeds of love and mercy
>   The heavenly kingdom comes.[5]

There is a tad of truth in this but a great deal of distortion, as if should people only be nice enough the kingdom would arrive. But

3. The victories over Moab and Edom may also be taken as a fulfillment of Num. 24:17-19.

4. For a plausible historical reconstruction of the events and wars of 2 Sam. 8 and 10, see Eugene H. Merrill, *Kingdom of Priests* (Grand Rapids: Baker, 1987), 255-60. He notes a possible alliance of Edom, Moab, and Ammon.

5. From 'Lead On, O King Eternal,' by Ernest W. Shurtleff (1862-1917).

surely the cross has taught us that no one defeats the dominion of darkness in a bloodless coup. Nor will history simply ooze into the kingdom of God. That kingdom will come at the last because Christ, David's seed, imposes it over all objection and opposition and conquers all his and our enemies.

The Wealth and Homage of the Kingdom (8:7-12)

These verses catalog the spoils and wealth that David collected from conquered or subservient peoples. Since the signal victories over Hadadezer (vv. 3-5) dominated the previous section, the present summary begins with Hadadezer's 'contribution':

> Spoil from Hadadezer, vv. 7-8
> Submission of /homage from Toi, vv. 9-10
> Consecration of spoil from the nations, vv. 11-12

So David amasses treasure: gold shields (some argue for 'quivers') from Hadadezer's officers (v. 7) and piles of bronze from his towns (v. 8);[6] articles of silver, gold, and bronze from Toi (Tou in 1 Chron. 18:9-10), king of Hamath, via his son Joram (v. 10); and all this added to the silver and gold taken 'from all the nations he had subdued' (vv. 11-12). Whether from Hamath or elsewhere David consecrated it to Yahweh; the wealth of the nations belonged to its rightful Owner (v.11). David surely set it apart for the 'house' his successor would build for Yahweh (7:13; 1 Chron. 22:14-16). David's kingdom is a forecast of the kingdom at the last: all the wealth of the nations will come to Yahweh (Isa. 60; Hag. 2:6-9; Rev. 21:24,26).

Don't miss the little note about Toi, king of Hamath (vv. 9-10). He seems to be smooshed in the middle of an archival sandwich and yet there is something distinctive about him: he does not have to be 'struck down' ($n\bar{a}k\bar{a}h$); vv. 1,2,3,5,13). Rather, when he hears how David has 'struck down' (vv. 9, 10) Hadadezer, he sends his son Joram to ask for terms of peace and to express his delight over David's trouncing of Hadadezer, for Hadadezer had been Toi's perennial antagonist. Toi exemplifies another pattern in the Bible's kingdom doctrine. If there are rulers and nations that war against

---

6. The site of Betah (or Tebah) is not known; Berothai is probably modern Bereitan, thirty miles north-northwest of Damascus (Youngblood).

Yahweh's kingdom (see previous discussion), there are also some who lay down their arms and seek peace under his kingdom (see, e.g., Isa. 45:22-23; 56:6-8; 66:18-24; Mic. 4:1-4; Jer. 3:17-18; Zeph. 3: 9-10; Zech. 2:10-11; 8:20-23).[7] Some nations must be subdued; others submit. Some remain rebellious, others are repentant. Some must be crushed, others are contrite. Apparently, some leaders of the nations will heed the counsel of Psalm 2:10-12:

> And now, you kings! Wise up!
> Accept instruction, you rulers of the earth!
> Serve Yahweh with fear
> and rejoice – with trembling.
> Kiss the Son, lest he become angry
> and you perish in your tracks...

Please understand. I don't mean to toy with Toi. I'm not saying Toi saw himself as an example of a right response to Yahweh's chosen king. He was probably more interested simply in having Hadadezer off his back. What I am saying is that the reactions of the surrounding peoples to David's kingship is a *pattern* of the reactions to Christ's kingship at the last. And in this picture Toi's response shows that a people need not be 'struck down' by Yahweh's appointed king if only they will submit to him. Though he himself is oblivious to the fact, Toi functions as a ray of hope. No nation can plead victimhood as if it had no alternative but to be crushed.

This point is not only political but personal. No one can claim to be so victimized by past or context that he has no hope before Christ.[8] Charles Colson retells the story of a young woman who confessed to her psychiatrist that she was exhausted by her lifestyle – an unending cycle of parties, drugs, sex, alcohol. 'Why don't you stop?,' her psychiatrist asked. She sat up immediately. The suggestion astounded her. 'You mean I don't have to do what I want to do?'[9]

---

7. These nations/peoples are not naturally disposed to submit to Yahweh's sway. A check of the passages and/or their contexts usually shows they submit because Yahweh calls, changes, or converts them.

8. Cf. Ezekiel 18, where Yahweh through the prophet is debunking victimhood.

9. Charles Colson, *Against the Night* (Ann Arbor: Servant, 1989), 58.

The Ideal and Order of the Kingdom (8:15-18)

By this section the writer(s) of 1–2 Samuel signals that he is closing off a major piece of his work. He uses such summaries at 1 Samuel 7:15-17 (closing the Samuel section), 1 Samuel 14:47-52 (closing the Saul section), and now (2 Samuel 8:15-18) to close the first David section (1 Samuel 15–2 Samuel 8), sometimes called the History of David's Rise. Like all of 2 Samuel 8, this section is no chilling narrative but more of a calm archive. Yet it does reflect both the ideal (v. 15) and the order (vv. 16-18) of the kingdom.[10]

I want to underscore the writer's résumé of David's reign in verse 15 (NIV):

> David reigned over all Israel,
> doing what was just and right for all his people.

He is saying that, on the whole, David exercised his royal office in the proper way. He asserts the general tone not the near perfection of David's rule. David was doing what a godly king was supposed to do (cf. Psalms 72 and 101). 'Doing what was just and right for all his people' – that is the ideal of the kingdom.

We may agree that all this is nice and we are glad that David was such a king, but, quite frankly, such a text does not reach out and grab us. But it should. Granted I am not the covenant king – nor even a small-time politician. I in no way share the same stature of office that David has as 'messianic' king in redemptive history. The same is true for you the reader. You do not rule the kingdom nor will you ever bring it. But you can *exemplify* the kingdom in whatever offices God has placed you (e.g., the 'office' of elder, father, mother, employer, employee, and so on). If you keep doing what is just and right toward the people connected with you in your various capacities, then the ideal of the kingdom is clear, the order of the kingdom is enjoyed.

My wife is from Kansas and she rather likes her native state. We have not lived in Kansas in over twenty years; currently we are settled in Mississippi. Just off our patio, however, is a small plot,

---

10. My exposition does not discuss David's cabinet appointees in verses 16-18. Hence on the problems of 'Ahimelech son of Abiathar' (v.17) and David's sons as priests (v.18), see Ronald F. Youngblood, '1,2 Samuel,' *The Expositor's Bible Commentary,* 12 vols. (Grand Rapids: Zondervan, 1992), 3:911-13.

perhaps fifteen by seven feet, loaded with samples of native Kansas plants, grasses, and flowers. Several years ago Barbara sent off for the basics of a 'Kansas garden'. We prepared the plot, souped up the soil a bit, and now Kansas visibly thrives outside our back windows. Barbara has made a bit of Kansas appear in Mississippi.

I suggest this text invites us to do the same. No, we are not Davidic kings; nor will we perfectly do what is just and right as Jesus will when he visibly and fully brings his kingdom at his second coming. But we ought to be planting kingdom righteousness in our own present plots, in whatever relationships or capacities we do have. Your task is not to leave doing what is just and right to David but to peel off that kingdom ideal and stick it over the circumstances of your own life; you must be doing what is just and right for all *your* people.

Part 2

A Servant under God's Rod

2 Samuel 9–20

11. Up With Covenant!
2 Samuel 9

Franklin Roosevelt made a speech in Pittsburgh in 1932 advocating restraint in government spending. Four years later he wanted to speak there in favor of government spending. He asked one of his advisors how he could manage an about-face without seeming two-faced. The counsel was straight-forward: Deny you made a speech in Pittsburgh in 1932.[1]

I suppose David could have done something like that. Now that his kingship was firmly in place and Saulide opposition (e.g. Abner and Ishbosheth, chs. 2–4) had been quelled or eliminated, he might have recalled his covenant with Jonathan (1 Sam. 20) and said, 'That was only a ceremony – passing between two halves of an animal; besides, that was over fifteen years ago.' David could have reasoned that considerations of dynastic security precluded showing favors to survivors of a previous, rival dynasty. However much David would have liked to honor his word, current circumstances forced him to renege.

Such, however, was not David's way. Instead he practiced covenant loyalty, and 2 Samuel 9 is the record of it. At first blush this chapter does not appear to be very theological or devotional. But, if I might anticipate, it has a good bit to teach us about covenant. Above all, 2 Samuel 9 asserts that life under the covenant gives you a firm place to stand and ought to evoke a sense of security, privilege, and wonder from you. Let us work through the narrative by means of three major observations.[2]

---

1. Paul F. Boller, Jr., *Presidential Anecdotes* (New York: Penguin Books, 1982), 271.

2. With 2 Samuel 9 we enter another major section of 1–2 Samuel. In-house jargon calls these chapters (2 Sam. 9–20, along with 1 Kings 1–2) the Succession Narrative, a section or document 'written to show how it was that Solomon, and not one of David's other sons, followed his father on the throne' (Robert P. Gordon, *I & II Samuel: A Commentary* [Grand Rapids: Zondervan, 1986], 41). The problem (as Gordon and others point out) is that the Succession Narrative doesn't focus on succession; see David M. Gunn, *The Story of King David,* JSOT Supplement Series 6 (Sheffield: JSOT Press, 1989), 82-84. Hence I dispense with the hypothesis. My rubric for these chapters is 'A Servant Under God's Rod', and I would break them down into the following broad sections:

The Power Covenant Exercises (9:1-4)

David's question was: 'Is there yet someone left in the household of Saul that I might deal with him in a *hesed*-way for Jonathan's sake?' (v.1).[3] You may wonder why I drag in covenant as the central theme of this passage. Because *hesed* (three times, vv. 1, 3, 7) is the devoted love promised within a covenant; *hesed* is love that is willing to commit itself to another by making its promise a matter of solemn record. So when David mentions *hesed* and 'for Jonathan's sake' we know he is alluding to the sacred commitment Jonathan had asked David to make in 1 Samuel 20:15: 'And you must not cut off your devoted love from my house forever, not even when Yahweh cuts off each one of David's enemies from the face of the ground.'[4] And David had gone on oath about that. Now he is preparing to fulfil that pledge.

David's officials locate a certain Ziba, a servant connected to Saul's family, and summon him for a royal interview. David inquires and Ziba informs him that there is still one of Jonathan's sons left, one who is 'stricken in his feet' (v.3). He is living in Lo-debar, east of the Jordan, under the patronage of Machir (v. 4). [5]

It has now been fifteen to twenty years since David had made that promise and entered into that covenant with Jonathan.[6] But it still controlled and directed his behavior: 'Is there anyone belonging

---

1. The fidelity of David's relationships, chs. 9–10
2. The morass of David's guilt, chs. 11–12
3. The trouble from David's house, chs. 13:1–19:8a
4. The turmoil in David's kingdom, chs. 19:8b–20:26

3. NJB nicely captures the connotation of *hesed* in its rendering here: 'to whom I might show *faithful love* for Jonathan's sake.' Cf. my discussion in *Looking on the Heart* (1 Samuel), 2:64-66. See also Katharine Doob Sakenfeld, 'Love (OT),' ABD. 4:377-80.

4. Perhaps 1 Samuel 23:18 indicates a renewal of this covenant promise. David had also assured Saul via oath that he would not eradicate Saul's family once he came to the throne (1 Sam. 24:20-22).

5. Exact location of Lo-debar is unknown. Umm ed-Debar, ten miles south/ southeast of the Sea of Galilee, is often proposed. See NBD, 2nd ed., 274-75.

6. We cannot reconstruct a gapless chronology. We only have some clues. We know Mephibosheth was five when he suffered his tragic injury when his father Jonathan was killed at Mt. Gilboa (2 Sam. 4:4; cf. 1 Sam. 31). David reigned for seven and a half years in Hebron before ruling all Israel from

to Saul's family left, to whom I might show faithful love for Jonathan's sake?' (v. 1, NJB). That solemn word, given in that solemn ceremony, under a solemn curse, constrained him to act with devoted love.[7] Nothing about it being a long time ago, about conditions being different, about it being only a formality. Here is the power covenant exercises – the promise made in the past directs fidelity in the present. Does this not press upon us the urgency of keeping all our covenants?

This is something our world and culture does not understand. I remember some years ago seeing the movie 'Out of Africa' – the natural scenery was breathtaking, the celluloid romance immoral. But in one scene the Meryl Streep and Robert Redford sit talking on the beach. She wants him to marry her. Redford's response is: 'Do you think I'll love you more because of a piece of paper?' That is the mentality. A covenant is a piece of paper, a mere, empty formality. And of course the movie line completely misses the point of a marriage covenant, for such a covenant never claims to regulate love's intensity but only its security. What the world does not see is that love that truly loves is willing to bind itself, is willing to promise, willingly and gladly obligates itself so that the other may stand securely in that love.

If you are a Christian, your life consists of covenant obligations, times when you have made sacred promises. In my own communion, we make vows when we publicly confess our faith before the congregation, when our children receive baptism, when someone assumes church office (elder, deacon), and, of course, when entering into marriage. One does not keep such vows because it is dramatic but because it is faithful. Sometimes you do not keep your covenants because you feel like it but simply because you promised.

Jerusalem (2 Sam. 5:5). David would likely consume a great deal of time consolidating his rule at home and abroad. If Mephibosheth already had a small son by the time David summoned him to court (the more natural reading of 9:12), he may have been twenty years old at this time. The episode in our text then could be as much as fifteen years after the debacle of Gilboa, and David's covenant with Jonathan (1 Sam. 20) could easily have been five years prior to Gilboa (cf. 1 Sam. 27:7). See Eugene H. Merrill, *Kingdom of Priests* (Grand Rapids: Baker, 1987) 252-53.

7. I do not mean to imply that David was moved only by a formal or legal motivation. One cannot read 'for Jonathan's sake' without sensing that love for the memory of his dear friend also stirs him.

The works of B. B. Warfield, the esteemed biblical theologian of old Princeton Seminary, are still known and read in the evangelical church today. What is not so well-known is the tale of his marriage. Warfield was pursuing studies in Leipzig, Germany, in 1876-77. This time also doubled as honeymoon with his wife Annie. They were on a walking tour in the Harz Mountains when they were caught in a terrific thunderstorm. The experience was such a shock to Annie that she never fully recovered, becoming more or less an invalid for life. Warfield only left her for his seminary duties, but never for more than two hours at a time. His world was almost entirely limited to Princeton and to the care of his wife. For thirty-nine years. One of his students noted that when he saw the Warfields out walking together 'the gentleness of his manner was striking proof of the loving care with which he surrounded her.'[8] For thirty-nine years. That is the power covenant exercises.

The Provision Covenant Makes (9:5-8)
These verses (especially verse 7) form the heart of this chapter. Let us make several literary observations that are germane to this point:

1. Mephibosheth's name first occurs in verse 6 (i.e., in this chapter; we already met the note about him in 4:4). To this point he has been spoken of generally as a 'son of Jonathan' or a 'man from the house of Saul'. Significantly, the writer introduces him as Mephibosheth, 'son of Jonathan, son of Saul'; he is a member of the old, rival regime.

2. When the writer passes on David's interviews with Ziba (vv. 2-4, 9-11a) he usually refers to David as 'The king'. However, when conversing with Mephibosheth (vv. 6-7) he is simply 'David'. Perhaps the writer intends to suggest a more personal touch with Mephibosheth?

3. The literary structure of the chapter seems to conspire in placing special stress upon David's statement in verse 7. Note the following proposal.

8. Stanley W. Bamberg, 'Our Image of Warfield Must Go,' *Journal of the Evangelical Theological Society* 34 (1991): 237-38, 240-41.

Structure of 2 Samuel 9

David's plans for kindness, v. 1
    King's conversation with Ziba, vv. 2-4
        (locating Mephibosheth)
                Mephibosheth's arrival and obeisance, vv. 5-6
                    Covenant protection and provision, v. 7
                Mephibosheth's obeisance and amazement, v. 8
    King's conversation with Ziba, vv. 9-11a
        (supporting Mephibosheth)
Mephibosheth's experience of kindness, vv. 11b–13

Here at the hinge and heart of the chapter David promises Mephibosheth: (1) protection ('Don't be afraid, for I will certainly act in a *hesed*-way with you on account of Jonathan your father,' v. 7a); (2) provision ('And I shall restore to you all the land of Saul your father,' v. 7b); and (3) position ('But you, you will always eat bread at my table,' v.7c). David's 'Don't be afraid' must have spelled relief to Mephibosheth, whose actions in verse 6 (falling on his face, showing homage, confessing his servant status) seem to betray apprehension. Mephibosheth knew he was a descendant of the previous rival king, and he knew what usually happened to such folks when the opponent became king. Restoring Saul's farm land to Mephibosheth and charging Ziba & Co. to work it would provide income for Mephibosheth (vv. 9-10). Perhaps Saul's estates had reverted to the crown; or it could be that Ziba had horned in and appropriated them for his use. We do not know. In any case, Mephibosheth's place was not to grovel like a servant at the king's feet but to sit at his table like one of the king's sons – a point mentioned four times (vv. 7,10,11,13).[9]

David's provision for Mephibosheth seems to have gone well beyond David's promise to Jonathan. At least a case can be made for this contention. In 1 Samuel 20:14 Jonathan foresees that he could still be alive when David comes to power. If so, Jonathan asks, 'Will you not treat me with the devoted love [*hesed*] of Yahweh that I not die?' Note: in such circumstances *hesed* would

9. Some (e.g., Hertzberg, McCarter) hold that not only kindness but wariness motivated David to have Mephibosheth eating at the royal board: David could then keep an eye on a possible claimant to the throne. But the text anchors David's motive in *hesed* for Jonathan's sake' (vv. 1,7) and we are safe to stick with that.

be shown by sparing Jonathan's life. Jonathan continues (1 Sam. 20:15), 'And you must not cut off your devoted love from my house forever.' Interpreting verse 15 in the light of verse 14 suggests that Jonathan's concern is that David will also show *ḥesed* toward Jonathan's descendants by sparing rather than liquidating them. Jonathan's covenant does not limit David to merely sparing Jonathan's family, but that seems to be its major concern.

Here in 2 Samuel 9, however, David goes far beyond any bare requirement. David doesn't merely spare Mephibosheth's life but heaps goodness on him. He not only protects his life but restores his inheritance. He not only saves him from the shadow of death but prepares a table for him. David's kindness goes beyond survival to sustenance. Mephibosheth is cared for by and with the king and will never face destitution. It takes no imagination but only faith to see that David's *ḥesed* is but a faithful reflection of Yahweh's – with whom there is no such thing as bare *ḥesed* (Ps. 23:1; John 1:16; 6:35; Rom. 8:32).

The Person Covenant Embraces (9:11b-13)

Here I want to consider the significance of Mephibosheth in the entire chapter, but I have referred to verses 11b-13 in particular since four of the seven references to Mephibosheth by name occur there. The king has placed Ziba under orders to manage Saul's estate for Mephibosheth, the 'son of your master' (three times in vv. 9-10).[10] Then there are four statements about Mephibosheth to close out the chapter, the last the most poignant: 'But Mephibosheth was staying in Jerusalem, for he ate regularly at the king's table – and he was lame in both his feet' (v. 13).

There are two elements of Mephibosheth's condition that are stressed in the text. The first is his *lameness*. Ziba had informed David that Jonathan's son was 'stricken in his feet' (v.3) and, as we have seen, the last line of the chapter (v. 13b) sadly reminds us of that. As a reader, you can hardly keep your heart from going out to Mephibosheth in pity, especially in light of that scrubby little note about him in 4:4. A tragic piece of data – for Israel nationally, for Mephibosheth personally. Though a prince's son, he is a helpless, dependent cripple.[11]

---

10. Ziba is quite wealthy in his own right, as his fifteen sons and twenty servants attest (v.10b).

But there is something worse about Mephibosheth – his *heredity*. He is 'the son of Jonathan, the son of Saul' (v. 6a). Mephibosheth is, quite simply, the wrong stuff. He is the enemy. He belongs to the previous regime. And yet he is spared – because of David's covenant oath to Jonathan (1 Sam. 20:14-16a). Though Mephibosheth is technically the enemy he is embraced in the safety of the covenant.

We need to go on a brief but relevant tangent. I must remind you that there was a certain miracle at the heart of the David-Jonathan covenant. Ordinarily, a new dynasty (David) would want no truck with sparing the former rival dynasty (Saul, Jonathan). Let me quote some of my comments on 1 Samuel 20:14-16a:

> When a new regime or dynasty came to power, the name of the game was purge. You needn't go wandering into the ancient Near East to confirm this. You can stay within the pages of biblical history and watch Baasha (1 Kings 15:27-30) or Zimri (1 Kings 16:8-13) or Jehu (2 Kings 10:1-11) to find out what happens to the remnants of the previous regime. The new king always needed to solidify his position. It was conventional political policy: solidification by liquidation. Everybody knew it; everybody believed it; everybody practiced it.[12]

Now perhaps we can understand why Mephibosheth must have been trembling (2 Sam. 9:6) when David summoned him. Mephibosheth's lameness was in his feet not in his brain. He knew what normally happened to the remnants of defunct dynasties. But David's 'Don't be afraid' (v. 7) signals that Mephibosheth will not receive the expected. Simply because of the covenant. Because David made an absurd promise that most sane politicians would never have made. He had promised *ḥesed* to the enemy, and that covenant was Mephibosheth's shelter.

Perhaps you can already see that we are slipping into deeper waters, that we are beginning to sense a parallel between David's devoted love for his 'enemy' Mephibosheth – the sort of thing that wasn't supposed to happen – and something like Romans 5:10, 'While we were enemies we were reconciled to God....' I am only

---

11. Note the place of the lame in the messianic era (Isa. 35:5-6; Jer. 31:7-9; Mic. 4:6-7) and what Jesus already does for them when he inaugurates that era (Matt. 11:2-6).

12. *Looking on the Heart,* 2:68

saying that you will never appreciate David's covenant love unless
you understand the source of it, the Author of it. In fact, is it not
Paul's purpose in Romans 5:6-10 to highlight the who-could-have-
guessed quality of God's love? Note his argument: 'While we were
yet helpless..., while we were yet sinners..., while we were
enemies...' (vv. 6,8,10). The first principle for grappling with the
marvel of God's love is to realize that he has no business – in a
sense – loving whom he loves. What I'm saying is that we are the
Lord's Mephibosheths, and there is absolutely no reason why we
should be eating continually at the King's table. And if we have
any sense, we won't be able to understand it either.

12. Foreign Folly
2 Samuel 10

Life offers any number of predictable situations to which we expect
equally predictable reactions, and we are aghast when the reaction
is anything but customary. Once Lefty Gomez, left-handed pitcher
for the New York Yankees in the 1930s, signaled for his catcher,
Bill Dickey, to come out to the pitcher's mound. They were in the
middle of a baseball game and the opposing team had the bases
loaded. Dickey knew Gomez wanted to discuss how to pitch to the
next batter. Instead Lefty asked Dickey if he had any extra bird
dogs back home in Arkansas. Dickey was totally flustered: Why
ask about bird dogs when the bases are loaded? Lefty 'explained':
'A friend of mine knows you hunt and asked me to find out from
you if I ever thought of it. Well, I just thought of it.'[1]

Our chapter revolves around another predictable situation, not
in baseball but in foreign affairs. Nahash, the king of the
Ammonites, had died; his son, Hanun, had succeeded him. David,
out of kindness and yet in accord with custom, sent several
diplomats to convey condolences to Hanun over his father's death
(vv. 1-2). It was a class act. Granted, it wasn't as if David cried
himself to sleep over Nahash's demise; and doubtless there was a
good degree of formality involved. Yet it was a nice touch – an
overt act of tribute for a departed leader. Even for all the formality,

---

1. Bruce Nash and Allan Zullo, *The Baseball Hall of Shame 4* (New York:
Pocket Books, 1990), 122.

it should be recognized as a gracious formality and acknowledged with courtesy. Yet one wonders if Hanun and his advisors did not have some of Lefty Gomez in them. Defying protocol they disgraced David's ambassadors by shaving off half (i.e., one side of) their beards, hacking off their garments all the way up to the buttocks, and running them out of town (v.4).[2] 'We can imagine them running the gauntlet through a mob of jeering men and women.'[3] Hanun should have stuck with convention. He had committed foreign folly. He had created a big stink.[4]

Hanun's outrage is the agitator that stirs the whole chapter. However, I want to back away from this Ammonite asininity itself to consider how we ought to approach this chapter as a whole.

Literary Observations
Let us first get the flow and content of the chapter in front of us via the following breakdown:

> Insane insult, vv. 1-5
> Critical moment, vv. 6-14
> > Assembly, 6-8
> > Difficulty, 9-10
> > Strategy, 11-12
> > Victory, 13-14
> Major subjugation, vv. 15-19

Second Samuel 10 appears to be a very compressed narrative. It seems to consist of the bones of battle reports with only a little narrative flesh on them. To be sure, Hanun's malicious etiquette (vv. 1-5) captures our interest; but the rest of the chapter doesn't

---

2. Hanun could hardly have inflicted a more shameful insult: the men's manliness was both marred (beard) and exposed (buttocks/private parts). Claus Schedl passes on an undated incident recorded by A. Musil of 'how the Bedouins who lived in the neighborhood of Hebron cut off half the beard of a drunken man, a jest which led to an all-out war between the two tribes involved' (*History of the Old Testament*, 5 vols. [Staten Island: Alba House, 1972], 3:211).

3. Hans Wilhelm Hertzberg, *I & II Samuel*, The Old Testament Library (Philadelphia: Westminster, 1964), 304.

4. So, literally, verse 6: 'The sons of Ammon saw that they had made themselves stink (*bā'aš*) with David.'

sport the graphic detail and fascinating close-ups that one finds in, e.g., 1 Samuel 17 or 2 Samuel 2:8-32. Even when Joab faces his logistic emergency (vv. 9-14) the account is very terse and clipped. Yet the chapter is not dull, for a careful reading shows the writer, for all his severe style, has preserved a note of crisis through the whole account. He does this with the five uses of the clause 'when [so-and-so] *saw that...*' (the verb $r\bar{a}'\bar{a}h$) + the particle ($k\hat{\imath}$). Note the following chart:

Text	Crisis	Action
v.6	Ammonites see that they stink with David	Hire Aramaean mercenaries
v.9	Joab sees battle is against him in front and rear	Divides troops
v.14	Ammon sees Aram has fled	Flee into their own fortified city
v.15	Aram sees that they are defeated	Gather a super-Aramaean army
v.19	Hadadezer's lackeys see they are defeated	Make peace with Israel

The chapter may be succinct but the crisis-reaction pattern both enlivens and unifies it.

Our major literary concern, however, has to do with the function of chapter 10 in its context. It certainly sets the stage for chapters 11–12. The Ammonite War serves as the historical background for the David-Bathsheba-Uriah fiasco (11:1, 6-17), and 12:26-31 brings closure to the Ammonite problem left hanging in 10:14. And yet chapter 10 also links up thematically with chapter 9, for here David wants to show *ḥesed* to the Ammonite Hanun (10:1-2) as he had shown *ḥesed* to the Saulide Mephibosheth (9:1,3,7).

Chapter 10 then points both forward and backward, but does it have its own witness? Its own word to say?[5] I hold that it does and would summarize that witness under the following heads.

---

5. Cf. Walter Brueggemann: 'Chapter 10 by itself has no great theological significance for us' *(First and Second Samuel,* Interpretation [Louisville: John Knox, 1990], 271).

Theological Witness

Prophetic Scenario

I propose, first, that 2 Samuel 10 functions as a prophetic scenario. Admittedly, at first sight there doesn't seem to be anything prophetic about these episodes. They simply depict what often happens. Political advisors sway a new king by insinuating he is surely not so naïve that he fails to see through David's condolence scam (vv. 2b-3).[6] That is what politicians do. Even the Ammonites' fiendish barbering and tailoring (v.4) are not that unusual, considering the source. Ammonites liked to scoop out the right eyes of subjugated peoples (1 Sam. 11:1-2) and slice open pregnant women (Amos 1:13) in order to dispose of two generations at once. So what's unusual about hacking a little hair and cloth? That's what Ammonites do. Nor is it strange that Aramaeans are meddling in trans-jordanian affairs and Ammonite ones in particular since, as a matter of fact, they would love to establish their control over the premier caravan route (called The King's Highway) running from Damascus in the north to Elath (and beyond) in the south.[7] Collecting road tolls helped their economy. That's just what Aramaeans do. It's all so typical.

Yet the typical can be prophetical. Since I discussed this matter more extensively in the exposition of 2 Samuel 8, I refrain from extended comment here. Suffice it to say that 2 Samuel 10 looks like a regionalized version of Psalm 2. As Hanun and Hadadezer's Aramaean confederates stir themselves up against David, so the kings and rulers of the world are bent on resisting the sway of Yahweh and his Davidic-messianic King (Ps. 2:1-3). Even after the initial defeat, Hadadezer has no better sense than to mount another, but all-out, massive assault (2 Sam. 10:15-18), which David smashes when he hits them at Helam.[8] Finally, Hadadezer's cronies

---

6. J.P. Fokkelman, *Narrative Art and Poetry in the Books of Samuel,* vol.1, *King David (II Sam. 9 – 20 & 1 Kings 1-2)* (Assen: Van Gorcum, 1981), 44.

7.Benjamin Mazar, 'The Aramean Empire and its Relation with Israel,' *The Biblical Archaeologist Reader, 2* (Garden City, NY: Doubleday, 1964), 131-33. On the caravan routes, see Yohanan Aharoni and Michael Avi-Yonah, *The Macmillan Bible Atlas,* 3rd ed. (New York: Macmillan, 1993), 17. Incidentally, for both maps and a helpful reconstruction of the order of events in 2 Samuel 8 and 10 (and 1 Chron. 18–19), see the same atlas, pp. 78-79.

8. Helam is a town or district about forty miles east of the Sea of Galilee. See ABD, 3:116-117. This was a major effort since Hadadezer drafted his allies

wise up (a la Ps. 2:10ff.) and seek terms of peace with David (2 Sam. 10:19).

It is far easier to see Psalm 2 being fulfilled when we eaves-drop on the prayer of the Jerusalem church in Acts 4:24-30 and hear the saints applying Psalm 2:1-2 to, among others, Herod and Pontius Pilate. We do not usually think of Hanun and Hadadezer in that way. We look on them as a bothersome episode on the eastern frontier that we must read about before we can get to the really sensational stuff about David and Bathsheba. But David is Yahweh's chosen king, and Hanun and Hadadezer & Co. have arrayed themselves against him. And they lost. Second Samuel 10 is but a miniature of Psalm 2 and proclaims: In spite of all resistance and hostility the Davidic king will rule. If we don't have that assurance, why go to the office on Wednesday?

Commendable Fidelity

This chapter begins like chapter 9 – by waving the word *hesed* at us (10:2; 9:1): 'David said, "I will act in a *hesed*-way with Hanun son of Nahash, since his father acted in a *hesed*-way with me." ' Nahash must have given David help when Saul was tracking him down. We do not know if there was some covenant or treaty relationship between Nahash and David. *hesed* may imply that. But there may have been no formal pact at all. *hesed*, with its double nuance of kindness and constancy, of love and loyalty, was an obligation that David in any case felt. David owed reciprocal kindness to Nahash and would express it toward Hanun his son.

I think the writer wants to cast David as the *hesed*-doing king.

---

from beyond the Euphrates and engaged Shobach, apparently a premier commander, to lead them. Readers can lose the sweat in the summary. Hence we need W.G. Blaikie's reminder: 'It requires but a very little consideration to see that the wars which are so briefly recorded in this chapter must have been most serious and perilous undertakings. The record of them is so short, so unimpassioned, so simple, that many readers are disposed to think very little of them. But when we pause to think what it was for the king of Israel to meet, on foreign soil, confederates so numerous, so powerful, and so familiar with warfare, we cannot but see that these were tremendous wars. They were fitted to try the faith as well as the courage of David and his people to the very utmost' (*The Second Book of Samuel*, The Expositor's Bible [Cincinnati: Jennings & Graham, n.d.], 155-56). It is difficult, by the way, to reconcile the tally and terms in v. 18 with its parallel in 1 Chron. 19:18.

In chapter 9 we entered (according to my outline) a new section of the Samuel materials (2 Sam. 9–10). At the very first David appears as the faithful king eager to act kindly/loyally toward Saul's family (ch. 9) and then as the grateful king careful to act kindly toward those outside Israel (ch. 10). At the beginning of this new section we have a double picture of David as the *ḥesed*-doing king. J.P. Fokkelman summarizes it nicely:

> 'Loyalty' [*ḥesed*] was, according to Ch.9, the principle which guided David with respect to a branch of Israel's former royal family and, thus, part of his domestic policy. According to Ch.10, David also wants to apply this key word as the guiding principle in his foreign policy, at this moment in particular with regard to the royal family of a neighboring country.[9]

I think the writer has his reasons for placing these two portraits of David-in-his-*ḥesed* before us, though I must admit I cannot prove my surmise. I propose, however, that the writer shows us these two glimpses of David in order to form a foil against which to see the David of chapters 11–12. Here is David acting kindly and loyally, there is David throwing kindness and loyalty to the winds. Here is David controlled by his covenants and his memories, there is David driven by his glands and his secrets. Here David spares and mourns life; there he tramples and destroys life.

But right now we are in chapter 10; right now the writer seems to be commending David. He not only acts kindly toward those within Israel (ch. 9) but toward those outside Israel (ch. 10). This is commendable fidelity.[10] Does not the apostle place the same claim in principle upon Christian believers in 1 Thessalonians 5:15? 'See that none of you repays evil for evil, but always seek to do good to one another *and to all*' (NRSV; emphasis mine). Isn't this the thrust of Jesus' argument based on the 'wideness in God's mercy' (Matt. 5:45-47)? In short, our *ḥesed* should include Ammonites and other pagans.

---

9. Fokkelman, *King David*, 43.

10. Some interpreters may accuse me of being too 'exemplary' here. My contention is that the writer intends to depict David as an example in this case. When an example is intended we should be 'exemplary' in our interpretation.

Unexpected theology

Finally, we must focus on the middle segment of this chapter (vv.6-14). Here David's army under Joab's command gets caught in a pincers movement while preparing to assault Rabbah, the capital of the Ammonites.[11] Faced with enemy fore and aft, Joab divided his troops. Those under his brother Abishai were to hold off the Ammonites, while those with Joab turned to face the formidable Aramaean contingents. The narrator is not eager to provide us with the stuff of a war movie. No details. The Aramaeans? 'They fled before him' (i.e., Joab; v. 13b). That's all. The Ammonites? They figured what was good for Aram was good for Ammon, so they fled behind walls (v.14).

The writer may stifle details of battle but gives ample space for Joab's speech to Abishai:

> If Aram is too strong for me, you must help me, and should the sons of Ammon prove too strong for you, I shall come to your help. Be strong and act like it on behalf of our people and the cities of our God. And Yahweh will do what he thinks good (vv. 11-12).

The speech therefore is important to the narrator.[12] The tension of this little section builds up to it; all one can say after it is: they ran.

Now only in Joab's speech do we meet an explicit theological note in this chapter. Only here do we hear of Yahweh. What bothers us is not this theological note but that Joab is the author of it. What are we to make of this iron-nerved, hard-bitten, vindictive, blood-spilling look-out-for-number-one military man (see 2 Sam. 2,3 and 20) suddenly spouting theology? Is this foxhole religion – turning pious under duress? A little faith coming out the mouth as the rope tightens on the neck? Surely the writer can't be serious, can he? Even if he is, can we afford to allow this rascal Joab to preach truth to us? Could Joab be right? Should we listen to him?

---

11. I assume the conflict occurred near Rabbah. Some hold that the city must be Medeba (see 1 Chron. 19:7, the parallel passage), about twenty miles south of Rabbah. But Medeba need only have been the assembly point for the Aramaean mercenaries, who, after Joab's army had prepared to engage at Rabbah, arrived to attack Joab's army in the rear. See further, Yigael Yadin, *The Art of Warfare in Biblical Lands,* 2 vols. (New York: McGrawhill, 1963), 2: 273-74.

12. See Fokkelman, *King David,* 48.

Why not? Why allow his unsavory character to eclipse the truth of his words? Can't even thugs speak truth?[13] I do not see anything wrong or misleading in Joab's exhortation. His final affirmation, in fact, is always the resting-place of God's beleaguered people: 'Yahweh will do what he thinks good.'[14]

I want to press the practical importance of this affirmation, for some who may finally be willing to let Joab be their teacher nevertheless see such a statement as a gasp of despair rather than an expression of faith. To the contrary, I hold that this affirmation is any believer's firmest solace in all life's uncertainties. Because of the personal, existential importance of the matter, I want to append part of Calvin's exposition:

> Well, if someone still claims that Joab did not show that he trusted in God, that he was not thoroughly assured of the promises of the Law, the reply to that is that God does not give particular promises about this or that to his children. We certainly have this point which should firmly persuade us that God will never abandon us, and that in the end he will show that our hope in him was not in vain, so that our faith will not be frustrated when it rests upon his mercy and his truth. Nevertheless, we must remain in suspense about many things. For instance, when we ask God for our daily bread, it is not that we are assured that he will send us a good harvest or a great vintage. We should leave that in his hands, and patiently await what pleases him. When we have any illness, we must rest well assured that he has not forgotten us, and that we have such access to him that, in the end, we will feel that he has looked on us in pity. The promise of God should be fully sufficient in regards to that. However, when we would like to have the word that today or tomorrow he will restore our health, we do not know – we are even in doubt of living or dying.

Calvin goes on to point out that Joab could have no absolute certainty of victory and deliverance in this Aramaean–Ammonite jam because he had no specific promise about that particular situation. Hence he concludes:

---

13. Karl Gutbrod certainly gives Joab a fair shake here: 'Joab understands not only his bloody calling, but also stands believing before the Lord' (*Das Buch vom Reich*, Die Botschaft des Alten Testaments, 2nd ed. [Stuttgart: Calwer, 1973], 135).

14. This line can be translated as an affirmation or as a wish/request ('May Yahweh do...'). I prefer the former (with NJPS and NIV).

We see, therefore, that Joab's uncertainty was not lack of faith, for we can certainly doubt, although we embrace the promises of God and hold them as absolutely certain and infallible. What we doubt are the things which are not clear to us. That is how he wants us to remain in suspense about many things and to leave it all to his secret counsel and his providence.[15]

There is a strange chemistry here: taking Joab's words into our dilemmas may make us both more confident and less certain. But, at some point, will we not see that if Yahweh will do what he thinks good, that will also be what *is* good for his people? If Joab stirs up our faith, we owe him our thanks.

13. Flesh and Blood
2 Samuel 11

Don't forget we are still at war. Well, David isn't, which gives rise to the story that takes up most of 2 Samuel 11–12. With the heading (11:1) and tailpiece (12:26-31) the writer reminds us that all this takes place during the war with Ammon. A new war year (11:1) gave Joab and the troops opportunity to put the finishing touch on Ammon with Operation Rabbah (cf. 10:14). The Ammonite war(s) holds all of 2 Samuel 10–12 together, but in chapter 11 the focus turns from the front lines in Ammon to the royal bedroom in Jerusalem. We will pick up the story there and restrict this study to chapter 11 to keep it manageable.

Literary Features

Before we consider the teaching of the chapter, I want to highlight some of its literary qualities. In some cases they help us interpret the text; in any case, we should appreciate literary artistry for its own sake.

First, chapter 11 moves at a slower pace than the preceding narrative in chapter 10. In the latter the writer seemed in a hurry to give us the facts, to summarize the situation, and to supply only necessary detail. Here, in chapter 11, however, the tempo slows, perhaps for a reason:

---

15. John Calvin, *Sermons on 2 Samuel*, trans. Douglas Kelly (Edinburgh: Banner of Truth, 1992), 464-65. I commend Calvin's whole discussion (pp. 463-69).

Whereas the progress of the Ammonite war is recorded in quick, sure strokes, almost too briefly, the events at the royal court are described in comfortable detail. In the one, it is only the course of the war that is important; in the other it is the exploration of human character.[1]

Secondly, chapter 11 reflects a great deal of restraint, a paradox when taken with the preceding point. The writer provides much circumstantial detail but severely restricts, for example, the actual words of Bathsheba and Uriah. David talks a good bit but Bathsheba's lines are limited to 'I am pregnant' (v.5) – only two words in Hebrew. Uriah, for all his importance in the story, only speaks in verse 11 (admittedly a significant speech), a speech expressing the acme of devotion and showing the reader that this Hittite is the only genuine Israelite in the whole chapter.

The writer's most apparent restraint, however, lies elsewhere: in his utter silence regarding the feelings of his characters. He does not clarify whether Bathsheba was baiting David, nor whether she considered the fling with the king an honor. The emphasis is on David and his deed. Nor does the writer offer a psychology of Uriah. Did Uriah refuse to 'go down to his house' because he suspected something was rotten in Jerusalem? Was this his way of wreaking vengeance on the king, of allowing him to stew in his own immoral juice? We do not and cannot know. The writer offers no help on this. He doesn't even indicate how Joab felt about David's 'sack Uriah' plan; he carried it out, perhaps improved on it. But whether he felt shock or smug satisfaction or something else we are not told.[2] The writer seems to silence all feelings in order to isolate David's actions.

Third, the writer litters his story with irony. For example, careful observance of the ceremonial law (Bathsheba's cleansing herself

---

1. Claus Schedl, *History of the Old Testament,* 5 vols. (Staten Island: Alba House, 1972), 3:230.

2. I have found Karl Gutbrod, *Das Buch vom Reich,* Die Botschaft des Alten Testaments, 2nd ed. (Stuttgart: Calwer, 1973), 139-41, very helpful on these items of literary restraint. Cf. also Hans Wilhelm Hertzberg, *I & II Samuel,* The Old Testament Library (Philadelphia: Westminster, 1964), 311; on Bethsheba (in 2 Sam.11), cf. Adele Berlin, *Poetics and Interpretation of Biblical Narrative* (Sheffield: Almond, 1983), 26-27, and Joyce Baldwin, *1 & 2 Samuel,* Tyndale Old Testament Commentaries (Leicester: InterVarsity, 1988), 244.

after her period, v. 4c)[3] is followed by blatant transgression of the moral law (David's adultery with her). Also, Uriah is disobedient (v. 9) to the king's order (v.8), but the most moving faithfulness (v.11) explains such disobedience. Or here is David incessantly asking and talking about *shalom* (peace, welfare, well-being) in verse 7[4] and yet doing all he wants and can to trash the shalom of a marriage and a servant's life.[5] Finally, Joab's instructions to the messenger (vv. 19-21) assume that King David has always been vigorously opposed to all unnecessary bloodshed in war.[6] Joab's remarks reflect David's policy never to risk heedlessly the lives of one's men. Here, however, David finds a few lives needlessly snuffed out to be a piece of welcome news.

The writer then seems to do all he can to keep the spotlight and the responsibility squarely on David, David the lustful adulterer (vv. 2-5) and gracious entertainer (vv. 6-13), the murderous schemer (vv. 14-15) and understanding commander (v. 25). Perhaps the easiest way for a reader to grasp the overall flow of the chapter is to follow David and his relationships:

> David and Bathsheba, vv. 2-5
> David and Uriah, vv. 6-13
> David and Joab, vv.14-25
> David and Yahweh, vv. 26-27

Other literary items can be mentioned as we discuss the teaching of the chapter.

Theological Witness

The Fallen Servant (11:1-5)
The writer places before us, first of all, a picture of the fallen servant. He intends us to see the David of 11:1-5 in stark contrast to the David of 9:1-3 and 10:1-2. At the beginning of these two previous

---

3. Cf. NJPS, 'she had just purified herself after her period,' taking v.4c, I think rightly, as a parenthetical aside showing why she had been bathing in v.2.

4. If *shalom* is translated as 'peace' in verse 7, one is faced in the last phrase with the anomaly of 'the peace of the war'!

5. Cf. Walter Brueggemann, *First and Second Samuel*, Interpretation (Louisville: John Knox, 1990), 274.

6. Gutbrod, *Das Buch vom Reich*, 141.

chapters we see David eager to show kindness to both Israelite and Ammonite. But the David of 11:1-5 has no kindness to show. Here it is not *ḥesed* but *eros* that drives him. Brueggemann captures the tone of the text:

> The action is quick. The verbs rush as the passion of David rushed. He sent; he took; he lay (v.4). The royal deed of self-indulgence does not take very long. There is no adornment to the action. The woman then gets some verbs: she returned, she conceived. The action is so stark. There is nothing but action. There is no conversation. There is no hint of caring, of affection, of love – only lust. David does not call her by name, does not even speak to her. At the end of the encounter she is only 'the woman' (v.5). The verb that finally counts is 'conceived.' But the telling verb is 'he took her.'[7]

This is the king Yahweh chose (1 Sam. 16:1-13); this is the man after God's own heart (1 Sam. 13:14).

The warning in this text reaches far beyond King David and touches all professed servants of Christ. How suddenly and fatally any of us can fall! There is a snip from Robert Robinson's hymn ('Come, Thou Fount of Every Blessing') that scares me, I think because I understand it:

> Prone to wander, Lord, I feel it,
> Prone to leave the God I love.

Maybe Robert Robinson understood it too. He had been converted under George Whitefield's preaching in 1752 and later became a Baptist pastor in Cambridge. Toward the end of his life he had again 'given way to frivolous habits,' as one account has it. One day during this period he was traveling by stagecoach. Another passenger, a lady and a total stranger, was going over some hymns and especially and persistently referred to 'Come, Thou Fount' as one that had brought her immense blessing. As she continued speaking Robinson became so agitated that he burst out, 'Madam, I am the poor, unhappy man who composed that hymn many years ago; and I would give a thousand worlds, if I had them, to enjoy the feelings I had then!'[8]

Don't look at verses 1-5 and stammer something about your being a New Testament Christian. What difference does that make?

---

7. Brueggemann, *First and Second Samuel,* 273.

8. W.J. Limmer Sheppard, *Great Hymns and Their Stories* (1923; reprint ed., Fort Washington, PA: Christian Literature Crusade, 1979), 159-60.

What immunity does that give you? If you begin to say, 'Oh, but I could never...,' then you have already taken the first step in your fall. Don't ever be surprised at what you are capable of. The only safe ground is to pray with Robert Robinson,

> O to grace how great a debtor
> Daily I'm constrained to be;
> Let that grace now, like a fetter,
> Bind my wandering heart to thee.

The Unvarnished Truth (11:6-25)

Before we come to the unvarnished truth I want us to get a feel for the whole narrative (vv. 2-25) from David's perspective. The story divides into two nearly equal parts:

> David frustrated, vv.2-13
> David successful, vv. 14-25

In the first section David is always the active one, always the one in control, but repeatedly frustrated. In verses 2-5 David saw, inquired, sent, took, and copulated. The woman returns home. But the palace 'secret' hits a snag: 'I am pregnant' (v. 5). In the next segment (vv. 6-11) David sends for (v. 6), asks (v. 7), orders (v. 8a), and lavishes a gift (v. 8b). He is in the driver's seat, in control. But he cannot control Uriah, who bunks among the royal servants (v. 9). David wonders why Uriah is so allergic to supper, shower, and sex (v.10b) and hears a reply that should have left his spirit in tatters (v. 11.)[9] Yet David has one more card in his hand. He gives Uriah final orders (v. 12), invites him for dinner, and makes him drunk (v. 13a). David is still the mover, the one in control. He puts Uriah under the influence but not under his influence, for Uriah staggers out to bed down in the servants' quarters again (v. 13b).

The core of David's whole scheme is to get Uriah home to spend a night with Bathsheba. Hence his order: 'Go down to your house' (v.8). But verses 6-13 emphasize the frustration of David's plan by repeatedly noting that Uriah did not 'go down to his house' (by narrator's report [vv. 9, 13], court gossip [v.10a], royal question [v.10b], or direct refusal [v.11]).

---

9. John Calvin has a graphic depiction of what David's response should have been (*Sermons on 2 Samuel,* trans. Douglas Kelly [Edinburgh: Banner of Truth, 1992] 500).

David, however, is up to the challenge as verses 14-25 show. He will have to make Uriah carry his own death warrant under royal seal. David is in control: he writes the letter and sends it via Uriah (vv. 14-15). Uriah must be liquidated and he is, for Joab and the Ammonites are most accommodating whenever it's only a matter of a little blood. In verses 14-25 all that matters is that Uriah die, and that big fact is mentioned repeatedly (vv. 15,17,21,24; also in v. 26). Oh, there will be the funeral at the national cemetery; and there will be the press releases eulogizing Uriah's exceptional military record and fanning anti-Ammonite sentiment. But Uriah is dead. And that is all that matters.

So David has persevered; he has succeeded. All of verses 6-25 centers on two facts: Uriah did not go down to his house and Uriah the Hittite is dead. And David engineered it. He had arranged it all.[10]

Such 'arrangements' do not usually surprise us. There was that day in October 1944 when Field Marshal Erwin Rommel was told, 'Everything has already been arranged in Berlin.' Rommel had been implicated in a plot against Hitler. Because of his services in Africa he was to be given the gentler, kinder option of taking poison. Should he not consent, who knows what might happen to his family after he was eliminated? This way they would be granted a pension. He only had to drive off with two generals, take the poison, and in fifteen minutes his wife would receive a call from a local hospital informing her that her husband had died of a cerebral embolism. It would be a lie. But it had been arranged. As had the state funeral. Hitler wired Frau Rommel asking her to 'accept my sincerest sympathy for the heavy loss you have suffered'. Hermann Goering, head of the Luftwaffe, joined the act, assuring the widow that 'the fact that your husband has died a hero's death as the result of his wounds… has deeply touched me'.[11] But everything had been arranged.

We expect such oppression and sham in Nazidom. And in a hundred other regimes. But this is Israel, this is David, the king in covenant with Yahweh (2 Sam. 7). The man after God's own heart

---

10. It may be, as some think, that Joab improved on David's plan. It would have looked too obvious had Joab hung Uriah out to dry by himself (cf. v.15b), but if there were a dozen or so funerals (vv. 17,24), who would be the wiser? Yet for the narrator the responsibility rests squarely with David.

11. William L. Shirer, *The Rise and Fall of the Third Reich* (Greenwich, CT: Fawcett, 1960), 1400-1401.

takes the sword after God's own people. Here is no theoretical descendant of David committing iniquity (2 Sam. 7:14b) but the covenant king himself, ruling with oppression and heartlessness. Here is the one who puts Mephibosheth at his table and Uriah in his grave. Welcome to Thugsville.

The unvarnished truth is that life for God's people can be like that even in the supposed kingdom of God. That kingdom is not safe even in David's hands. It is only safe when Jesus Christ rules and will rule with justice and righteousness. Yet until Jesus publicly enforces that just regime at his second coming, it will not be unusual for God's people to suffer even within (what claims to be) the kingdom of God. I do not care to enter a church and kingdom debate here. But, clearly, Christians today find much of their kingdom life within their church, and it is beyond sadness when the leadership in such churches rules with harshness and severity, crushing rather than comforting Christ's flock, suffocating rather than sustaining.

The Bottom Line (11:26-27)

Apparently it's all over but the weeping. Bathsheba (but note how the writer deliberately calls her 'the wife of Uriah', v.26a) receives the letter of notification and condolence from the army and engages in the usual mourning rites (v. 26b). We don't know whether her grief was perfunctory or acute; the writer gives no hint about how she *really* felt. But mourning periods always end, at least official ones do, and after Bathsheba's David has her brought to the royal household as his wife, where she bears David a son. Hence nine months have passed, and that is that.

Well, almost. There is the bottom line: 'The thing David had done was evil in Yahweh's eyes' (v.27b). My literal translation is deliberate. If one also translates literally David's message to Joab in verse 25 the contrast becomes clear. David soothed Joab with 'Don't let this thing be evil in your eyes.'[12] 'Certainly reverses are lamentable in this business, Joab, but you mustn't brood over them; they're part of the territory, as we say; you must brush them off and press on.' But Yahweh will not brush it off. David may take a casual view, but 'the thing…was evil in Yahweh's eyes'. And that is the bottom line.

---

12. Most English translations give more idiomatic renderings of verse 25 and/or verse 27b and thereby obscure what jumps out of the Hebrew.

The force of this 'bottom line' comes from the fact that it is literally the bottom line, the last line of the chapter. The writer relates his whole sordid tale of lust and sex and deceit and murder without pausing to make marginal moral notations along the way. He details every step of the story as if God was nowhere involved. David (as we said above) was in control. This silence about God, however, only serves to accentuate the lone statement in verse 27b. It is as if David can vent his glands and weave his cover-up without any interference – until he runs smack into the judgment of God. It was evil in Yahweh's eyes. That's what Yahweh thought of it.

The way the narrative is written, then, tells us that the silence of God does not indicate the absence of God. 'His eyes gaze upon, his eyelids test, the sons of men' (Ps. 11:4b). Because evil runs on in its successful course does not mean God is not watching it. And yet there is the mystery, and there is the problem some may feel with 2 Samuel 11. Like much injustice, the evil of 2 Samuel 11 goes on unimpeded as if God is not there. We are told at last that it was 'evil in Yahweh's eyes'. But if Yahweh hates injustice, why did he not prevent it here? If he hates oppression, why did he not stop it? To steal mourners' words at Lazarus' grave – could not his God have kept Uriah from dying? (cf. John 11:37).

Our story does not resolve this mystery. It only insists on a clarity: Yahweh may be silent but he is not sightless. 'The thing David had done was evil in Yahweh's eyes.' David may have Bathsheba's flesh and Uriah's blood, but he will have to face Yahweh's eyes.

14. Grace Greater Than All Our Sin
2 Samuel 12

In 2 Samuel 11 David is in control; he is the prime mover; he gets things done. David totally dominates the action from the palace roof (11:2) until he crashes into the unyielding standard of Yahweh's righteousness (11:27b). As expected, Yahweh and his word dominate chapter 12. We expect retribution, punishment, judgment on David. And that is here. But we have the sense that we have traveled beyond judgment in 2 Samuel 12 into the Land of Grace. I think that is the right perspective, and I will develop the teaching under the theme of grace, God's something-for-nothing-when-we-don't-deserve-anything.

The Pursuit of Grace (12:1a)

'And Yahweh sent Nathan to David.' Without those words we would be in for a bleak and hopeless story. The first line of chapter 12 dispels any notion that Yahweh is a passive onlooker. The verb 'sent' ($\check{s}\bar{a}lah$) is a signal. This verb occurs twelve times in chapter 11 (vv.1,3,4,5,6 [3 times], 12,14,18,22,27), where everyone sends – David sends, Bathsheba sends, Joab sends. Now Yahweh sends (12:1a). He has gone into action. Yahweh sends Nathan to David.

Of course we know what that will mean, for we have cheated and read the rest of the story. But we must not run ahead too soon; we need to dally on those opening words for they speak of the vigilance of grace; they show us that grace pursues and exposes the sinner in his sin. They teach us that Yahweh will not allow his servant to remain comfortable in sin but will ruthlessly expose his sin lest he settle down in it. You may succeed in unfaithfulness; but Yahweh will come after you. What immense and genuine comfort every servant of Christ should find in the first six words of this chapter! Not that God's pursuing grace is enjoyable. But what if grace did not pursue? What if Yahweh abandoned us when we succeed at sin?

The Savvy of Grace (12:1b-7a)

Nathan relates a sample case to David. David is the supreme judge in the land, and this story stirs his judicial juices. Perhaps David took this as an actual case Nathan had gotten wind of and was passing on in generic form. I don't know. The story is frequently called a parable, but we don't know if David thought so. Nathan didn't say that; he didn't begin with 'David, this is a parable – this is only a parable.' Nathan was too smart for that. He simply told him the story.

A fascinating story! After meeting the two men (v.1b), we hear the description (vv. 2-3) and the deed (v.4). The description is interesting. In depicting what the respective men *had,* one line suffices for the rich man (v.2), while four times as much space is needed to tell of the poor man (v.3). The poor man has far more than flocks and herds; he has a family circle and the warmth of home life.[1] But the rich man has a guest (v.4). And guests must be

fed. The rich man loathes the thought of liquidating even one of
his assets. Maybe it was while the poor man and his children were
hard at work in the fields that he went by and filched the lamb. He
'took' it (v.4b) – just as the king had 'taken' Bathsheba (11:4).
And he barbecued it for his guest.

David exploded. He was seriously religious – uttered an oath
'by the life of Yahweh' (v. 5b) – and gravely judicial – the culprit
was a 'son of death', i.e., deserved to die. Oh, there was restitution
to pay (four sheep for one; v. 6a and Exod. 22:1); but the judge saw
more than a mere property offense here. There was an attitude
beneath the act, a heartlessness, a cruelty (v.6b). Nathan had David
right where he (and Yahweh) wanted him.

Nathan's story is the turning point in the whole narrative of 2
Samuel 11–12. Even the general structure of the text seems to
suggest this:

> David sends Joab against Ammon, 11:1
> Sexual relations with Bathsheba – pregnant, 11:2-5
> Manipulating Uriah, 11:6-13
> David's successful scheme, 11:14-27
> The story that reveals, 12:1-7a
> Yahweh's severe word, 12:7b-15a
> Submitting to God, 12:15b-23
> Marital relations with Bathsehba – birth, 12:24-25
> Joab summons David against Ammon, 12:26-31

Some map out the structure so that 11:27b stands at the center of
the two chapters,[2] but I think what I have sketched here is just as
defensible.

Nathan's story then is (or is close to) the hinge of the narrative.
Yet we are not so concerned with Nathan's story as with his strategy,
for his strategy is the method of grace. Let me state what is both
obvious and significant: 'You are the man!' is the punchline not
the introduction. That may disappoint some readers. They may
prefer more of a John-the-Baptist approach (cf. Mark 6:18). But
Nathan knew what stout defences mind and mouth can muster

---

1. See also Walter Brueggemann, *First and Second Samuel,* Interpretation
(Louisville: John Knox, 1990), 279.

2. See Ronald F. Youngblood, '1,2 Samuel,' *The Expositor's Bible
Commentary,* 12 vols. (Grand Rapids: Zondervan, 1992), 3:927.

against a frontal assault. So instead of sitting down and calling
David a filthy womanizer and a cruel murderer he began with, 'Sir,
I want to tell you about a situation...' He so suckered the king into
the case that David judged himself (12:5-6). Just because Nathan's
a prophet doesn't mean he can't be sharp. But it's more than Nathan.
Nathan's strategy is nothing but the ingenuity of grace. His
technique is the godly scheming of grace that goes around the end
of our resistance and causes us to switch the floodlights on our
own darkness. Some of you may need to repent – you've thought
all these years that only the Serpent was subtle (Gen. 3:1)!

I assure you there is nothing unethical about such grace. That's
why I called it 'the godly scheming of grace'. I recall a clip in a
farming magazine that told about the debate over (what would
become) the Soil Conservation Act. It was 1934 and Senator Bennett
was chairing hearings over the matter. It is said that at one point
the senator delayed the hearings a day. The reason? He had been
tracking a Southern Plains dust storm that was on its way up the
Ohio Valley heading for the East Coast and Washington. When
hearings were resumed the next day and the dust storm had arrived,
Senator Bennett had the group take a little time off the record,
push back from the posh mahogany table, and amble over to the
windows of the Senate Office Building for a look at Washington's
midday twilight! Bennett's alleged comment was: 'Gentlemen, that
is Kansas blowing by.' The senator indicated that 'everything went
nicely' after that. There was nothing unethical about the senator
delaying the hearings a day; it was just wise.

Now that is how Nathan dealt with David. He did not accuse or
harangue. He simply upped David's blood pressure over that
ruthless rich fellow and David accused himself. Nathan only had
to make the identification (v.7a). Alexander Whyte was right:
Nathan's sword was within an inch of David's conscience before
David knew that Nathan had a sword.[3] That is the holy craftiness
of grace. If God determines to bring you back to repentance, what
chance do you have against grace like that? Grace is far more than
amazing; it's smart.

---

3. Alexander Whyte, *Bible Characters,* 2 vols in one edition (reprint, Grand
Rapids: Zondervan, 1967), 1:245.

The Fury of Grace (12:7b-12)
David has delivered his verdict (vv. 5-6), and now Nathan
announces Yahweh's word (vv. 7-12). These verses are of major
importance for the whole narrative; the reader will see how verses
10-12 control the rest of 2 Samuel. Nathan's judgment speech breaks
down into three segments:

> Grace, vv. 7-8
> Accusation, v.9
> Retribution, vv. 10-12

Yahweh begins with grace. For sin to appear as lurid as it should
it must stand in the blaze of grace. Treachery may only appear
hideous when viewed against the fidelity it has despised. So Yahweh
itemizes his grace to David (vv. 7-8):

> *I* anointed you king over Israel,
> and *I* delivered you from the hand of Saul;
> then I gave you your master's house
>> and your master's wives into your possession,
> and I gave you the house of Israel and Judah;
> and if that were too little I would give you all the more.[4]

In this way Yahweh stresses the senselessness of David's sin. David
was hardly deprived. Yahweh had loaded him with benefits. David
really was the 'rich man' – he had no need to take both a man's
wife and his life. No wonder Yahweh erupts with a 'Why?!' in
verse 9.

Verse 9 specifies the king's sin but with an interesting emphasis.
The Hebrew text places special stress on the direct objects by placing
them before the verbs.

> *Uriah the Hittite* you struck down with the sword;
> *His wife* you took as your own wife;
> But *him* you killed with the sword of the sons of Ammon (v.9b)

---

4. The first two occurrences of 'I' are emphatic in the Hebrew. I take the
giving of 'your master's wives' as a conventional way of speaking; it seems
that control of the predecessor's harem passed to the new king. In any case,
Saul's wives were accounted a part of his 'house' (v.8a).

In this way the text emphasises that David not only committed iniquity but destroyed persons. He sinned against Yahweh and ruined people. In view of all this verses 10-12 announce the judgment: (1) For the sword against Uriah 'the sword will not turn away from your house forever' (v.10a); and (2) because David took Uriah's wife Yahweh will 'take your wives before your eyes and give them to your companion,' whose sexcapades would be as public as David's were secret (vv. 11-12). This 'trouble from [David's] house' is a primary theme of 2 Samuel 13-20.

I have called this section the 'fury of grace'. But one cannot understand Yahweh's fury unless one catches Yahweh's view of David's sin. That view is expressed by the double use of the verb *bāzāh* (to despise, treat with contempt) in verses 9 and 10. 'Why have you despised the word of Yahweh by doing evil?' By his adultery and murder David had despised Yahweh's commandments, his word. He treated them as though they didn't matter. To despise Yahweh's word, however, is to despise the One who has given the word; to trample on his commandment is to trample on the Commander. Therefore, in verse 10 Yahweh cries: 'You have despised *me*' (emphasis mine).

Franz Joseph Haydn was cheerful in both his disposition and his music – but not because of his wife. Patrick Kavanaugh tells us that 'Haydn's new bride had so little regard for his composing genius that she cut up his manuscripts to use for hair-curling papers.'[5] Was she merely expressing her contempt for his music? Certainly not. Her contempt for his music was only the visible sign of her contempt for *him*. And Yahweh always sees that – he sees the true significance of sin both in David and in us. If we can grasp that, perhaps we can begin to understand, at least intellectually, the fury of grace.

It is nothing less than that. If David, a mere mortal sinner, has the moral capacity to fly into a rage over Nathan's rich man (vv. 5-6), how much more will Yahweh over David's deed? So he should. This is the gracious God who sends Nathan to David, and he is the furious God who is outraged because his servant has despised him. Part of God's grace consists in his informing us of his fury. Sometimes we try to de-claw grace. But grace is not niceness;

5. Patrick Kavanaugh, *The Spiritual Lives of Great Composers* (Nashville: Sparrow, 1992), 21.

otherwise (one is tempted to say), grace would no longer be grace. We forget the words of the hymn: ''Twas grace the *taught my heart to fear*....' Grace is not merely favor; it is also the fury that precedes the favor.

The Miracle of Grace (12:13-14)

The law tells us what David deserved – death (cf. Lev.20:10; Deut. 22:22); but grace shows us what David received – forgiveness and commuting of the death sentence (v. 13b). Readers may become cynical at this point, yammering about David's getting off easy. Please don't do that – unless you want to condemn yourself. We will do better to wade through the text.

First, note David's *confession:* 'I have sinned against Yahweh' (v.13a). Some may consider this confession too brief. After all, David only says two Hebrew words and Nathan gives him an assurance of pardon. Does David get off too easily? Is he only expected to say the right formula? We would prefer him to wallow in his guilt and plead, beg, and agonize over the possibility of pardon. If only he would writhe in obvious misery. We should know better, but we still assume that intensity of repentance contributes to atonement.

Simplicity, however, marks David's confession: 'I have sinned against Yahweh.' And precisely this simplicity makes it commendable rather than defective. The Berleburg Bible (1726 – 29) says it well:

> The words are very few, just as in the case of the publican in the Gospel of Luke (xviii.13). But that is a good sign of a thoroughly broken spirit.... There is no excuse, no cloaking, no palliation of the sin. There is no searching for a loophole,... no pretext put forward, no human weakness pleaded. He acknowledges his guilt openly, candidly, and without prevarication.[6]

Let us pause to observe how David here differs from Saul in 1 Samuel (cf. 1 Sam. 15). This text implies that the state of a man's heart is revealed in his response to the criticism of the word of God. In this David stands in contrast to Saul; he is sensitive to the divine critique. To be the man after God's own heart is not to be

---

6. Cited in C.F. Keil, *Biblical Commentary on the Books of Samuel* (1875; reprint ed., Grand Rapids: Eerdmans, 1950), 391.

sinlessly perfect but to be, among other things, utterly submissive to the accusing word of God.[7]

Secondly, consider David's *assurance*: 'Yahweh himself has put away your sin – you will not die' (v. 13b).[8] There is no reason for that statement; it was not what the law called for; the forgiveness was wholly gratuitous. I think even the church has lost the marvel of such forgiveness. We have by and large the vending machine view of forgiveness rather than the miracle view. We pop in our penitence token and out comes the assurance of pardon. In public worship we mumble through our prayers of confession, admitting we 'have left undone those things which we ought to have done, and we have done those things which we ought not to have done', even calling ourselves 'miserable offenders'. But it's all in the script, in the church bulletin. It's another thing for it to seize our mind, to convulse our emotion. Rarely do we respond as the Marquis of Argyll, who, on the night before his execution, claimed that God was 'just now saying to me, "Son, be of good cheer; thy sins are forgiven thee," ' and upon repeating those words burst into tears and retired to a window to weep there.[9] Instead we have lost the goosebumps on our souls. Having a God 'who passes over rebellion' (Mic. 7:18) should make us shudder with joy.

In this miracle of grace note, thirdly, David's *substitute:* 'However, because you have totally scorned (the enemies of) Yahweh in this matter, that son that is born to you will surely die' (v. 14).[10] Yahweh forgives the guilt of sin but inflicts the consequences of sin. He cleanses sin's defilement but may continue

---

7. On being 'after his [Yahweh's] heart', see V. Philips Long, *The Reign and Rejection of King Saul: A Case for Literary and Theological Coherence*, SBL Dissertation Series 118 (Atlanta: Scholars, 1989), 92-93.

8. On the Hebrew text here, cf. J.P. Fokkelman, *Narrative Art and Poetry in the Books of Samuel*, vol 1, *King David (II Sam. 9-20 & I Kings 1-2)* (Assen: Van Gorcum, 1981), 87.

9. Thomas McCrie, *The Story of the Scottish Church from the Reformation to the Disruption* (1875; reprint ed., Glasgow: Free Presbyterian, 1988), 257.

10. I have included 'the enemies of' because this is the idiom of the text; I have placed the words in brackets to indicate the meaning. Scorning the enemies of Yahweh simply means scorning Yahweh himself; the expression in the text is a euphemism used in place of the more direct terminology. For Egyptian parallels, see K.A. Kitchen, 'Israel Seen from Egypt: Understanding the Biblical Text from Visuals and Methodology,' *Tyndale Bulletin* 42:1

its discipline.[11] For David, Yahweh's forgiveness was both marvelous and costly – the child would die. It is as if the child will die in David's place. There was no doubt that David was the one under the threat of death. David himself had judged Nathan's rich man a 'son of death' (v.5). Yet Nathan had assured David that he would not die (v. 13). But a death would occur. The child to be born would die (v. 14b). It is as if the child is David's substitute. I do not intend to read New Testament meanings back into an Old Testament text. I only want readers to note the pattern here, for there are some of us who know this paradox of forgiveness that is both free and costly, because a son of David has been our substitute.

The Sense of Grace (12:15b-25)

The child became critically ill – Yahweh struck the child (v. 15b). But the saga of grace is not finished, for sometimes we receive more grace in God's strokes than in his favors. This section focuses on the behavior of David, a man clearly in the grip of grace. I want to fasten on this main concern, but readers should not ignore the writer's literary craft in telling the story. The following outline shows both the content of the story and the art of the writer.

> The son Yahweh struck, v. 15b
>> David's humiliation, v.16
>>> Servants' perplexity, vv. 17-18
>>>> David's question, v. 19
>>> David's 'restoration,' v. 20
>>>> Servants' perplexity, v.21
>>>>> David's answer vv.22-23
> The son Yahweh loved, vv. 24-25

(1991): 116. Normally the OT uses the direct expression (see the use of this verb, $nā'as$, to scorn, disdain show contempt, in, e.g., Num. 14:11, 23; 16:30; Deut. 31:20; Isa. 1:4).

11. Cf. Walther Eichrodt (*Theology of the Old Testament,* The Old Testament Library, 2 vols. [Philadelphia: Westminster, 1967], 2:455): '[T]he reality of divine forgiveness did not in all circumstances have to be proved by earthly blessings. If God received the sinner back into favour, one might expect the natural outcome of this to be a change in his earthly fortunes; but the two things were not understood as simply identical. God's pardon was valuable and meaningful in itself, as is shown with increasing clarity by the fact that men could speak of forgiveness which did not just do away with the

Now in this segment David's behaviour both scares and baffles his servants. David throws himself into supplication: 'David pleaded with God for the child. He fasted and went into his house and spent the nights lying on the ground' (v. 16, NIV). He turns deaf ears to his aides' pleas to eat. His intensity petrifies them; when the child dies, they can't bring themselves to tell him. Who knows if David will prove suicidal? But David is anything but dense; he senses something has happened. His direct question brings a straight answer (v.19). When he hears the news, he picks himself up, takes a shower, splashes on some after shave, changes into clean clothes, and goes off to the tabernacle to worship. Then he comes home and tells the cooks how hungry he is (v.20). His servants are dizzy trying to understand him. Why not fast and weep after the death? Why so wildly unconventional? And so on. So David explains:

> While the child was alive, I fasted and wept, for I thought, 'Who knows? Yahweh may show grace to me and the child will live!' Yet now he has died. Why should I go on fasting? Am I able to bring him back again? I am on my way to him, but he will never return to me (vv. 22-23).[12]

That explains David's relentless intercession. David thought that maybe Yahweh's sentence (v. 14b) was not his last word. Maybe, David thought, he's stirring me to pray. It all rests on David's thinking, his assumption, about God. 'I thought, "Who knows? Yahweh may show grace to me!"' See how well David knows his God! Showing grace is Yahweh's forte. And who can tell what a God like that may delight to do in this case? Who can imagine how gracious a God of all grace wants to be to us in our sins and messes? For David grace is not a doctrinal concept but the peculiar bent of God's nature.

There is that story of the always-impoverished philosopher in the court of Alexander the Great. Being in dire financial straits

---

punishment, but went hand in hand with it, as in the descriptions of Jacob's fortunes or of the affliction of David because of his crime against Uriah.'

12. I do not think we should press v.23b as a glowing expression of hope. By 'I am on my way to him' David means that he too is going to die, i.e., enter the realm of death where his infant son has gone. I am not saying David had no hope beyond death (see Ps. 16:8-11; 17:15); I am only saying *this text* does not express it. See, however, the remarks of Calvin (*Sermons on 2 Samuel*, trans. Douglas Kelly [Edinburgh: Banner of Truth, 1992], 592-93).

again, where better to go than to Alexander, his master and
conqueror of the world? Alexander gave him a commission to
receive from his treasurer whatever he wanted. He promptly
demanded, in Alexander's name, ten thousand pounds. The treasurer
was aghast; he refused to give it. He went to Alexander with the
matter – the request was unreasonable, the amount absurd.
Alexander heard his treasurer out, then replied: 'Let the money be
instantly paid. I am delighted with this philosopher's way of
thinking; he has done me singular honor; by the largeness of his
request, he shows the high idea he has conceived, both of my
superior wealth and my royal munificence.'[13]

In this case Yahweh did not grant David's plea, but that fact
does not negate the rightness of David's thinking about God. One
wonders – reverently – if Yahweh a la Alexander may have said, 'I
like this king's way of thinking…' You see, David does not merely
have a grip on grace; grace has gripped him. Doesn't this text then
give hope to any fallen believer? You are conscious of your failures,
repentant of your sins, yet have no ground in yourself to expect
mercy, no reason to expect favor. You wonder if for the rest of
your days you are doomed to exist within the confines of God's
frown. But *if* you have more than a doctrine of grace, if you have a
sense of grace – if you think of Yahweh as David did, you will
walk on in the light of hope. This passage does not mean to help
you excuse the guilt of your sin but to help you get beyond the
despair of your sin.

Endnote (12:26-31)
We almost forgot the Ammonites. The story of David's sin had
begun with the note about Joab's foray against Ammon (11:1).
Now the writer returns to Rabbah, which Joab has brought to the
brink of capitulation (vv. 26-27).[14] Proper convention calls for the
king to strike the finishing blows (vv. 29-30). David subjugates
Ammon and imposes forced labor (v. 31).[15]

---

13. John Whitecross, *The Shorter Catechism Illustrated from Christian
Biography and History* (rpt. ed., London: Banner of Truth, 1968), 170-71.

14. For more detail see Joyce Baldwin, *1 & 2 Samuel,* Tyndale Old Testament
Commentaries (Leicester: InterVarsity, 1988), 245.

15. Verse 31 is difficult. The NIV is probably close: 'brought out the people
who were there, consigning them to labor with saws and with iron picks and

Yet coming back to the Ammonites after reading all of 11:2–12:25 does strike a reader as anti-climactic. Perhaps that is intended. After the writer has walked you through the sin and shame and severity of the whole story, perhaps he wants you to think that the Ammonites really don't matter that much. Comparatively. Of far more weight is the obedience and holiness of Yahweh's anointed. The conflict with Ammon was won, but the real battle was lost. It reminds one of Robert Murray McCheyne's reflection on his role as pastor: 'My people's greatest need is my personal holiness.'

The terrible failure of David is important to our writer. Throughout 1–2 Samuel the writer introduces the leaders of Israel: Eli and sons, Samuel, and Saul (not to mention the would-bes like Eliab and Abner). All of them are flawed in some way. Eli's sons and Saul severely so; even Samuel falls short in some respects (cf. 1 Sam. 8:1-2, 5; 16:6-7).[16] And now David, the covenant king. Just because David is Yahweh's beloved and chosen king does not mean he retains the kingdom by any merit but only by grace, for he is a 'son of death'. In 1–2 Samuel *all* human leadership is flawed, which means that the kingdom – if there is to be one – can only be established and maintained by grace. Hence 1–2 Samuel makes us lift our eyes to wait for the Messianic King.

15. All in the Family
2 Samuel 13

As soon as she received word from the king, she was on her way. Her half-brother Amnon was down sick, and she was to go play cook and nurse. She was a beauty and a king's daughter, but she knew how to work. Scarcely in the door, she became a flurry of industry: she 'took dough, kneaded it, made cakes in his sight, and baked the cakes'; then she 'took the pan and dished them out before him, but he refused to eat' (vv. 8b,9b, NASB). Too sick to eat? To weak to feed himself? Anyway, Amnon dismissed all his attendants;

---

axes, and he made them work at brick making.' The saw-pick-axe work details could have been assigned the task of ripping down Rabbah's fortifications. See further, P. Kyle McCarter, Jr., *II Samuel,* The Anchor Bible (New York: Doubleday, 1984), 311,313.

16. On the latter passage see my comments in *Looking on the Heart: Expositions of the Book of 1 Samuel,* 2 vols. (Grand Rapids: Baker, 1994), 2:27-30.

he wanted her to feed him. No problem. She took up the food, came into his bedroom, got close enough so as not to slop the food – and Amnon's hands locked on her wrists. Terror takes a second or two. In ten minutes Tamar's whole life lies in tatters.

Our chapter is a mess: lust and rape, hate and murder. But we will jump right in. We will deal with the literary aspects of the text as we discuss its teaching. The primary question is: what does the writer of 2 Samuel 13 want to highlight for us? I suggest three major emphases.

The Perversion We Ought to Abhor (13:1-22)
This first half of chapter 13 has received close attention from literary critics, who have shown that it is a very carefully crafted story that places Amnon's unthinkable deed and inexplicable change from lust to loathing at the very heart of the narrative. George Ridout[1] has set it out this way:

A. Amnon is in love with Tamar (vss. 1-4)

  B. Tamar comes to Amnon's house and
    bakes bread for him (vss. 5-9a)

    C. Amnon orders his servants out,
      that he might be alone with Tamar (vss. 9b-10)

      D. Amnon commands Tamar to come lie with
        him; she pleads with him but to no avail (vss. 11-14a)

        E. Amnon rapes Tamar, and his love for her
          turns to hate (vss. 14b-15a)

      D[1]. Amnon commands Tamar to get out; she pleads
        with him but to no avail (vss. 15b-16)

    C[1]. Amnon calls a servant back and orders him to lock Tamar out
      (vs.17)
  B[1]. Tamar leaves Amnon's house,
    mourning her fate (vss. 18-19)

A[1]. Absalom hates Amnon for having raped Tamar (vss. 20-22)

---

1. George Ridout, 'The Rape of Tamar: A Rhetorical Analysis of 2 Sam 13:1-22,' in *Rhetorical Criticism: Essays in Honor of James Muilenburg*, ed. Jared

However, right now I want to focus on Tamar rather than Amnon.
Readers will sense their sympathy welling up for Tamar, especially
when they hear her two desperate pleas (vv. 12-13, 16; see D. and
D¹ in Ridout's structure).

Looking back over the story, we see her trapped (vv.5-11),
ignored (vv. 14a, 16b), raped (v.14b), despised (v.15), banished
(v.17), and ruined (vv. 18-19, 20b). We must do what Amnon did
not do: listen to Tamar. The writer's viewpoint comes through
Tamar's pleas, and we must hear her if we are to form a proper
estimate of Amnon's deed.

As Amnon held her in his vise-like grip and invited her
submission, Tamar blurted out her reaction:

> v.12   No, my brother, do not violate me!
>   For things like this are not to be done in Israel;
>   don't do this godlessness!
>
> v.13   And I – where could I take my disgrace?
>   And you – you would be like one of the
>   godless wretches in Israel!
>   And now – please speak to the king,
>   for he will not hold me back from you.

Amnon had called her 'my sister' when demanding a little
afternoon sex. She rejected the idea with, 'No, my brother!' This
relation was a problem (already broached in verse 1). Rape was
shameful enough; but this was more than rape. It was incest and
was explicitly forbidden in the covenant law (Lev. 18:9, 11; 20:17;
Deut. 27:22).[2] Hence Tamar called it *nĕbālāh* (godlessness) and
argued that if Amnon did this he would be like one of the *nĕbālîm*

J. Jackson and Martin Kessler (Pittsburgh: Pickwick, 1974), 81. See also
Charles Conroy, *Absalom Absalom!: Narrative and Language in 2 Sam 13-20*, Analecta Biblica (Rome: Biblical Institute Press, 1978), 17-42; and Jenny
Smith, 'The Discourse Structure of the Rape of Tamar (2 Sam. 13:1-22),' *Vox
Evangelica* 20 (1990): 21-42.

2. Some scholars hold that 2 Samuel 13 has to do with rape not incest, primarily
because they date (wrongly, in my view) the laws of Leviticus and
Deuteronomy later than David's time and allege they were not in effect prior
to the time of 2 Samuel 13. But see Jacob Milgrom, *Leviticus 1-16*, The Anchor
Bible (New York: Doubleday, 1991), 3-13, for the antiquity of Leviticus-
Numbers materials. Some object that if Amnon's deed was incestuous one

in Israel. A *nābāl* (singular) is not a 'fool' as we think of fools (though English versions have traditionally translated it that way), but a wicked pervert or a 'godless wretch' (see Isaiah 32:6 for a sketch). A *nābāl* will do *něbālāh*, flagrant godlessness (the term can refer to such sexual offenses as rape, single [Gen. 34:7] or repeated [Judg. 20:5-6], premarital unchastity [Deut. 22:21], homosexual relations [Judg. 19:23-24]).[3]

Tamar not only called the deed by its right name but pled with Amnon to consider the consequences, both for her and for him (v.13a). She was certainly right about her case. He was stronger; he 'laid her' (v.14). When he finished, he said two words in Hebrew: 'Get up, get out' (v. 15b). Tamar protests: kicking her out now is a greater wrong than violating her (v. 16). But Amnon has neither ears nor heart. He calls in and orders his attendant, 'Get this woman out of my sight' (v. 17, TEV). Strictly, the word 'woman' is not in the Hebrew text. He says, 'Get this out,' as if Tamar were a bit of impersonal trash to be put out at the kerb. Manhandled again and dumped outside, 'Tamar put dust on her head and rent the ornamented tunic she was wearing; she put her hands on her head, and walked away, screaming loudly as she went' (v.19, NJPS).[4] Her brother Absalom's words (v. 20a) must have been cold comfort; he could hardly restore to her what Amnon had taken from her.[5] She lived in Absalom's household, and one word summed up her life: 'desolate', or as Keil renders it, 'laid waste'. The writer wants to win your sympathies for Tamar. He wants you to see the deep

---

cannot explain Tamar's plea for him to ask the king for permission to marry her (v.13b). But one can explain it. First, Tamar is desperately struggling to prevent Amnon's rape; she is clutching at straws in an emergency and cannot be expected to speak as a paradigm of legal precision. And secondly, she likely knew, as various texts indicate (vv. 5-7, 24-27; 1 Kings 1:6), that David was permissive to a fault with his children. If cajoled he might well permit a relation that was otherwise prohibited.

3. See the discussion in P. Kyle McCarter, Jr., *II Samuel*, The Anchor Bible (New York: Doubleday, 1984), 322-23. See also his argument that Amnon's offense was incestual rape and that the laws of Leviticus 18 were in effect at this time (pp. 323-24).

4. On the significance of tearing her robe, see Shimon Bar-Efrat, *Narrative Art in the Bible*, JSOT Supplement Series (Sheffield: Almond, 1989), 270.

5. Karl Gutbrod, *Das Buch vom Reich*, Die Botschaft des Alten Testaments, 2nd ed. (Stuttgart: Calwer, 1973), 161.

sinfulness of Amnon's deed and the sadness of that sinfulness in Tamar's condition. He wants you to abhor this perversion.

That is the tricky part, for we don't abhor it that much. We find it interesting. We become like spectators entranced with the disaster of others. In 1979 we were living in Jackson, Mississippi. About Easter time the Pearl River flooded and engulfed hundreds of homes in five to six feet of water. Local authorities had problems with people who wanted to drive near the flooded area – not to work, not to help, but simply to sight see. There seems to be a subtle pleasure folks get from seeing the misery of others. That can happen to us in 2 Samuel 13. We may be fascinated with Amnon's scheming without hating his wickedness; we may be entranced – as many are – with the literary artistry of the story without grieving Tamar's ruin. There is a perversion in us; we are so unholy we find it supremely difficult genuinely to hate sin.

The Persons We Ought to Observe
The focus on biblical characters in biblical narrative usually leads biblical interpretation astray. The Bible's stress, after all, is on God's words and deeds. However, in 2 Samuel 13 the writer so graphically depicts the cast that we might be pardoned for thinking that he wants us to take a close look at them. The writer portrays each of the four major male characters as deficient in some way.

Amnon – Passion Without Love
Amnon 'loved' his half-sister Tamar (v.1b) and 'became frustrated to the point of illness on account of his sister Tamar, for she was a virgin, and it seemed impossible for him to do anything to her' (v.2, NIV). The word translated 'virgin' is *bĕtûlāh*, a word that denotes a young woman of marriageable age rather than a virgin as such.[6] Tamar then is sexually mature. Hence Amnon's frustration – Tamar is both beautiful and, in Amnon's view, ready. However, for some reason (perhaps royal daughters were under protective oversight) he can see no way 'to do anything to her' (v. 2b).

The last statement of verse 2 is scary. Amnon wants to do something to Tamar. Not much doubt about what Amnon has in mind. I am not impressed by those who argue that Amnon, as David's oldest son, seduced Tamar to strengthen his claim to the

---

6. See TWOT, 1:137-39, and TDOT, 2:338-43.

throne.[7] Were that the case, Amnon would have clung to Tamar long-term – instead of trashing her immediately. Rather, Amnon is simply, as Tamar suggested, godless (v.13). Amnon has far more glands than brains (which is why he needed Jonadab, vv. 3-5).

Yet even Amnon can figure out what he wants to do with Tamar when he is finally alone with her (vv. 10-11). Would Amnon's reaction have been different if Tamar had willingly co-operated? Who knows: I doubt it. In any case, Amnon had a hearing problem (v.14a) and forcibly raped her. The writer has crafted his story so that this most tragic moment stands at the center of it (see the structural layout given earlier in this chapter); but he could do nothing to prepare us for the shock we meet:[8]

> Then Amnon hated her with a very intense hatred; in fact, the hatred with which he hated her was greater than the love with which he had loved her. So Amnon said to her, 'Get up! Get out!' (v.15).

Amnon's was no passing disgust; he turned a deaf ear to Tamar again (v.16b), threw her out and locked her out.

We are only shocked momentarily, for now we see that Amnon's 'love' was only lust, and we know lust and hatred are natural bedfellows. Amnon has multiplied himself thousands of times in contemporary music videos and rap music, where we meet 'remarkably one-dimensional characters, ruled entirely by their all-powerful genitalia'.[9] Such media glamorize the hard, bitter, sadistic sex they promote – but also expose it for those who have eyes to see. But teenagers and sixth graders seldom do.

Jonadab – Wisdom without Principle (13:3-5, 32-35)

Jonadab was Amnon's friend and David's nephew (v.3a) and 'a very wise man' (v. 3b). By 'wise', the writer means 'skillful' or 'sharp'. Jonadab immediately showcases his sharpness. He notices and inquires about Amnon's condition: 'Why, O son of the king, are you so dejected morning after morning? Won't you tell me?' (v.4a). Amnon must have been suffering an extended depression, plainly visible to those near him. When Jonadab hears of Amnon's passion for Tamar, he suggests to Amnon a plan for fulfilling his

---

7. See article 'Jonadab' in ISBE, 2:977, and ABD, 3:936.

8. Conroy, *Absalom Absalom!*, 32.

9. Michael Medved, *Hollywood vs. America* (New York: Harper, 1992), 104.

designs upon Tamar (v. 5). Thus Jonadab is 'wise'; he knows all the angles, knows how to work the angles, knows how to make anything succeed – even the rape of a cousin. Jonadab is the consummate politician: he gets things done.

Not only that, but he knows what is going on. He has clear insight into events and circumstances. In verses 32-35, in the panic following Amnon's murder, Jonadab was the only cool head at the palace. First reports had it that Absalom had butchered all the king's sons (vv. 30-31). But in the mayhem Jonadab assured David that only Amnon was dead. He even knew why: it was Absalom's long-considered revenge for Amnon's ravishing of Tamar (v.32). Jonadab was right (vv. 34-35) – as usual.

Jonadab is perhaps the most dangerous man in the whole fiasco. Amnon's evil is relatively restricted; he will always be in bed with someone, tending his hormones. But Jonadab has the skill to leak evil everywhere. He is dangerous because he has skill without scruple, wisdom without ethics, insight without integrity. He reminds me of the anecdote about the Vicar of Bray, who was Catholic under Henry VIII, Protestant under Edward VI, Catholic again under Queen Mary, then a Protestant in the reign of Queen Elizabeth. Someone critized him as bringing shame and scandal on his calling. The vicar replied, 'I cannot help that; if I changed my religion, I am sure I keep true to my principle, which is, to live and die vicar of Bray.'[10]

That is Jonadab: nothing succeeds like success; nothing impedes like standards. Jonadab can show you how to raise needed funds for your Christian institution or how to rape a scrumptious female; whichever you want. Here is a caution light blinking at us, as Calvin clearly saw:

> Therefore, when we see that the Spirit of God stated here, as a reproach, that Jonadab was a prudent man, and that he so forgot himself as to be a pimp for his male cousin, disgrace his female cousin, and be disloyal to his uncle, the king – it all warns us to pray that if God has given us some prudence, he would also add integrity and sincerity so that we may keep ourselves from craftiness.[11]

---

10. John Whitecross, *The Shorter Catechism Illustrated from Christian Biography and History* (reprint ed., London: Banner of Truth, 1968), 78.

11. John Calvin, *Sermons on 2 Samuel,* trans. Douglas Kelly (Edinburgh: Banner of Truth, 1992), 619.

Nor is this merely a 'secular' problem. Many of us have observed that in the church those with the greatest gifts pose the gravest threat, for unless their gifts are wrapped in godliness they multiply disaster among Christ's flock.

David – Anger without Justice (13:21)

'And King David heard about all these things....' David heard how Amnon had used him, had weasled his permission for Tamar to come to his house. He heard how Amnon had abused Tamar, how he had disposed of her, how she was seen and heard running and screaming through the streets with robe ripped. He perhaps heard how she was now a destroyed woman, existing in her brother Absalom's house. David 'heard about all these things, and he was very angry'. That's good. But that was all. And that's bad. David was irate; he was furious; he could scarcely contain his rage. But, unfortunately, he did.

I say unfortunately, because there was something right about David's fury. It should have led to a righteous result. His anger should have led to justice. Amnon should have been punished and Tamar exonerated. Instead Amnon is not held accountable, Tamar receives no redress, and Absalom is handed a plausible excuse for revenge. David heard. He was very angry. And he did nothing.[12]

Of course, legions of expositors say that David found himself a prisoner of his own folly. After all, how could he call Amnon to account when he himself had violated Bathsheba and eliminated her husband (chs. 11–12)? Hardly a solid basis for exercising moral authority. And yet such an argument does not negate David's responsibility. He holds nevertheless the office of magistrate – one might say – both in his kingdom and in his family. As both father and king he is charged with maintaining justice, whether he is personally compromised or not. One may understand David's failure to act; one may not, however, excuse it. So Amnon remains an unpunished felon, Tamar languishes as damaged goods, and

---

12. Verse 21 is longer in LXX, which REB follows: 'When King David heard the whole story he was very angry; but he would not hurt Amnon because he was his eldest son and he loved him.' Similarly, NRSV and NJB. A Qumran fragment and Josephus seem to assume a text like LXX. I am not yet convinced LXX reflects the original text and still prefer the more abrupt reading of the received Hebrew text.

Absalom becomes a seething vigilante.[13]

Karl Gutbrod has captured, sadly but accurately, the picture of David in this narrative: 'A second Eli, this David, who places his fatherly love higher than the will and justice of the Lord' (cf. 1 Sam. 2:29).[14] He certainly does not mimic Yahweh's kingship or he would be a stronghold for the oppressed and bring the way of the wicked to ruin (Pss. 9:7-9; 146:5-9).

Absalom – Hatred without Restraint (13:22-39)

As often noted, the first narrative in chapter 13 begins with Amnon's love and ends with Absalom's hatred (vv. 1, 22). Absalom hated Amnon, because Amnon had abused Absalom's sister. But Absalom's hatred was a sophisticated, high-class hatred. He gave no public clue of his animosity, nor did he take any hostile action toward Amnon. Absalom's was a cool, patient hatred, a rage that could wait. After two years the moment arrived. Absalom was having a sheep-shearing party (v.23) – it would be a perfect time to shear sheep and butcher Amnon. This episode (vv. 23-39) constitutes the second narrative of the chapter and somewhat parallels the development of the first narrative. The reader can both observe this development and obtain an overview of verses 23-39 in the following scheme:[15]

Absalom's sister, v. 1
    Amnon, Jonadab, and David: getting Tamar accessible, vv. 2-7
        Amnon's rape of Tamar, vv. 8-17
            Reaction: grief, tearing garment, vv. 18-19
                Solace from Absalom, v.20
                    Reactions of David and Absalom vv. 21-22

Absalom's sheep-shearing, v.23
    Absalom and David: getting Amnon accessible, vv. 24-27
        Absalom's murder of Amnon, vv. 28-29
            Reaction: grief, tearing garments, vv. 30-31
                Solace from Jonadab, vv. 32-33, 34-35
                    Reactions of David & Absalom & others, vv. 36-39

---

13. There are some who think that Jonadab and Absalom were actually co-conspirators willing to sacrifice Tamar, thereby wreck Amnon, and pave Absalom's way to the throne (cf. Ronald F. Youngblood, '1, 2 Samuel,' *The Expositor's Bible Commentary*, 12 vols. [Grand Rapids: Zondervan, 1992], 3:959). It is an interesting reconstruction but, I think, not likely.

It all took place up at Baal-hazor, about fifteen miles north of Jerusalem.[16] Absalom had invited King David and his staff, but David had declined, citing the excessive expense Absalom would incur (vv. 24-25). So far, so good. Absalom then cajoled David to permit Amnon's presence (vv. 26-27). The plan was to wait until Amnon loosened up during happy hour, then, at their master's word or signal, Absalom's henchmen were to wipe out Amnon (v.28). Everything went off like clockwork (v. 29a). Naturally, panic reigned until all the facts were in (vv. 29b-36). Absalom fled (vv. 34,37, 38) but Amnon was dead – and that is all that mattered.

Of course our danger is that we may think Absalom embodies some restricted number of social whackos who plot and pull off sinister and/or highly visible crimes. We consider him a rare bird, driven by a consuming malice to destroy people. Like Gaetan Dugas, the French Canadian flight steward sometimes identified as Patient Zero, the initial carrier of the AIDS virus in the United States. Before he died in 1984, Dugas calculated he had had sexual episodes with some 2,500 partners in New York and California bathhouses, motels, bars, and restrooms. Even after doctors informed Dugas he had a fatal, sexually transmitted disease, he went on infecting dozens of partners. After each liaison he would tell them, 'I've got gay cancer.'[17]

We reason, however, that premier haters like Dugas and Absalom are in a class by themselves. But it is not so; Absalom is not the rare exception but the universal rule. Absalom is everyman. Remember the apostle's lurid description of us B.C. (before Christ) in Titus 3:3:

> For we also were once foolish, disobedient, being deceived, living as slaves to all sorts of passions and pleasures, *spending our lives in malice and envy, hated and hating one another* (emphasis mine).

There is no hope of escape except through the 'goodness and generosity of God our Savior' (Tit. 3:4). Apart from that, we share Absalom's nature whether or not we duplicate his deed.

---

14. Gutbrod, *Das Buch vom Reich,* 161.

15. After working out this structure I discovered that Robert Polzin had also noted some of the same parallels; see *David and the Deuteronomist* (Bloomington: Indiana University, 1993), 134-35.

16. On the site location, see ABD, 1:552.

17. Charles Colson, *Against the Night* (Ann Arbor: Servant, 1989) 67.

Here then are these four portraits in the text. The tragedy, however, appears when we look beyond the separate depictions to the whole picture: *no one* is doing righteousness in Israel.

The Perspective We Ought to Keep

We have come all the way through 2 Samuel 13, where disaster follows disaster, and life in David's kingdom rushes along, driven by lust, conniving, weakness, and hatred. A shattered woman remains ignored by justice and unrestored by murder. And God is never mentioned in the whole affair. What is Yahweh doing in all this? Has the kingdom he established lurched out of control, its course subject only to the whims and sins of men?

We know on our part how our designs elude our control. When entertainer Martha Raye died she left money to the People for the Ethical Treatment of Animals, an anti-fur organization. She also left her seventh husband, Mark Harris, about $1.5 million. He in turn plans to become a fashion designer, to design and market his own line of furs. PETA went up in arms, its director asserting that Martha Raye would roll over in her grave if she knew Harris was using her money to finance his furry folly. But Martha could exercise no control.

That is sometimes the impression we have of Yahweh's kingdom and/or of his rule in history. It all seems like a macrocosm of 2 Samuel 13, with everything bashing and bouncing along and God seemingly not in residence. But, of course, that is not true of 2 Samuel 13. We have already been given the clue for this chapter in 12:10-12. Yahweh had told David that 'the sword would not depart from your house' and that he was 'raising up disaster against you from your own house' (12:10,11). Is this not what has begun to happen in chapter 13? Many have pointed out the appropriateness of the disaster: Amnon's sexual escapade with Tamar corresponding to David's with Bathsheba, and Absalom's contrived murder of Amnon paralleling David's of Uriah. In this sordid episode, then, Yahweh is *fulfilling his word of judgment* against the house of David. Humanly speaking everything seems to be going aruck; yet Yahweh is fulfilling his word. Not that it is pleasant – anything but. Yet Yahweh has not hung out a vacancy sign over his universe or his people. He is there, bringing his word to pass. Sometimes only that assurance keeps his people sane.

16. The Manipulators
2 Samuel 14

Like 2 Samuel 13, chapter 14 falls into two major sections:

Vv. 1-22:   How Joab gets action to bring back Absalom
Vv. 23-33: How Absalom gets action to receive royal favor

And the scheming (as in chapter 13) continues: Joab uses a crafty female from Tekoa, while Absalom hatches his own bold plan using unskilled labor. But there is no real joy in the text, for it is not the prodigal but the murderer who returns. And the father's kiss is not the prelude to celebration but a cue for foreboding.[1]

Apparently David had little enthusiasm for Absalom's return from exile and still less for reconciliation with him. One would never get this idea from our English versions, for in 13:39 and 14:1 they tell us, almost with one voice, that 'the spirit of the king longed to go to Absalom' and that 'the king's heart longed for Absalom' (e.g., NIV). Certainly 13:39 is difficult, but the verb $k\bar{a}l\bar{a}h$ is generally stronger then 'to long' or 'yearn'; it means to come to an end, to be used up. The verse may then be saying that 'the king's enthusiasm for marching out against [Absalom] was spent' (McCarter). The expression 'to go out to' (McCarter's 'march out against') can be used in a hostile sense (Deut. 28:7). In 14:1 there is no verb 'long/long for'. That verse simply says Joab knew that the heart of the king was either 'upon Absalom' (i.e., he was thinking about him) or 'against Absalom' (he remained hostile to him), the latter being perhaps more likely in light of Daniel 11:28.[2] Any idea of longing in 14:1 must be imported from 13:39. If David was already yearning for Absalom, Joab's whole stratagem in chapter 14 becomes unnecessary. Why all the subtle maneuvering if all David requires is a little nudge to send him off doing what he already wants to do? But if David remains 'against' Absalom, one can

---

1. Karl Gutbrod, *Das Buch vom Reich,* Die Botschaft des Alten Testaments, 2nd ed. (Stuttgart: Calwer, 1973), 173.

2. On this whole matter, see C.F. Keil, *Biblical Commentary on the Books of Samuel* (1875; reprint ed., Grand Rapids: Eerdmans, 1950), 404-406; A.F. Kirkpatrick, *The Second Book of Samuel,* The Cambridge Bible for Schools and Colleges (Cambridge: CUP, 1897), 141-42; and P. Kyle McCarter, *II Samuel,* The Anchor Bible (New York: Doubleday, 1984), 344.

understand Joab's lining up his best guns. Verse 24 clearly shows David was in no mood to welcome Absalom back with open arms.

I must admit 2 Samuel 14 puzzles me. It is not so difficult to understand what the chapter reports; but I have the eerie feeling that these episodes may not be about what they seem to be about. It all reminds me of a story Paul Boller passes on about Adolph Sabath of Illinois, chairman of the House Rules Committee from 1940-52. One of the committee members, Eugene Cox of Georgia, wanted to vote on a resolution to change the committee's rules so that any member of the committee could call up bills for votes even over the chairman's objection. Sabath was in his eighties and he begged Cox not to pass the resolution. With faltering voice he told Cox he had a weak heart, and then pleaded, 'Mr. Cox, this will kill me, if you pass this resolution. The humiliation! It will kill me!' Cox retorted that he didn't care, that Sabath had dallied on this far too long. Instantly, Sabath pitched forward out of his chair, fell at Cox's feet, and lay motionless there. Cox panicked, exclaiming, 'I've killed him!' Cox and other Congressmen carried Sabath into the nearest office, laid him on a large leather couch and ran for a doctor. Ohio's Clarence Brown was left with Sabath. After a minute or two Brown saw Sabath open one of his eyes and scan the room. Brown was aghast: 'Why you old rascal! There's nothing wrong with you!' Sabath shot back, 'Well, Mr. Cox didn't get his resolution, did he?'[3] So there seemed to be a death, but there wasn't. And that is the way 2 Samuel 14 strikes me. There seems, for example, to be a lot of wisdom in this story. But is there? Or is it only a matter of appearance? We will try to arrive at valid teaching points by posing our questions of the story.

Is This Wisdom?

As Amnon relied on the advice of 'wise' Jonadab (13:3), so Joab solicits the help of a 'wise woman' from Tekoa (ten miles south of Jerusalem) to press upon David his argument for the return of Absalom. The pattern of the episode is easy to trace:

---

3. Paul F. Boller, Jr., *Congressional Anecdotes* (New York: Oxford, 1991), 64.

Joab may have 'put the words in her mouth' (v. 3), but this woman had her own finesse with words. She summarizes her distress: she's a widow; had two sons; they were fighting out in the field; there was no one to intervene; one struck the other – the blow proved fatal (vv. 5-6); now the rest of the clan is clamoring for the remaining son to be turned over to be executed for taking his brother's life (v.7). But, the widow alleges, her relations have their own agenda. She quotes their sentiments in verse 7: 'Then we will get rid of the heir as well' (NIV). Their passion for justice is only a cover for their greed. If they execute the remaining son, then not only will she be without support or help but her husband will be left without heir or descendant, and, at the widow's death, his property would become available to extended family. Under a guise of justice they plot injustice. Would the king please intervene?

David seems willing to come down on her side in the case (v. 8). Should anyone keep badgering her about this, she need only bring him to David and the bother would cease (v.10). The woman, however, seems to want David to go on oath about immunity for her son (v. 11a), which the king promptly does (v. 11b).

The woman now asks for a point of personal privilege (v.12) and raises an accusing question (v.13). The king is being two-faced. He has decreed that the woman's banished son should be restored, but he has not moved a finger to restore his own banished son.[4] Mortality may be unavoidable (v.14), but it is God's way to preserve and restore life: 'But God does not take away life; instead, he devises ways so that a banished person may not remain estranged from him' (v. 14b, NIV). No sooner does the woman deliver her broadside than she cushions the blow by reverting to her own situation (vv. 15-17), explaining again her reason for appealing to the king. Some

---

4. She may also be assuming that Absalom is heir to the throne and that by depriving Israel of the heir David wrongs and acts 'against the people of God' (v.13a).

scholars think verses 15-17 are dislocated – why would the woman revert to her own case after reaching the main point? But they miss the woman's subtlety. She brings up her own situation again because she doesn't want David to think that her main point is the main point.

> First, the woman means to give the impression that her own personal problem is the reason for her appearance and the case of the exiled king's son is mentioned only incidentally, as a related instance. By the construction of her address she means to make what is, of course, her main concern, the case of Absalom, seem to be a subsidiary matter.[5]

David, however, is wise (cf. v.20) and can smell the difference between main points and sub-points. 'Isn't the hand of Joab with you in all this?' (v. 19, NIV). She replies, 'By your life, my lord the king, there is no going to the right or going to the left from all that my lord the king has stated' (v.19b), which, being interpreted, means 'Yes'. After the exposé, however, David does acquiesce to Joab's desire (vv. 21-22).

Joab's scheme succeeds, then, through the offices of the wise woman from Tekoa. But is his/her wisdom really wisdom? The argument appears plausible: the widow has two sons (parallel to Amnon and Absalom); one killed the other (as Absalom killed Amnon); the life of the killer is forfeit unless special provision is made for his security. And so on. Yet the cases are not parallel. The widow's sons get into a fight somewhere off by themselves; one thing leads to another, and the blows of the 'winner' prove fatal to the other. Perhaps the woman has not given us enough

---

5. Hans Wilhelm Hertzberg, *I & II Samuel*, The Old Testament Library (Philadelphia: Westminster, 1964), 332-33. Cf. also Robert P. Gordon, *I & II Samuel: A Commentary* (Grand Rapids: Zondervan, 1986), 268: 'It is true that here she reverts to the fictitious situation of verses 4-11, yet we should not assume that she intended dropping her disguise in verses 12ff., when she drew the parallel between her own circumstances and those of the king. It would have suited Joab well if the woman's wise counsel had been heeded without her having to give herself, and Joab, away. In verses 15-17, therefore, she returns to her own problem and her reasons for bringing it before the king, with, perhaps, the implication that it was her own distressing experience which had awakened her to the dangers in the situation involving David and Absalom.'

detail, but what she does relate suggests the slaying was not intentional or with malice aforethought; it was the sad result of an occasion of mutual hostility. It would then fall under the category of manslaughter (cf. Num. 35:6-34; Deut. 19:1-13; Josh. 20). Absalom's disposal of Amnon, however, was a methodically planned, long-calculated act of carefully nursed hatred (13:22-29). It was murder, not pure but simple. And it cried out for justice not clemency.

Both Nathan (2 Sam. 12) and the woman of Tekoa tried to grip David by their stories, but W.G. Blaikie exposes the difference between them:

> But there was a world-wide difference between the purpose of the parable of Nathan and that of the wise woman of Tekoah [sic]. Nathan's parable was designed to rouse the king's conscience as against his feelings; the woman of Tekoah's, as prompted by Joab, to rouse his feelings as against his conscience.[6]

To appeal to God's mercy (v.14) in a case that requires his justice is not wisdom but sentimentality.

So where is wisdom in 2 Samuel 14? It is everywhere and nowhere. There is much wisdom yet little wisdom in this chapter. There is a planning wisdom on Joab's part (vv. 1-3), one that can conceive and orchestrate a scheme to achieve his ends. There is a persuasive wisdom in the woman's story (vv. 4-17), as she deftly weaves David's situation into her own, suggesting that David is less compassionate than God (v. 14b).[7] There is a perceptive wisdom on David's part (vv. 18-20), a sharpness that can sniff out what hands and minds are at work behind the scenes. We might even pull in Absalom from the last section, for he exhibits that pragmatic wisdom that knows how to get things done (i.e., non-responsive persons will pay attention to you if you burn up their barley fields, vv. 29-31).

There are all sorts of scheming and ingenuity in this narrative. Joab, the woman from Tekoa, and Absalom seem to be the

---

6. W.G. Blaikie, *The Second Book of Samuel*, The Expositor's Bible (Cincinnati: Jennings & Graham, n.d.), 208.

7. On the woman's expertise, see J.P. Fokkelman, *Narrative Art and Poetry in the Books of Samuel*, vol. 1, *King David (II Sam. 9–20 & I Kings 1–2)* (Assen: Van Gorcum, 1981), 141.

manipulators who know how to make things happen. There are all the trappings of wisdom yet such a dearth of wisdom. David can detect Joab's hand (v.19), but can he deal wisely with Absalom? Perhaps his own memories (2 Sam. 11) haunt his will to act. Nevertheless, he could have allowed Absalom to be banished for good; better, he should have executed justice on Absalom. Ironically, Absalom's own words suggest as much (v.32b). But David no longer acts; he is acted upon. In this chapter David reacts rather than rules; he does not reign but consents (v. 21); he appears decisive (v.24) but caves in (v.33). Is this wisdom?

This chapter should haunt the church, not to mention the individual, believing or unbelieving. It is possible to have all the signs of wisdom – plans, strategies, accomplishments – and yet be utterly devoid of it.

Is This Providence?

I want you to place yourself immediately after 14:33 and look back at the whole story from Absalom's viewpoint. David's kiss signifies Absalom's restoration to royal favor.[8] This moment looked impossible five years before (13:38; 14:28).

His cool, calculating murder of Amnon seemed to have dashed whatever ambitions Absalom may have had (13:23-39). He had no choice but self-imposed exile (13:37-38). Three years of it. It looked like Absalom's vengeance had sabotaged his future.

But then Joab went to work on David with his pro-Absalom scheme (14:1-17). We don't know if Joab had any contact or correspondence with Absalom in Geshur. Not unlikely, but the text doesn't say. So David relents and Absalom is permitted to return to Jerusalem without retribution (14:21-23), though David insists on stiff-arming him (v. 24). Joab, for whatever reason, ceases to be an ardent advocate; in fact, he doesn't even return Absalom's calls (vv. 28-29). But Absalom knows it will only take one fire on the farm to get Joab's attention (vv. 30-31) and to press his case with the king again (vv. 32-33). Why should he be an exile in Jerusalem as in Geshur? Absalom lays down the challenge to David: either receive me or execute me. Absalom's ultimatum was a risk. But it

---

8. There is no reason to assume that David's kiss conferred the right of succession on Absalom; it only signified reconciliation and restoration to royal favor. So, rightly McCarter, *II Samuel*, 350.

was a calculated risk. If David were minded to impose justice he would not have permitted Absalom's safe return in the first place (vv. 21-23). Absalom was right – a little groveling and it was all over (v.33). Now he is on site to make a play for the throne (2 Sam.15).

Absalom could be nominated for comeback of the year. Looking at chapter 14 from Absalom's viewpoint, it all seems to be a marvelous piece of providence, whereby what he forfeited by liquidating Amnon he now recovers and stands poised for his next opportunity. What Absalom had seemingly sacrificed forever was now amazingly restored to him. It seems 'all things work together for good,' i.e., for Absalom.

I have asked readers to project themselves into what could have been Absalom's point of view. I do not claim that Absalom actually thought in terms of God's providence – though he could *talk* that way when it suited him (15:7-8). In any case, it looks like providence was smiling on Absalom. And wicked men can be quick to appeal to divine providence to justify their course.

It was July 20,1944. A military conference was in progress. A briefcase had been left under the table. Suddenly it exploded with a blazing sheet of flame. Some moments later Adolf Hitler, the intended victim, was staggering outside the debris, singed and tattered, but surviving with only temporary paralysis in his right arm and a punctured eardrum. Mussolini was scheduled to arrive soon, so Hitler hurried off to meet the train. Hitler brought Mussolini back to the Wolf's lair to show him the damage. 'Frankly, Duce,' Hitler confessed, 'I regard this event as the pronouncement of Divine Providence.' When Mussolini admitted he had had a marvelous escape, Hitler retorted: 'Marvelous? It's more than that. It's God's intervention. Look at this room, at my uniform. When I reflect on this, I know nothing will happen to me. Clearly it is my divine task to continue on and bring my great enterprise to completion.'[9]

We may dispute such Hitlerian hermeneutics and can understand how even his perverted mind might draw such inferences from the episode. And we may recall 12:10-12 and think that this 'providence' of chapter 14 is not really for Absalom's advancement but for David's judgment. And even for Absalom's judgment – we

9. Robert Leckie, *Delivered from Evil: The Saga of World War II* (New York: Harper & Row, 1987), 731-32.

know this if we've snitched and read chapter 18. But the slice of life we see isolated in chapter 14 can give faith fits. For here is a man driven by hatred, guilty of murder, who has friends in high places and gall to force the issue, who comes off scot-free. So it sometimes appears that evil men are blessed with success, approved by heaven, and free from justice. Leukemia doesn't kill their kids; cancer doesn't decimate their wives; drunk drivers don't mangle their families; down-sizing doesn't eliminate their jobs; hail doesn't ruin their crops (see Job 21:4-16; Ps. 73:3-12). Is that providence? Are they under God's smile? Go and worship (Ps.73:16-17) before you answer that.

Is This Leadership?

One wonders why verses 25-27 intrude into this story. I say 'intrude' because these verses seem to be free-standing and break the flow of the narrative. They are not strictly necessary. The narrative flows smoothly and naturally when we read verse 28 immediately after verse 24. Verse 24 ends by informing us that 'Absalom went round to his house, but he did not see the king's face', and verse 28 recaps and continues with: 'So Absalom lived in Jerusalem for two years, but he did not see the king's face.' Why then this clip about Absalom's good looks (v. 25), hair care (v.26), and family (v. 27)? Here is Mr. Israel, the darling of the media, the choice of photographers, enchanted with his own locks,[10] with three sons and a beautiful daughter,[11] the latter appropriately named after her gorgeous aunt (13:1).

A veteran reader of 1–2 Samuel, however, comes to verses 25-27 with some dread, for they conjure up shades of other leaders, or potential leaders, of Israel who were long on image and short on substance. One can hardly read verses 25-27 without hearing an echo of Saul, 'an impressive young man...a head taller than any of

---

10. One can't be sure how much weight to give Absalom's hair harvests; preferences range from two-three (McCarter) up to five to six pounds (Gordon).

11. The mention of three sons here seems to conflict with 18:18. Many assume that Absalom's sons may have died very young, leaving him without a male heir. Matthew Henry proposed that Absalom had no child for a long time and erected the monument of 18:18 because he despaired of having one; however, post-monument, three sons and a daughter arrived (*Commentary on the Whole Bible*, 6 vols. [New York: Revell, n.d.], 2:517).

the others' (1 Sam. 9:2, NIV; see also 10:23-24), or without
remembering how Eliab so gripped Samuel's imagination that the
prophet almost anointed a second 'Saul' (1 Sam. 16:6-7). Not that
Yahweh looks on physical attractiveness or impressiveness as a
*dis*qualification (1 Sam. 16:12 knocks that notion on the head); but
physical presence before men without internal submission to God
makes for leadership disaster. We should be uneasy then when we
come upon verses 25-27, for they tell us that here is another Saul,
and chapter 15 will make clear that, unfortunately, Absalom is not
so reticent as Saul about laying hold of the kingdom.

Matthew Henry's observations on this Absalom note are both
concise and comprehensive:

> All that is here said of [Absalom] is,
> 1. That he was a very handsome man....
> 2. That he had a very fine head of hair....
> 3. That his family began to be built up....

Henry aptly remarks, 'Nothing is said of his wisdom and piety.'[12]
And we ask: Is this leadership?

The answer is, I suppose, both yes and no. Our media and politics
have operated on Absalom's approach for so long that we expect
little else. Our times insist on style over substance, cosmetics over
content, manner over matter. It hardly surprises us that a president
who cultivated a public image of warm, devoted family life would
also, with his secret service agents, plod the tunnels under New
York's streets, flashlights in hand, on the way to a waiting sexual
liaison in another hotel or apartment; nor are we surprised to learn
that this was a pattern from his first day in office.[13]

Such image-reality gaps have been the case among
political leaders for centuries, but, as Jesus says to his church, 'It is
not to be like that among you' (Mark 10:43). Yet it seems it is.
Douglas Webster describes the 'Fortune 500 pastors' desired for
contemporary American congregations as being

---

12. Henry, 2:517.
13. Thomas C. Reeves, *A Question of Character: A Life of John F. Kennedy*
(New York: Free Press, 1991), 235-44.

winsome, charismatic, executive like pastors who exude warmth and
success. Known more for their humor than for their spirituality, today's
market-sensitive pastors are relationally savvy.... Instead of eliciting
deep feelings of guilt as the old revivalists did, these pastors lift the
spirit, promote optimism and make people feel good about
themselves.[14]

By contrast, when listing some of the standards for elders in the
church, the apostle stresses character over charisma and personal
godliness over public giftedness (1 Tim. 3:1-7). Woe to the church
that falls into the Absalom trap.

Once Absalom is back (v.24) he dominates the narrative. We
read of his appearance (vv. 25-27), his antics (vv. 28-32a), his daring
(v. 32b). Absalom takes over the narrative just as he will take over
the kingdom.

17. Politics and Faith
2 Samuel 15

During 1942 and afterwards Red Cross packages began to arrive
for prisoners held in German concentration camps. When at one
point the International Red Cross asked for an accounting, it turned
out that at Buchenwald alone some seven carloads (= twenty-one
to twenty-three thousand packages) were unaccounted for. Some
of the prisoners who survived to see the collapse of the Third Reich
were highly amused watching the SS officers feverishly clearing
revealing and empty Red Cross cartons from their offices in April
1945.[1] The packages had not been intended for SS officers, but the
SS took them anyway. They seized what did not belong to them.

That is what is happening in 2 Samuel 15: Absalom is seizing
what does not belong to him – the kingdom. But it doesn't seem so
bad, for Absalom does not use SS methods. He has finesse and
flair and knows how to work the crowd. The evil is the same but
far more winsome.

Our chapter breaks into two major divisions, the rebellion of
Absalom and the exile of David.

---

14. Douglas D. Webster, *Selling Jesus: What's Wrong with Marketing the
Church* (Downers Grove: InterVarsity, 1992), 120.

1. Eugen Kogon, *The Theory and Practice of Hell: The German Concentration
Camps and the System Behind Them* (New York: Berkley, 1980), 128.

Rebellion: The Art of Politics (15:1-12)

As the poster boy of Israel's now generation (14:25) Absalom took care to primp his image (15:1). The chariot, horses, and lackeys would not necessarily excite suspicion; they may have been chalked up to the flash and dash and showmanship of a prince.

But Absalom wasn't merely showing off. He worked the crowd. He made a point to be up early and standing outside the courthouse (i.e., the gate), starting conversations with those coming and waiting to have their cases decided. Absalom would inquire about his new friend's hometown, furrow his brow in apparent concentration as he listened to the fellow's dilemma, periodically injecting a grunt of empathy, then indicate how cogent he thought the case was ('Your claim is right and just,' v.2, NJPS). In fact, Absalom never met a plaintiff with whom he didn't agree.

That was only part of Absalom's caring approach. After granting the cogency of someone's case, Absalom would interject the tragic note, the 'unfortunately' clause. It was important to exacerbate dissatisfaction with the system (i.e., David). In spite of your convincing case, Absalom would sigh, 'there is no one assigned to you by the king to hear it' (v.3, NJPS). Absalom may mean to bemoan the delay of justice – a fellow's case gets stuck in the backlog of the court docket until the king can finally hear it.[2] Absalom saw a way through the logjam, oddly enough centered around himself: 'O that I were appointed judge in the land! And *to me* every man who had a case and needed a judgment would come, and I would get him his rights' (v. 4; emphasis in Hebrew). Absalom didn't have to make those hard and often unpopular judgments; he only had to *claim* he would. He only had to suggest he wanted to have a government that cares.

---

2. 'The cases brought to the king would normally be those which were beyond the competence of local elders, doubtless including complaints against the state' (Robert P. Gordon, *1 & II Samuel: A Commentary* [Grand Rapids: Zondervan, 1986], 270). Gordon also seems to caution against assuming wide-spread dissatisfaction with David's regime. That is what Absalom wants to insinuate and arouse, but he has his own axe to grind and can hardly be trusted for an accurate state-of-the-kingdom report. Joyce Baldwin rightly calls Absalom's complaint in verse 3 'misleading, even deceitful, in its intention, because these people have come to put their case before the king, and it is clear from the way the woman of Tekoa was received (2 Sa. 14:4-7) that the king dealt personally with those who asked for his ruling' (*1 & 2 Samuel*, Tyndale Old Testament Commentaries [Leicester: InterVarsity, 1988], 257).

Absalom also perfected his common-man technique. Since he was the king's son people would normally begin to go through the usual procedures of deference (bowing, etc.). But Absalom dispensed with such high brow moves and treated all his greeters with the marks of equality and affection (vv. 5-6a). Politicians still do this. An office-seeker will loosen his tie, unbutton his collar, roll up his sleeves, don a farmer's hat with 'Dekalb' on the front, brave the slop by the hog pen, put one foot up on the fence rail, and be photographed in earnest conversation with an Iowa farmer about the latter's needs and problems. That photograph is meant to say, 'See! Here's a fellow who gets down where the people are – down with the hogs and the corn; he's not isolated in some air-conditioned office in Des Moines.' That was Absalom's technique. Should someone suggest the Hilton for lunch, Absalom would say, 'Naw, Burger King's fine with me.' He was down where the people are.

And it worked! 'Absalom duped the men of Israel' (v. 6b). Literally, this verse says Absalom 'stole away the hearts of the men of Israel'. This idiom, however, does not refer to capturing the affections but to duping the mind, as when Jacob 'stole Laban's heart' (Gen. 31:20, 26), i.e., deceived him.[3] Naturally, as a suave politician, Absalom added a little religious veneer (15:7-9) for a finishing touch.[4]

In Absalom's successful coup we begin to see something both clearly and dimly. We can see clearly how Yahweh's word in 12:10-12 is reaching fulfillment: Absalom and his carefully crafted rebellion constitute the threatened disaster out of David's own household (12:11a). Yet Absalom's deed is a wrong and despicable act of rebellion against Yahweh's kingdom. Absalom has no qualms about putting forth his hand against Yahweh's anointed (contrast David in 1 Sam. 24 and 26).[5] Side by side we have the truthfulness of God's word (12:11) and the wickedness of Absalom's act. And the latter fulfils the former. Yet Absalom will be held accountable

---

3. See TWOT, 1:168, and P. Kyle McCarter, Jr., *II Samuel*, The Anchor Bible (New York: Doubleday 1984), 356. On the scope of Absalom's support throughout Israel, see T.N.D. Mettinger, *King and Messiah*, Coniectanea Biblica (Lund: CWK Gleerup, 1976), 121-23.

4. In using religion Absalom places himself beside Saul (1 Sam. 15:30-31) and Israel (1 Sam. 4:3).

5. On the significance of anointing I refer again to the very helpful discussion by Gerard Van Groningen, *Messianic Revelation in the Old Testament* (Grand Rapids: Baker, 1990), 23-28.

for his wickedness. How do we put all this together? Here we see dimly. And yet the biblical preachers never flinched over this mystery. Peter packed both sides of it into one sentence in his Pentecost sermon: 'This Jesus, delivered up according to the definite plan and foreknowledge of God, you crucified and killed by the hands of lawless men' (Acts 2:23). God ordained it and you are guilty for doing it. It is mystery, but a mystery is not irrational, only insoluble. And where we cannot explain we can nevertheless adore.

Exile: The Arena of faith (15:13-37)

It is time to run. When David receives word of Absalom's success (v. 13) he orders flight: 'Get up, and let's flee, or there will be no escape for us from Absalom; hurry and go, lest he hurry and overtake us, and scatter disaster upon us, and strike the city with the edge of the sword' (v.14).[6] This account of David's exile covers 15:13–16:14 and features encounters with various individuals. Readers will soon note that the narrative of David's return (19:9-43) follows the same pattern. To show this – and to provide a visual map for all of 2 Samuel 15–20, we will sketch the general structural pattern.

Pattern of 2 Samuel 15–20

```
Revolt, 15:1-12
          Exile, 15:13-16:14
                    Ittai
                    Zadok
                    Hushai
                    Ziba
                    Shimei
                              Decision for Absalom, 16:15–17:23
                              (In response to Ahithophel and Hushai)
                                        Conflict, 17:24-18:18
                                        News, 18:19-33
                              Decision for David, 19:1-8
                              (in response to Joab)

          Return, 19:9-43
                    Judah
                    Shimei
                    Ziba
                    Mephibosheth
                    Barzillai

Revolt, 20:1-22
```

The writer seems to use the story of David's flight as a vehicle for highlighting David's faith. We will trace the practical teaching of this section under that theme.

Faith is supported by the gifts of God (15:19-23)

David paused at the last house and watched as his supporters filed past (vv. 17-18). He stopped Ittai the Gittite, a mercenary from the Philistine city of Gath. Who knows if David may have been testing him? Even so, David's proposal is magnanimous:

> Why are *you* going with us? Go back and stay with the king, for you are a foreigner, and you are also an exile from your place. You came only yesterday, and today should I make you wander around with us when I must go wherever I can? Go back and take your brothers back with you; and may Yahweh deal kindly and faithfully with you (vv. 19-20).[7]

David will not allow Ittai to act under compulsion. He had only been in David's service a brief time. Why should he share in David's sudden disaster? David graciously releases Ittai to serve the new regime and to enjoy a normal life.

But Ittai will have none of it:

> By the life of Yahweh and by the life of my lord the king, wherever my lord the king is – whether it means death or life – there your servant will be (v.21).

Ittai uses a double oath (by the life of Yahweh ... of my lord the king) to put his answer in bold print, to underscore how seriously he means his words. David had urged him to 'go back and stay

---

6. Abandoning the city was kind: '[T]he king decides to evacuate the city, not only to save himself and his men, but also so as not to expose Jerusalem to the devastation which would take place were it really besieged and captured' (Hans Wilhelm Hertzberg, *I & II Samuel,* The Old Testament Library [Philadelphia: Westminster, 1964], 341). It was also wise: if David remained in Jerusalem, how could he tell loyalists from waverers? By going into exile he could be sure that only avid supporters would accompany him.

7. On the text of verse 20, see S.R. Driver, *Notes on the Hebrew Text and the Topography of the Books of Samuel,* 2nd ed. (1913; reprint ed., Winona Lake, Ind.: Alpha, 1984), 314; LXX helps us restore the last clause.

with the king', i.e., Absalom (v. 19), but Ittai insists only David is the king (note his two uses of 'my lord the king' in v.21). He holds nothing back from David – even his children (v.22) share the hazards of Ittai's fidelity and David's dubious future. One can scarcely hear Ittai's devotion to David (v.21) without remembering Paul's preoccupation for Christ:

> I eagerly expect and hope that I will in no way be ashamed, but will have sufficient courage so that now as always Christ will be exalted in my body, whether by life or by death (Phil. 1:20, NIV).

Ittai is an island of fidelity in a sea of treachery. The irony is clear: David's own son, 'whom he had loaded with undeserved kindness, was conspiring against him, while this stranger, who owed him nothing in comparison, was risking everything in his cause.'[8] And one wonders if our writer intends to contrast Ittai the faithful Philistine with Ahithophel the treacherous Israelite (v.12). David's trusted and treasured counselor (16:23) dropped him and threw his weight behind Absalom.[9] But here is Ittai, the foreigner, who sticks closer than a brother (Prov. 18:24), and who, with his men and all their children, tramps off after David to share his deliverance or his doom.

The text does not say how Ittai's tenacity affected David. It must have impressed him for he entrusted Ittai with a place of leadership in the battle against Absalom's troops (18:2). And it must have been a welcome support for David's faith. Ittai is to David in the Old Testament what Onesiphorus is to Paul in the New (2 Tim. 1:16-18) – not particularly well-known, but doggedly faithful in dire need. Paul was deeply moved by Onesiphorus' fidelity: 'He often refreshed me and was not ashamed of my chains' (2 Tim. 1:16b). And Jesus appreciated similar support from the apostles. For all their misunderstanding and bungling, they had remained with him and, at the Last Supper, he gratefully acknowledged their companionship: 'You are those who have continued with Me in my trials' (Luke 22:28, NKJV). One of God's

---

8. W.G. Blaikie, *The Second Book of Samuel,* The Expositor's Bible (Cincinnati: Jennings & Graham, n.d.), 232.

9. Perhaps the anguish of Psalms 41:9 and 55:12-14, 20-21 reflects Ahithophel's betrayal.

ways of supporting you is to give you a friend who stands with you in the darkest hour. Ittais are God's gifts.

Faith is free in the will of God (15:24-29)

David also enjoys major support among the clergy. Zadok and Abiathar, the priests, are ready to share David's banishment. Nor are they alone, for the Levites, under Zadok's orders, have brought the ark of the covenant along (v.24). Absalom may have the city but he will not have the priests – nor the sign of Yahweh's presence. David, however, will have none of this:

> Take the ark of God back to the city; if I find grace in Yahweh's eyes, he shall bring me back and allow me to see both it and his residence; but if he says, 'I do not delight in you' – here I am – let him do to me as seems good to him (vv. 25-26).

Liberty leaps out of those words. David will not consent even to the appearance of a 'have ark, have God' mentality. He will not repeat the fiasco of 1 Samuel 4:3. David says his restoration (should there be such) does not depend on whether he has Yahweh's furniture but on whether he has Yahweh's favor. All rests on grace (v. 25b).[10] He submits to Yahweh's sovereign sway – Yahweh will show grace or he will not delight in me. Should it be the latter, 'Here I am – let him do to me as seems good to him' (v.26). No gimmicks, no superstitions, no rabbit foot religion, no conning God by pilfering the ark. This is not weak resignation but robust submission. Here is the freedom of faith in the will of God. All depends on him: 'if I find grace in Yahweh's eyes,... but if he says, "I do not delight in you...".' How much sheer relief there is in this, for David does not bear God's load of what-will-happen-to-me. I must not *use* God (the ark) but *submit* to him, and he will do as he pleases.

Now watch how truly free faith is! There are some who say that if you really hold to God's sovereignty (i.e., take wild positions

---

10. Karl Gutbrod (*Das Buch vom Reich*, Die Botschaft des Alten Testaments, 2nd ed.[Stuttgart: Calwer, 1973], 184-85) compares David's flight from Saul (1 Sam. 18ff.) and his flight from Absalom. As in the former David owed his final deliverance not to his own energy or skill but solely to the Lord, so in the latter rescue from his suffering depends only on the caring mercy of God. David must leave his future wholly and entirely with the Lord.

like David just did), then you'll sit on your hands and do nothing. That is not true. To share such a Davidic faith in or grip on Yahweh's sovereignty *does not stifle but releases human resourcefulness and ingenuity.* Notice verses 27-28. As soon as David plops himself wholly into God's hands (vv. 25-26), he nevertheless forms a fifth column within the city.

> David said to Zadok the priest: 'Do you see? Go back to the city in peace – and Ahimaaz your son and Jonathan, Abiathar's son – both of your sons with you. See, I am waiting at the fords of the wilderness until some word comes from you informing me (vv. 27-28).

This activity is not a bit inconsistent with the statement of verses 25-26. It only demonstrates that complete submission to God's sovereignty still permits you to use your head, to work actively. But without the idolatry. You do it without the feverish anxiety of having to play God. It may sound strange, but people who hold the faith of verses 25-26 find liberty and relief and energy in it, especially in the darkest hours. There are people who know what I mean.

Faith is encouraged by the providence of God (15:31-37)
Now we hear that David received the bad news about Ahithophel (v. 31a; see v. 12). Immediately David shot up an ejaculatory prayer: 'Please make Ahithophel's counsel foolish, O Yahweh' (v.31b). There was good reason for David's concern : having Ahithophel as your counsellor was like having Bear Bryant for your football coach or Michael Jordan on your basketball team. Ahithophel was sharp; he had no peer; savvy and success oozed from his advice (16:23). Hence David met the dreaded report with instant prayer.

We no sooner hear David pray than we see the answer to his prayer, an answer that has two feet, torn clothes, and dirty hair (v.32). It was Hushai the Arkite, David's special confidant.[11] Apparently David himself senses that Hushai may be Yahweh's answer to his cry, as his proposal to Hushai suggests:

---

11. So Gordon, *I & II Samuel*, 276. The term 'friend' in verse 37 probably refers to an official capacity (Friend of the King) not merely to a personal attachment. See also McCarter, *II Samuel*, 372.

If you cross over with me, you will be a burden to me. But if you go back to the city and say to Absalom, 'O king, I will be your servant; as I was your father's servant, so now I will be your servant' – so you will frustrate for me Ahithophel's counsel (vv. 33-34).

David went on to inform Hushai of the information highway he already had in place in Jerusalem (vv. 35-36), and so Hushai, hopefully after a shower and a change, plods into Jerusalem to dupe Absalom (v. 37). Hushai was not needed for companionship but for espionage.

Here we have met Yahweh's delightful providence again! How it must have heartened David. No sooner does he pray than Yahweh begins to answer his prayer – and that in a way no scriptwriter could have guessed. Our prayers deal with the what; God's answers deal with the what and the how and the when. And how the how can surprise us!

This situation reminds me of a dilemma Don McClure related from his missionary service at Pokwo in Ethiopia in the 1950s. After dark of an already long day McClure was called back to the river bank. Two women had brought a young girl in a canoe through the rain. The girl was lying in bloody water, and, as the two women lifted her out of the canoe, she looked up piteously at McClure. He saw her trouble: an umbilical cord had not been removed and trailed behind her as they hauled her out of the boat on to the ground. The day before she had given birth to a stillborn baby; the placenta would not detach itself. This sad girl did not look to be more than thirteen. She'd lost so much blood she was too weak to stand. McClure stooped down to gather the terrified girl in his arms, take her to the house, and do what he could for her. However, as he lifted her and straightened up, she grabbed his neck and screamed in pain, and one of the women cried, 'It is out!' McClure explains:

And so it was. In the dark the great Dr. McClure had stepped on the trailing cord when he stooped to pick her up, and in his lifting her with his foot still firmly planted on the umbilical cord, the whole placenta had pulled free. I daresay this was the only case on record where a placenta was removed in this manner.[12]

---

12. Charles Partee, *Adventures in Africa: The Story of Don McClure* (Grand Rapids: Zondervan, 1990), 312-313 (quote from p. 313).

McClure confessed he did not know what he would have done if God in his grace had not helped that poor girl. Who would've guessed God's providence would embrace a clumsy foot?

Who would have guessed that the prayer David just uttered would be answered through this disheveled civil servant Hushai? Actually, Yahweh did not answer David's prayer precisely but substantially: Yahweh didn't turn Ahithophel's counsel into foolishness but – as chapter 17 will show – turned Absalom into a fool to reject it. And he did that through Hushai.

David prays. Yahweh sends Hushai. He did not zap Ahithophel with a stroke or have someone poison his wine or cause him to die in a five-chariot crack-up on the Jerusalem-Hebron Freeway. Yahweh's answer is unguessable – as providence frequently is. Yet it seems so natural – as providence frequently does. But how it encourages our faith when once we look back and can see it.

For all the hints of faith it is still a dark day in Israel. Admittedly, David is suffering for his sins (12:10-12), but he is nevertheless the rightful king. But the rightful king has been rejected and plods up the Mount of Olives weeping (v.30). The scene will be repeated. The Descendant of David, the rightful king according to 7:12-16, will be seen on the Mount of Olives (Luke 19:37), and he will be weeping (Luke 19:41-44) not so much over his rejection as over the doom of those who have rejected him.

18. In the Presence of My Enemies
2 Samuel 16

As 2 Samuel 15:13-37 depicts three encounters with David's friends, so 2 Samuel 16 focuses on three of David's enemies, whether subtle or blatant. So Ziba, Shimei, and Ahithophel (ch. 16) prove to be the opposite numbers of Ittai, Zadok, and Hushai (ch. 15).

I know I am oversimplifying (which, however, is not a mortal sin). Structurally, chapter 16 seems to belong to two different segments of the narrative: 16:14 closes off the account of David's exodus (15:13–16:14), while 16:15 opens another section that focuses on Absalom's deception (16:15–17:23).[1] And yet chapter

---

1. See Ronald F. Youngblood, '1, 2 Samuel', *The Expositor's Bible Commentary*, 12 vols. (Grand Rapids: Zondervan, 1992), 3:1005-6, for a structural proposal embracing 16:15–17:29.

16 can be viewed by itself, consisting of two distinct narratives, which in turn consist of two sections:[2]

Verses 1-14:   David
                      Ziba's slander, vv. 1-4
                      Shimei's cursing, vv. 5-14

Verses 15-23:   Absalom
                      Hushai's flattery, vv. 15-19
                      Ahithophel's counsel, vv. 20-23

Before moving to the exposition I want to be explicit about how we are to regard David. David is not just anybody; he is Yahweh's chosen king (1 Sam. 16:1-13). Hence to rebel against David as king is to rebel against Yahweh and *his* kingdom. David must not be viewed as an individual but in terms of his office, in his vocation as Yahweh's covenant king. Absalom's coup then was not the only option available for an advocate of change in a society that didn't have democratic elections; it was rebellion against Yahweh's anointed servant (cf. 1 Sam. 24:6; 26:9-11). This is not to deny David's sinfulness or the judgment he now suffers (even via Absalom). David is both under Yahweh's election and under Yahweh's judgment and yet remains Yahweh's appointed servant. And to despise, oppose, and betray him is to despise, oppose, and betray the God who appointed him. For the principle, see John 5:23b and Luke 10:16.

Now let us meet the king's enemies.

Ziba, The Man Who Manipulates (16:1-4)
It sounds uncharitable to dub Ziba an enemy when he graciously (it seems) meets David with donkeys, bread, raisins, summer fruit, and wine (v.1).[3] Ziba assures David that the provisions are for the relief and refreshment of the king's loyalists on their arduous journey (v.2). The supplies are hardly inexhaustible, but they constitute something rather than nothing and point to the thought-

---

2. See the fine discussion by Zvi Adar, *The Biblical Narrative* (Jerusalem, 1959), 156-60.

3. The NIV may be right in translating 'a string of donkeys' as opposed to the traditional pair. See discussion in Youngblood, *Expositor's Bible Commentary*, 3:999.

fulness of the giver. David wondered about Mephibosheth: 'Where is your master's son?' (v. 3a; Hebrew 'son' is often elastic – it can denote a grandson or a more distant descendant). Ziba was quick on the draw: 'Why, he's staying in Jerusalem, for he said, "Today the house of Israel will restore to me the kingdom of my father" ' (v. 3b). David didn't like that. After all he'd done for Mephibosheth (2 Sam. 9)! He made a snap decision. It had to be quick. His people had to make tracks. He transferred all Mephibosheth's property to Ziba (v. 4a). Ziba was, of course, grateful (v.4b).

What are we to make of Ziba's allegation about Mephibosheth in verse 3 – especially in light of the very different account Mephibosheth gives David in 19:24-30? It's simple: Ziba lied through his teeth. It was a bit risky, but in the present hyper-situation he knew David had no opportunity to check his story. And Ziba was obviously pro-David; the loaded donkeys were tangible evidence of that. And in the pressure of the moment David made an impulsive decision. One can understand that: David's mental circuits were surely loaded.

A little thinking, however, punches a few holes in Ziba's slander. It would have been passing ludicrous for Mephibosheth to suppose that Saul's line would be reinstalled when the whole groundswell was for *Absalom's* kingship. And, though Ziba here shows his Davidic colors, he and his men stay behind at the farm (cf. 19:17-18). They do not go with David. Ziba likely had a hunch that David would survive Absalom's threat; hence his show of support. But suppose Absalom made good? No problem. Ziba is not exiled with the former king but working the farm ready to live under a new regime. Ziba is a manipulator – he capitalizes on David's trouble in order to line his own pockets.[4] What moved Ziba was not loyalty to Yahweh's king but greed for his own gain.

You have heard of the horrible winter the Continental Army suffered at Valley Forge. Clothes were so threadbare and blankets

4. Should David come out on top and discover his slander, Ziba will still be secure, for, though he may be exposed as a liar, he did help the king when he was down; and David could hardly ignore that. For corroboration of my view of Ziba, see Robert P. Gordon, *I & II Samuel: A Commentary* (Grand Rapids: Zondervan, 1986), 276-77; Karl Gutbrod, *Das Buch vom Reich,* Die Botschaft des Alten Testaments, 2nd ed. (Stuttgart: Calwer, 1973), 194; and Hans Wilhelm Hertzberg, *I & II Samuel,* The Old Testament Library (Philadelphia: Westminster, 1964), 345.

so rare that the troops often sat up all night rather than fall asleep and freeze to death. Lafayette saw there soldiers whose legs had frozen black – they were taken to 'hospitals' for amputation. Why such suffering? It was not the severe winter, for the winter was mild by Pennsylvania standards. But soldiers went hungry because 'nearby farmers preferred to sell to the British in Philadelphia for hard cash'. The army was half-naked because merchants in Boston refused to 'move government clothing off their shelves at anything less than profits ranging from 1,000 to 1,800 percent'.[5] The colonies swarmed with Zibas. The hardship of others was their opportunity for success.

Zibaism can be both blatant and subtle, and we must beware of bewailing the grosser samples of such avarice and manipulation lest we be oblivious to their polite forms. The essence of Ziba's approach was to make an impression, an image; and profit from it. Why, I have had to ask myself, do I tell a troubled friend, in conversation or letter, that I am praying for him? No one can deny that such assurances can genuinely encourage other believers in their distresses. And sometimes that is my purpose: I want him to know he is not forgotten. But that is not the only reason. Enter Ziba. If I make a point to communicate such concern such friends will likely think well of me, perceive me as a caring person, and, though there are no big bucks in it, my Christian stock will go up a bit. Thus my piety serves myself. Why don't I simply pray for that friend and not tell him? Why, then there would be nothing in it for *me.* I agree with old Rabbi Duncan, who, looking back on decades of his life, confessed, 'I have never done a sinless action during the seventy years.'[6]

Shimei, The Man Who Curses (16:5-14)

At Bahurim, a little to the east of Jerusalem, David and his entourage run into a human volcano, Shimei, a descendant of Saul's family. He pelted David & Co. with abuse, stones, and dirt (vv. 5,6,13). Apparently Shimei threw his rage and rocks at David from the side of a hill across from or above David's route (v. 13), close enough

5. Robert Leckie, *The Wars of America,* 2 vols. (New York: Harper & Row, 1968), 1:181.

6. A. Moody Stuart, *The Life of John Duncan* (1872; reprint ed., Edinburgh: Banner of Truth, 1991), 150.

to be damaging, far enough to be safe. He lambasted David as a raunchy killer and a worthless jerk (v.7b). Shimei never had believed David's protests of innocence over the deaths of Abner and Ishbosheth. (2 Sam. 3,4). He was sure David was the brains behind that convenient violence; his protests were so much political posturing (v. 8a).[7] Shimei was both theological and pitiless (a combination others have duplicated). He seems to know exactly what God is doing: Yahweh is paying David back for all the Saulide blood he shed and giving the kingdom into Absalom's power (v.8a). In gleeful fury he adds, 'Look at you – in your disaster!' (v.8b).[8]

Shimei's trash-talking soon becomes tiresome. Abishai, Joab's brother, turns to David and so much as says, 'We don't need this!' (=Why should this dead dog curse my lord the king?', v.9a) and asks permission to 'go over and take off his head' (v.9b). Abishai proposes this because he has observed that people without heads do not curse. But David will have none of it (v.10a), and offers a strange rationale:

> If he curses, and if Yahweh has said to him, 'Curse David,' then who can say, 'Why have you done that?' (v.10).

Hence David's order (and conviction) was: 'Leave him alone, and let him curse, for Yahweh has ordered him' (v.11). Shimei's venom comes at Yahweh's direction. Instead of going for Shimei's jugular David looks for relief elsewhere:

> It may be that Yahweh will look upon my iniquity and return to me good in place of his cursing today (v.12).

Let us punch the stop button and consider that statement. There is a text problem in verse 12. What is it that David wants Yahweh to see/look upon? There are at least three possibilities:

---

7. Cf. J.P. Fokkelman, *Narrative Art and Poetry in the Books of Samuel*, vol. 1, *King David (II Sam. 9–20 & I Kings 1–2)*, (Assen: Van Gorcum, 1981), 198. Fokkelman argues that the clause 'in whose place you became king' (v.8) shows that Shimei is not referring to the affair of 2 Samuel 21:1-14 but 'to the Saulide losses [Abner, Ishbosheth] at the end of Saul's reign and shortly thereafter'.

8. Heb., *wĕhinnĕkā bĕrā 'ātekā*; NIV: 'you have come to ruin.'

1. 'Upon my affliction' (or distress, suffering). This reading is reflected in the ancient versions (e.g., LXX); most all English translations follow this option.[9]

2. 'Upon my eye/eyes.' This is a marginal reading in our Hebrew text and appears in a few Hebrew manuscripts. The medieval Jewish commentators construed it as 'upon my tears,' eyes being the source of tears.

3. 'Upon my iniquity.' This is the reading of the traditional Hebrew text.[10]

Why such differences? Because the Hebrew words for affliction, eye, and iniquity look very similar and can be easily confused. How do we decide among these? Count noses by checking translations? Then we would decide for option 1. Actually, there are only two possibilities, for option 2 as explained really blends with option 1. So, is it affliction or iniquity? I am in favor of iniquity (i.e., as the correct reading). Why? Because 'affliction' seems to fit so well. Let's pretend that 'affliction' was in fact the original text. Who would ever want to change it? It fits so naturally; it's just the word one would expect. What copyist would ever puzzle over it? If 'affliction' were original, I can't imagine these other variant readings arising. But pretend that 'iniquity' was the original text. That jars a bit. Yahweh looking on iniquity and returning good? One can imagine scribes scratching their heads over that one. It would only be natural to suppose the word was a slight mistake for the much more natural and similar looking 'affliction'. One can certainly understand how affliction would conquer iniquity in this text. Hence I think 'iniquity' is the original reading.[11]

---

9. As do NASB and NIV; these two, however, give no footnote to clue the reader that a text problem exists.

10. The Hebrew word ('āwôn) can mean the iniquity itself, the guilt of it, or the punishment for it. Cr. TWOT, 2:650-51. Here NJPS translates 'my punishment', stressing the last.

11. In this I agree with a number of commentators; e.g., Keil, Erdmann (in *Lange's Commentary*), Hertzberg. So too Walter Brueggemann, 'On Coping with Curse: A Study of 2 Sam 16:5-14,' *Catholic Biblical Quarterly* 36 (1974): 181. For more detail, Carmel McCarthy, *The Tiqqune Sopherim,* Orbis Biblicus et Orientalis 36 (Göttingen: Vandenhoeck & Ruprecht, 1981), 81-85. Very helpful, though I disagree with her final decision. It should also go without

I have just argued that 'iniquity' is the original reading because it does not seem to fit so well. That's true for chapter 16. But I also think 'iniquity' is correct because it *does* fit so well, i.e., in the larger context. If one reads the whole narrative theologically and comes to chapter 16 realizing that *12:10-12 controls all of 2 Samuel 13–20*, then David's use of 'iniquity' in 16:12 fits perfectly. David then recognizes that the cursing is what he deserves, not, as Shimei holds, for bleeding Saul's house, but for his sin of chapters 11–12. David was assured of immediate forgiveness but warned of ongoing consequences, and, in his view, Absalom's revolt and Shimei's abuse are part of those consequences.

I drag readers through this textual problem because I think the correct reading has enormous practical import. Here in 16:12 is the secret of David's peace. Not in having Shimei's head on a platter but in this astounding statement: 'It may be that Yahweh will look upon my iniquity and return good to me.' Let that sink into your gray matter. David has a deep-seated confidence in a God of unguessable grace, who has a tendency to replace cursing with goodness! He assumes that Yahweh has this strangely wonderful way of looking upon guilt and yet returning blessing instead of curse. He senses that though the mouth of God has declared his punishment (12:10-12), the eye of God may long to spare him from it.

How can David even begin to think this way? Where did he get such an outlandish idea? Note that he is not sure of this. He says, 'Perhaps...', or 'It may be...'. David confesses Yahweh's freedom in this matter; he may or he may not. But can't you see that David could never have said, 'It may be' – he could never have even conceived the possibility unless he had already laid hold upon the known character of his God? How can he even dream this unless he actually knows a God like that? You just can't imagine how deep and warm and longing God's compassion is for you even when he disciplines you for your sin. But David would try, because he knew him.

'It may be that Yahweh will look upon my iniquity and return good to me...' What an instinct for God. What a holy hunch! Should this word not come as special hope to Christians who believe they've made a royal curse-job of their lives, Christians who at some point,

saying that 'my iniquity' means David's own iniquity and *not* 'the iniquity done to me'.

sometimes with open eyes, have smashed God's commandments
and defied his standards, and then suffered miserably for it?
Repentance and forgiveness have come yet they are sure God only
regards them with grudging toleration, and sometimes they doubt
the toleration. They are, they think, doomed to the junk yard of
Christian existence. But what if they can get a glimpse of David's
God? What if they can say 'It may be' of him? What if they have a
God who can look at guilt and return good?

Shimei is the man who curses, but David has told us that Yahweh
is the God who may reverse the curse. In fact, he has (Gal. 3:13).

Ahithophel, The Man Who Betrays (16:15-23)

Ahithophel is the Judas Iscariot of the Old Testament. Some may
think that a harsh judgment. After all, doesn't a fellow have a right
to work for whomever he wants? Can't he, if he wants to, swing
his loyalty from David to Absalom (15:12, 31)? Answers: No and
no. David is not one of many possible employers but Yahweh's
chosen king. Ahithophel has no more right to forsake David than a
true disciple has to forsake David's Son (cf. John 6:66-71).

Reference to Ahithophel in verses 15 and 23 wrap this section
of the chapter; the focus is on Ahithophel. Yet there is a short clip
depicting Hushai's commitment to Absalom (vv. 16-19). Absalom
is seemingly duped by Hushai's carefully chosen words. Hushai
meets Absalom with a double 'Long live the king!' (v.16). This
formula is not a casual wish but 'an acclamation by which royal
authority is officially recognized and assented to' and is likely an
abbreviated oath of allegiance.[12] One might assume that by 'the
king' Hushai means Absalom – Absalom doubtless did. Yet who
knows but that Hushai was thinking of David? When Absalom
pressed Hushai on his loyalty to David (v.17), Hushai insisted that
he would belong to and remain with the one whom Yahweh, the
people, and all the men of Israel had chosen (v.18). Absalom, like
Haman (Esther 6:6), assumed Hushai referred to him, but Hushai
could as easily have been describing David.[13] In any case, Hushai

12. P. Kyle McCarter, Jr., *II Samuel*, The Anchor Bible (New York: Doubleday,
1984), 384; see further, T.N.D. Mettinger, *King and Messiah*, Coniectanea
Biblica (Lund: CWK Gleerup, 1976), 131-37.

13. For possible irony and double meaning in Hushai's words, see Charles
Conroy, *Absalom Absalom!*, Analecta Biblica (Rome: Biblical Institute Press,

assures Absalom that there is nothing more natural than his serving the son of David (v.19). This episode may hint at Hushai's eventual success, but right now Ahithophel enjoys center stage. The big action comes in verses 20-22.

Absalom requested advice (v.20) and Ahithophel was ready: 'Have sex with your father's concubines whom he has left to care for the palace, and all Israel shall hear that you have made yourself stink [lit.] with your father, and the hands of all who are with you shall be made strong' (v 21). And so it was. They set up a portable bedroom on the palace roof, and Mr. Virility performed his mighty acts (v.22). Had it been three thousand years later all the news networks would have had their vans on the scene and their zoom lenses trained on the tent. All Israel knew what was going on in there.

It was a watershed event. It seems that a king's harem used to pass to his successor (cf. 2 Sam. 12:8), although this need not mean the new king had relations with these women. It may well have been a paper transaction. But possession of the king's harem was a title to the throne, and Absalom made this a matter of show-and-tell here.[14] By actually having sexual relations with David's concubines Absalom told all Israel he was burning his bridges behind him; there was no turning back; he meant business; he had no intent or hope of reconciliation with David. Such decisiveness would galvanize Absalom's supporters (v. 21c).

No doubt then about Ahithophel's intent: the counsel and deed of verses 20-22 was meant as the initial blow to topple David's kingship. And yet the careful reader senses something more. True, the writer does not use the ancient equivalent of underlining in these verses. He does not intone, 'Thus was fulfilled the word Yahweh had spoken through Nathan the prophet....' No, he does not make his point blatantly. He doesn't need to be blatant since the reader who comes upon 16:20-22 automatically resurrects 12:10-12 in his mind. Who can forget verses 11b-12 of that passage?

1978), 114, and Joyce G. Baldwin, *1 & 2 Samuel,* Tyndale Old Testament Commentaries (Leicester: InterVarsity, 1988), 264.

14. Roland de Vaux, *Ancient Israel,* 2 vols. (New York: McGraw-Hill, 1965), 1:116. Fokkelman (*King David,* 250) notes that 'the same prince who was full of holy [?] indignation at his brother's sexual violence [chap. 13] perpetrates a sexual crime against his father in 16:22'.

I will take your wives and give them to another man before your very
eyes and he shall sleep with your wives under this very sun. You acted
in secret, but I will make this happen in the sight of all Israel and in
broad daylight (NJPS).

A reader then can see that Ahithophel's advice that is meant to
overthrow David's kingdom nevertheless carries out Yahweh's
judgment upon David's sin. Ahithophel's scheme to remove
Yahweh's chosen king nevertheless fulfils Yahweh's previous
word. That is why there is hope for God's people in this text, even
though it depicts a judgment upon the covenant king, for the text
(16:20-22 with 12:10-12) is saying that the betrayer is yet in the
hand of God. His act of treachery only executes Yahweh's word.

We often face this blessed and ultimately encouraging mystery
in the Scriptures. It reminds one of Lee's entrenched position at
Fredericksburg in 1862 and of how General Burnside ordered the
Federal troops across the river and to the attack. I believe it was on
that occasion, as Confederate guns mowed down attacking Yankees
in droves, that Lee turned to Longstreet to remark, 'It is well war is
so horrible – else we would grow much too fond of it.' Burnside
did what he wanted to – or thought he must – do; his was a free
decision to assault the Confederate lines; and yet his assault was
an exact fulfilling of Lee's will, who had chosen and fortified that
position precisely so that Burnside would walk into his trap.

This dynamic was at work in the scheme of Ahithophel's New
Testament counterpart. The tradition of the Lord's Supper probably
refers to Judas' work in its opening words: 'The Lord Jesus, in the
night he was being handed over...' (1 Cor. 11:23; the verb is
paradidōmi, to hand over, usually here translated as 'betray').[15]
And yet Paul uses the same verb elsewhere with God as the subject:
'He who did not hold back his very own Son but *handed him over*
for us all...' (Rom. 8:32). On the one hand Judas wickedly hands
over the Son of God, but, actually, God hands over his Son, and,
mysteriously, Judas' scheme only carries out God's design. This is
perhaps the ultimate humiliation for all who oppose God and his
kingdom. This truth is clear whether or not you can fit all its pieces

15. See C.K. Barrett, *A Commentary on the First Epistle to the Corinthians*,
Harper's New Testament Commentaries (New York: Harper & Row, 1968),
266; and F.F. Bruce, *1 and 2 Corinthians*, The New Century Bible
Commentary (Grand Rapids: Eerdmans, 1980), 111.

together. It is the word of 2 Samuel 16: the betrayer only carries
out Yahweh's word. And that can prove solid solace to the people
of God when we are in the presence of our enemies.[16]

19. His Kingdom Cannot Fail
2 Samuel 17

The third stanza of Charles Wesley's 'Rejoice, the Lord Is King'
begins, 'His kingdom cannot fail, he rules o'er earth and heav'n;
The keys of death and hell are to our Jesus giv'n', while the final
line of Luther's 'Mighty Fortress' dogmatizes that 'His kingdom
is forever.' Whether we prefer the joyous lilt of Wesley or the
heavier majesty of Luther, the assurance is the same: No one,
nothing, can overthrow or terminate Yahweh's kingdom plan. Yet
in the muck and goo of history the stability of Yahweh's kingdom
looks much 'iffier' than that, for there are all sorts of Absaloms
and Ahithophels running loose ready to muscle through their own
kingdom plans. That is why when Bible readers come to 2 Samuel
17 they must keep their fingers on the promise of 1 Samuel 28:17,
of 2 Samuel 3:18, 5:2, and 7:12-16. The right perspective is crucial.
One must not focus on character studies or personal tragedies here;
the chapter reports a threat to the kingdom of God and to God's
appointed king. Not to worry though; Luther and Wesley are right.
So is Daniel: 'the God of heaven will set up a kingdom...and it
shall stand forever' (Dan. 2:44, NJKV). That text can rightly hang
over 2 Samuel 17, a chapter that simultaneously shows Yahweh's
kingdom under attack *and* the consolations his people still have in
such times.

The Hiddenness of Yahweh's Sovereignty (17:1-14)
The first consolation arises from the fact of Yahweh's sovereignty.
Yahweh is in control. The saints must have that assurance. If his
sovereignty seems invisible, they can live with that, providing they
are sure that he is there.

---

16. Some hold that Bathsheba was Ahithophel's granddaughter (inference
from 2 Sam. 11:3 and 23:34) and that his animosity to David arose from
David's violation of her. I do not hold this view. Among other things, it is too
flimsy to suppose there was only one Eliam (see ref. cited).

At first blush it appears that human manipulation will control the kingdom. Ahithophel is offering Absalom some crucial advice (vv. 1-4). I say crucial because of 16:23. We must ignore the chapter division to understand 17:1-4. If we breeze directly from 16:23 (Ahithophel's advice was almost divine) to 17:1-4, then we already sense how critical Ahithophel's advice is for Absalom's success. Ahithophel proposes a four-step plan in which he assumes the major risk:

1. Ahithophel will select a sizable body of troops and pursue David immediately ('tonight'; v.1).

2. He will strike while David's people are tired and exhausted, terrifying them and driving them off in a rout (v.2a).

3. Ahithophel will execute only David (v.2b).

4. With David eliminated Absalom will receive the loyalty of David's supporters, who will have no reason to continue the conflict (v.3).[1]

Absalom and the elders of Israel are impressed (v.4). What could be better than the plan of Ahithophel who always knows best?

I can't understand it. Why did he do it? Why did Absalom make that fateful inquiry in verses 5-6? Why that first step in his slide into the pit? In any case, Absalom decided he wanted to hear from Hushai as well. He may not have trusted Hushai fully, but he was curious about what he might say. And he stupidly handed Hushai a tremendous advantage. He did not simply ask Hushai what should be done in the present situation, but he divulged to him Ahithophel's whole plan (v. 6) and asked for his opinion, review, and comment. In this way Hushai knew exactly what he was up against and what his agenda must be.[2] Simply knowing Ahithophel's proposals was an advantage to Hushai, for now he could try to punch holes in them.

---

1. The textual difficulties in verse 3 do not obscure Ahithophel's primary point.

2. J.P. Fokkelman, *Narrative Art and Poetry in the Books of Samuel*, vol 1, *King David (II Sam. 9–20 & I Kings 1–2)*, (Assen: Van Gorcum, 1981), 214.

Hushai seems to shoot himself in the foot with the very first words of his extended remarks (vv. 7-13),[3] when he says, literally, 'No good, the counsel which Ahithophel has counseled.' That's gall. It is almost like saying the pope doesn't know anything about Catholicism. Hushai, however, both shocks and softens, for he immediately adds 'this time' to his stricture. Thus Hushai acknowledges Ahithophel's consistent expertise and only disputes his present proposal. Even the best of us can miss the train now and then.

We can appreciate Hushai's craft by hearing the various appeals he uses. He appeals to *logic* (vv. 8b-9a). No one could dispute the obvious – David is 'a man of war', an experienced fighter. That being the case, 'he will not spend the night with the troops' (v.8b, NIV) but will be hiding off by himself, maybe in some pit. Hushai means: Ahithophel means well, but he simply hasn't thought this through; it sounds fine to say he'll only kill David. But come on, wake up! There's no way you could kill just David – you couldn't even *find* him!

With logic Hushai mixes an appeal to *caution* (vv.9b-10). Imagine, Absalom, Hushai seems to say, what could happen if Ahithophel goes against your father with this commando force of his. Should David's men draw first blood, it might spook your bravest troops into panic. You must reckon, you know, with the intimidation factor, 'because everyone in Israel knows' – and this includes your men, Absalom – 'that your father is a great soldier and that his men are hard fighters' (v. 10b, TEV). You could have a major disaster on your hands solely because you didn't take time to prepare properly. Why leave such an important opportunity to chance? There's a difference, you know, between audacity and stupidity.

3.Robert Alter, in *The Art of Biblical Narrative* (New York: Basic Books, 1981), contrasts Ahithophel's urgent brevity with Hushai's deliberate loquacity: 'In the story of Absalom's rebellion, Ahitophel's [sic] militarily correct advice takes about forty words in the Hebrew. It consists mainly of a chain of jussive verbs – "Let me pick men... let me set out... let me pursue David tonight" (2 Sam. 17:1) – which perfectly expresses both the content and the mood of Ahitophel's counsel. There is not a moment to lose, the only course is to hit David hard before he can regroup his forces, and the statement itself has no time for fancy rhetorical maneuvers. By contrast, Hushai's counsel is three and a half times as long, and makes itself felt at virtually every point as a brilliant rhetorical contrivance, abounding in persuasive similes....' (p. 74).

Perhaps Hushai's most convincing argument is his appeal to *vanity*. Ahithophel knew how to be successful against David, but Hushai knew how to be successful with Absalom. Hushai gently appealed to Absalom's vanity at the very beginning: '*You* [emphatic in Hebrew] know your father and his men...' (v.8a), as if to say, Whatever short-sighted assessments others (read: Ahithophel) may make of the situation, you are not one to be duped, for you are fully aware of what you are facing. But Hushai's overt appeal to vanity comes in verse 11 when he begins to disclose his own program for David's demise: reinstate the draft; amass a huge army; let all Israel be gathered 'to you, with you yourself leading them into battle' (v. 11b, NIV).[4] A quick glance at Ahithophel's proposal in verses 1-3 highlights the contrast. There we hear a barrage of first person, singular verbs:

> Let me pick twelve thousand men and set out tonight in pursuit of David. I will come upon him when he is weary and disheartened, and I will throw him into a panic; and when all the troops with him flee, I will kill the king alone. And I will bring back all the people to you (vv. 1-3a, NJPS).

Ahithophel knows how to execute successful revolts but Hushai knows how to stroke thirsty egos. Let Absalom personally lead a real army; let him swagger out in all the pomp and pageantry of war. Hushai made Absalom the center of everything, which fell precisely in line with Absalom's own philosophy of life. Hushai made Absalom the focus, after which he subtly identified himself with Absalom's cause (note the 'we' – verbs in vv. 12-13). So Ahithophel is smart but Hushai is cunning; Ahithophel directs but Hushai pampers. Ahithophel can win Absalom's victory but Hushai can nourish Absalom's arrogance. Ahithophel gives better advice,

---

4. Cf. here Shimon Bar-Efrat, *Narrative Art in the Bible*, JSOT Supplement Series (Sheffield: Almond, 1989), 233: 'But the effort to give prominence to Absalom reaches its culmination in the solemn pronouncement, "and that your presence (literally, your face) go to battle". The same expression, namely, the same synecdoche combined with the same verb, appears in reference to God in Exod. 33:14,15: "My presence will go with you", "If thy presence will not go with me." This means that Absalom himself in all his glory will head this enormous army and lead it into battle. Hushai plays on Absalom's desires and aspirations, directing his words towards the delusions of grandeur and excessive self-love of the ambitious prince.'

but Hushai offers more convincing advice.

Finally, Hushai includes an appeal to *vengeance* (vv. 12-13). Hushai proposes the total eradication of David and his loyalists. Why rest content with wiping out David alone as Ahithophel prefers? Why such half measures? Why spare any pro-David elements? Wouldn't the new regime be far more secure if we didn't mollycoddle the opposition but wiped it out root and branch?

Hushai's mix of apparent reason and graphic imagery works its magic. Absalom & Co. issue a revised decision: 'The counsel of Hushai the Arkite is better than the counsel of Ahithophel' (v. 14a; see v.4). Hushai's finesse, however, cannot account for this reversal. There is a secret behind it, and the writer shares it in verse 14b:

> Now *Yahweh* had ordained to nullify the good counsel of Ahithophel, in order that Yahweh might bring disaster upon Absalom.[5]

That is the explanation for the whole story, for all this which has occurred so naturally, so humanly, so freely. Yahweh had ordained it. That may raise some questions for you. But remember: Yahweh's sovereignty is not meant to give you philosophical problems but spiritual comfort. And the primary characteristic of his sovereignty in this passage is its hiddenness. There are no trumpets, no turmoil, no billboards or bumper stickers. No glitzy, frenetic commercials like car dealers blast out on television. Only this quiet text, this discreet aside (v. 14b). The plot against Yahweh's king has gone to pot. Why? Yahweh had ordained it.

More often than not that is the manner of God's work. His sceptre

---

5. The first occurrence of 'Yahweh' is emphatic in the Hebrew. When the text calls Ahithophel's counsel 'good' (*ṭôbāh*) it speaks in practical not moral terms, i.e., it was good in the sense that it would have worked, been effective. Verse 14 is obviously the theological heart of the chapter. It may also be the literary center of verses 1-23, as in the following pattern:

Ahithophel's advice, vv. 1-4
   Absalom's inquiry, vv. 5-6
      Hushai's counsel, vv. 7-13
         Yahweh's secret, v.14
      Hushai's report, vv. 15-16
   David's informants, vv. 17-22
Ahithophel's end, v.23

is unseen, his sovereignty hidden behind the conversations and decisions and activities and crises of our lives. We see only grocery lines and diaper changes and school assignments; but through and over and behind it all Yahweh rules. He is not absent but neither is he obvious. Sometimes we must be told that lest we become too enamoured with our Hushais.

The Excitement of Yahweh's Providence (17:15-22)

You must remember that you know a secret: verse 14b. You know what Yahweh had decided about Absalom and what ruin Yahweh intends to bring upon him. The writer knows this and you know this because he has told you. But verse 14b is the writer's aside to you, the reader. The folks in the drama do not have this information. Hushai, for example, does not have it. In fact, Hushai didn't even know the decision of Absalom and his brass about his own advice (v.14a). He had been dismissed before they had conferred and reached their decision.[6] Hushai could only tell David what he and Ahithophel had both said and urge him to act on the assumption that Ahithophel's advice would be followed (vv. 15-16). All the *dramatis personae* then are in the dark; Yahweh's sovereign purpose really is hidden. Which is why verses 15-22 function as subtle consolation for God's people. They contain a little episode of Yahweh's providence, a small story about how Yahweh is for his servant, in this case David. Sovereignty is hidden, but providence brings sovereignty out where we can get a glimpse of it. Though the scales have turned, as it were, in verse 14, we often are not aware of it. But an episode like verses 15-22 gives us some hints. We may prefer to do without the nailbiting, but that goes with the turf.

We have then this pins-and-needles paragraph that relates how Hushai's news finally reaches David. The news was essential. As noted, Hushai could only pass on Ahithophel's advice and his own advice and tell David to prepare for the worst, i.e., Ahithophel's plan (v.16). Yet David also needed to know Hushai's counsel, for, should Absalom for some reason prefer it, David must then be prepared for a massive onslaught.

The incident is related in a concise and orderly way with the

---

6. A point Matthew Henry noted long ago (*Commentary on the Whole Bible*, 6 vols. [New York: Revell, n.d.], 2:534).

tightest tension at the center of the story (vv. 18-19). Note the
following structure:[7]

> Hushai's intelligence report given, vv. 15-16
>> Jonathan and Ahimaaz – waiting, v. 17a
>>> Maidservant – communication, v.17b
>>>> Lad – exposure, v. 18a
>>>>> The well, v.18b
>>>> Woman – concealment, v.19
>>> Servants – frustration, v.20
>> Jonathan and Ahimaaz – going, v.21a
> Hushai's intelligence report received, vv. 21b-22

Both structurally and literally the well is the lowest point of the
narrative!

The tension rises as the maidservant goes out to En-rogel, the
spring a short way south of the City of David where Jonathan and
Ahimaaz wait (v.17a).[8] Will David's undercover network succeed?
Nothing unusual about a woman going to a spring for water. But
one of Absalom's cronies sees them and reports to Absalom (v.18a).
Jonathan and Ahimaaz know they are being tracked. At Bahurim
(16:5) just east of Jerusalem they slink into a friendly citizen's
place and lower themselves into the well in his courtyard. His
obliging wife throws a canvas over it and some grain over the
canvas; everything looks normal and no one's the wiser (vv. 18-
19). But Absalom's posse arrives and demands the whereabouts of
Ahimaaz and Jonathan, for whom the woman stories. They had
already gone on, she assures them (v.20a).[9] Absalom's stoolies
continue the pursuit to the point of futility and turn back; the priests'
sons then come up for air and a run to David (vv.20b-21).

The episode is both a narrow escape and a small sign that

---

7. Some time after tracing out this structure for verses 15-22, I came upon one
done by Fokkelman, *King David,* 224, along similar lines.

8. On En-rogel, see ISBE 2:104, 1007.

9. The woman's words are a bit obscure to us: 'They have passed over the
(*mîkal*) [brook?] of waters.' Apparently she referred to a nearby wadi or
stream. We needn't bog down over the woman's ethics here. She deceives
Absalom's men. The narrative simply reports that but makes no moral
judgment about it. The writer does not want to stop and teach morality but to
hurry to tell you about a close shave.

Yahweh is at work for David. It reminds me of a story Spurgeon told of a godly minister running from his persecutors, finding a hayloft, and plunging himself beneath the hay. The soldiers came soon, swords and bayonets thrusting and testing the hay for the 'scoundrel'. The lord's servant even felt cold steel on the sole of his foot – the mark remained for years. Yet his pursuers did not discover him. Afterwards a hen came and laid an egg every day right near the place where he was hidden, and 'so he was sustained as well as preserved until it was safe for him to leave his hiding-place'.[10] That might not seem like much. You may not care much for raw eggs. But what a clear sign that God had not forgotten his servant. And it beats eating hay. Little providences can be grand encouragements.

The End of Yahweh's Enemy (17:23)
Suddenly we are reading the obituary of Ahithophel:

> When Ahithophel saw that his advice had not been followed, he saddled his donkey and set out for his house in his hometown. He put his house in order and then hanged himself. So he died and was buried in his father's tomb (v.23, NIV).

It is such a matter-of-fact description. The writer doesn't go into any literary hysteria or sensationalism. His step-by-step report probably reflects Ahithophel's own mind-set: calculated and deliberate. Perhaps some of the locals saw Ahithophel come bumping into Giloh (cf. 15:12) that afternoon.[11] His family remembered his going straight to his desk as though business matters were on his mind. Later they found him. The suicide was vintage Ahithophel – efficient and methodical.

Motive? The text only says 'Ahithophel saw that his advice had not been followed.' This might imply that Ahithophel had planned to be the power behind the throne. When, however, Absalom considered his counsel as an option rather than a mandate, Ahithophel realized that he would be an 'also ran' in the new regime; hence in bitter disappointment he opted out. More likely, however, the text hints that Ahithophel could see the handwriting on the

---

10. C.H. Spurgeon, *Lectures to My Students* (reprint ed., Grand Rapids: Zondervan, 1962), 403.

11. Giloh was probably 20-25 miles south/southwest of Jerusalem, likely south and west of Hebron; Gary A. Herion, 'Giloh (Place)', ABD, 2:1027.

wall; he saw doom written over Absalom's cause as soon as the pretender rejected his advice. Given time to recoup, David's crack troops would decimate Absalom's forces, after which Ahithophel would be executed for the traitor he was. It was crystal clear to Ahithophel. He was no dummy – at least in some things.

The report of Ahithophel's end, while tragic, nevertheless fortifies the faith and hope of God's people. As noted in our introductory remarks to 2 Samuel 16, Ahithophel is not merely a government official who committed political folly but an adversary of Yahweh's chosen king and, therefore, an enemy of Yahweh and his kingdom. And now they are carrying Ahithophel out to bury him. This is the man who lifted up his hand against Yahweh's appointed king. His end is a sign of what will happen to all the enemies of that King and kingdom. You cannot attack the kingdom of God without – sooner or later – being crushed by the power of God. The Ahithophels and Adolfs, the Hamans and Himmlers, the Sennacheribs and Stalins all rot and perish in the junk yards of history, because Yahweh stands guard over his kingdom and its subjects.

The Steadfastness of Yahweh's Servants (17:24-29)
If Yahweh's king has enemies and traitors, he also has friends and supporters. That is the testimony of this last section of the chapter.

Actually, verses 24-29 may more properly belong to chapter 18, for here the scene shifts east of the Jordan, the scene of the showdown between David's loyalists and Absalom's insurgents. However, we may also treat them with chapter 17 without distorting their witness.

Verse 24 picks up the narrative from verse 22. David comes to Mahanaim, Ishbosheth's old capital (2:8), probably on the north bank of the River Jabbok, about thirty air miles north and a bit east from where he likely crossed the Jordan. Then the writer catches us up on Absalom and his army: their crossing (v.24b), their captain (v.25), and their camp (v.26). That done, he brings us back to Mahanaim to witness what happened there upon David's arrival (vv. 27-29).

The writer organizes his vignette around the who (v.27), what (vv. 28-29a), and why (v. 29b). And a fascinating collage of whos it is: Shobi, the Ammonite from Rabbah, quite probably the brother

of the lame-brained Hanun (2 Sam 10) in whose place David
appointed Shobi as his vassal; Machir the son of Ammiel from Lo-
debar, who had been very sympathetic to Saul's clan, since he had
provided a haven for Mephibosheth (2 Sam. 9:4-5); and Barzillai,
the wealthy but fading octogenerian (2 Sam. 19:31-37) from
Rogelim.¹² These arrived with an impressive inventory (the whats:
beds, basins, pottery ware, wheat, barley, flour, parched grain,
beans, lentils, honey, curds, sheep, cheese from the herd ([vv.28b-
29a])¹³ and a transparent sympathy ('For they said, "The people
are hungry and tired and thirsty in the wilderness," 'v.29b).

One of these men is a pagan (Shobi), one a former Saul loyalist
(Machir), and another a long-time senior citizen (Barzillai). Here,
however, they are Yahweh's servants because they stand beside
Yahweh's appointed king. And they do so at some risk: the battle
had not yet been fought; the issue had not been decided; indeed,
Absalom was likely to marshall overwhelming numbers against
David. But these men come out in the open; they stand by David;
they choose the one Yahweh has chosen. Each of them had plenty
to lose since all were doubtless wealthy landowners. Nevertheless,
in spite of the risks, all that mattered, it seems, was to remain loyal
to the one to whom they owed allegiance.

During the War with Mexico and the assault on Chapultepec, a
battery under command of Lt. Thomas J. (later Stonewall) Jackson
came under a punishing fire. Some of the horses were killed, and
the gunners deserted the guns to find shelter behind an embankment.
But Lt. Jackson remained at the guns, urging his men back. Years
later Jackson's pupils at Lexington, Virginia, were inquiring about
this episode. One of them, astonished, asked, 'Major, why didn't
you run when your command was so disabled?' Jackson's quiet
response was: 'I was not ordered to do so. If I had been ordered to

---

12. For your mental map: Rabbah was located some twenty-two miles east of
the Jordan River, some twenty-five air miles southeast of Mahanaim; Lo-
debar may have been nine miles south of the Sea of Galilee (east of the Jordan,
of course); cf. C.E. DeVries, 'Lo-debar', ISBE, 3:151; Rogelim cannot be
definitely located. For overall orientation see *The Macmillan Bible Atlas,* 3ʳᵈ
ed. (New York: Macmillan, 1993), 84.

13. The main verb (*higgîš,* to bring near, present) does not occur until the
middle of verse 29; the list of personalities and provisions precedes it.
Fokkelman notes that the 'length of the enumeration in v. 28 [and 29] expresses
the extent and the depth of the allies' loyalty' (*King David,* 235).

run, I should have done so; but I was directed to hold my position, and I had no right to abandon it.'[14]

That was the situation with Shobi, Machir, and Barzillai: Israel had a covenant king, and they had no right to abandon him. Nor did they. It should require no imagination to see that, covenantally, the Christian disciple stands in the same relation to the Lord Jesus Christ, the son of David and Yahweh's appointed King. No matter how heavy the assault upon his authority and rule, no matter how much he is demeaned or despised, we are under orders to go on confessing him (Matt. 10:32-33) and supporting his subjects.[15]

True, 2 Samuel 17 shows God's kingdom under attack – but also under protection. There is solace in that for the people of God. Our ultimate security does not rest on any immunity from personal disasters or on any guarantee that our own nation will never fall but only in the fact that the God of heaven has set up a kingdom and it shall stand forever.

20. The Sad Triumph
2 Samuel 18:1–19:8

May 6, 1864, the Battle of the Wilderness: Federal troops had broken through the Confederate lines, but their success was momentarily stalled by point-blank artillery fire. General Lee himself was there with his cannoneers as they poured double-shotted grape and canister at the Federal ranks. Soon, however, Lee knew these guns would be overrun unless reinforcements arrived. Then he saw them – a lead brigade of Texas troops! Lee was ecstatic. As they prepared to counter-attack Lee spurred Traveller forward among them; he was preparing to lead the counter-charge himself. The troops

---

14. Mary Anna Jackson, *Life and Letters of General Thomas J Jackson* (1892; reprint ed., Harrisonburg, VA: Sprinkle, 1995), 42-45

15. Note the suggestive comments of C. Chapman on Shobi, Machir, and Barzillai: 'The sacred historian was doubtless guided by a principle of selection when he inserted the names of these three men in a book that is to abide through all time. It was the will of God that reference should be made to their conduct. Thus has God expressed approval of their regard for his anointed. In the same way our Saviour gave honour to the sympathy of the woman who poured on him the box of ointment, by declaring that what she had done should be told in all the world for a memorial of her (Matt. xxvi.13)' (*II Samuel*, The Pulpit Commentary [London: Funk and Wagnalls, n.d.], 426).

stopped, refused to go forward, and began chanting, 'Lee to the rear! Lee to the rear!'[1] They cherished a warm affection for their general and recognized that his life was too valuable to their cause to be risked in the thick of battle. And so it was at Mahanaim. David's troops would not allow David to risk himself on the field of battle. Should Absalom's forces gain any advantage they would – without doubt – zero in on the king. David was worth ten thousand of them – and so he must stay behind in the city (18:2b-4).

Literary Features

Before moving to exposition I want to highlight several literary features of the narrative, which may help us to understand how the writer views the events he is describing. The content of the narrative is straightforward:[2]

> Preparation, 18:1-5
> Description:
> > Summary, 18:6-8
> > Detail, 18:9-18
> Communication, 18:19-32
> Reaction, 18:33–19:8

---

1. Shelby Foote, *The Civil War, A Narrative*, vol. 3, *Red River to Appomattox* (New York: Vintage Books, 1974), 166-70.

2. Interestingly, one could argue that 2 Samuel 16:15–18:33 breaks down into a parallel pattern. Note:

A. 'King' comes to Jerusalem, 16:15-23
> B. Directions from Ahithophel, 17:1-4
> > C. Defeat of Ahithophel, 17:5-14
> > > D. Drama of two messengers, 17:15-22
> > > > E. Suicide, 17:23
A. King comes to Mahanaim, 17:24-29
> B. Directions from David, 18:1-5
> > C. Defeat of Absalom, 18:6-18
> > > D. Drama of two messengers, 18:19-32
> > > > E. Grief, 18:33

Both A-sections have two parts, the first speaking of the opposition (16:15-19, 17:24-26), the second of the support (16:20-23, 17:27-29). The last

However, let us consider the writer's manner of telling his story.

First, we can detect the *focus of attention* by the way the writer all but ignores the battle as a whole. In verses 6-8 he gives an ever so brief synopsis of the battle itself (place, losers and casualties, and circumstances) and then takes ten verses (vv. 9-18) to turn his zoom lens on Absalom's disastrous encounter with David's troops.[3] 'Now Absalom happened to meet David's men…' (v. 9a, NIV) – that episode preoccupies our writer. He does not want to give you a comprehensive and detailed account of the battle; rather he wants to tell you about how Absalom met his end. If space is a criterion of interest, then he also wants to highlight David's anxiety for news of Absalom and his reaction to such news (18:24–19:8).[4]

Secondly, note the *portrayal of characters* in the story. To summarize:

> Absalom is central
> Joab is dominant
> David is passive

In one sense Absalom has been central for a long time – ever since 13:1. His presence hangs heavily over chapters 13–14, all the way to 15:12. In 15:13–16:14 the focus is on David, but, come 16:15ff., Absalom takes the limelight again. In the present story, however, David makes Absalom central with his request to his three commanders: 'Deal gently with my boy Absalom, for my sake'

---

sentences (17:14b and 18:18) in the C-sections form an interesting combination. In both the subject stands first in the sentence, the one disclosing the divine secret (17:14b), the other the human irony (18:18). I do not press this, for other structural patterns are possible. At the least, however, such patterns imply these accounts were not sloppily compiled but carefully crafted.

3. No one can pinpoint the 'Forest of Ephraim' (v.6), site of the battle. But it must have been east of the Jordan and not overly far from Mahanaim. To argue that the Forest of Ephraim must be in the territory of Ephraim west of the Jordan, as Keil does, ties the whole account into geographical knots.

4. Cf. Charles Conroy, *Absalom Absalom!*, Analecta Biblica (Rome: Biblical Institute Press, 1978), 45-46: 'Though the reader has been told already at 17,14b that things will go ill for Absalom, this anticipation does not prevent the narrator from telling of Absalom's end as a story with moments of complication, retardation, and resolution. The narrator's interest is clearly in Absalom's end and even more in the effect this has on David, while the battle between the two armies is told very briefly (18, 6-8).'

(18:5, NJPS). This sentiment is both remembered by one of the troops (v.12) and repeated by David in his question to the messengers, 'Is my boy Absalom safe?' (vv.29,32,NJPS). My boy Absalom. Hence the narrator's close-up of Absalom's fate (vv. 9-18) only reinforces David's own concern (vv. 5,12,29,32). But note: though Absalom is central, he is not in control. He never speaks, he is only acted upon. He is central but mute.

Joab, however, is in control, if any human character can be said to be in control. Joab is dominant. Joab disposes of Absalom (18:14-17); Joab sends and directs messengers (18:19-23); Joab reads the riot act to the king (19:1-7); and, looking ahead, Joab will be the one who eliminates a rival and squelches another rebellion (20:4-22). Joab is the one who does the deeds and calls the shots. By contrast, David is passive. He gives a command (18:5), but it is not followed; he waits and hopes (18:24-27); he questions and grieves (18:29-33). David is king, but he is not in control.

Finally, we should be aware of the *twists of irony* in this story. The whole episode seems to be twisted. Looking at our story in isolation, everything happens that shouldn't happen. David makes a request (18:5) which, however unrealistic, is crassly ignored (18:14-15); Israel's rave poster boy (14:25-27) gets trapped in the most undignified dilemma (18:9);[5] the monument Absalom meant to commemorate his fame (18:18) is eclipsed by one that perpetuates his infamy (v.17);[6] Joab's intent for the Cushite to reach David first is frustrated when Ahimaaz takes a more circuitous but rapid route and outdistances the Cushite (18:19-32); news of victory

---

5. The mule seemed to be the royal saddle animal in David's time (2 Sam. 13:29; I Kings 1:33, 38,44); hence Absalom's mule deficiency may pack some symbolism, as Conroy suggests: 'The mule was a royal mount; losing his mule Absalom has lost his kingdom' *Absalom Absalom!*, 60). See also P. Kyle McCarter, *II Samuel,* The Anchor Bible (New York: Doubleday, 1984), 406.

6. No one knows how to reconcile 14:27 (three sons born to Absalom plus a daughter, Tamar) and 18:18 (Absalom has no son). It may be the sons predeceased Absalom, a plausible suggestion since the sons' names are not given in 14:27 though the daughter's is (so Robert P. Gordon, *I & II Samuel: A Commentary* [Grand Rapids: Zonderven, 1986], 285). See also chapter 16, note 11, above. The monument of v. 18 cannot be identified with the traditional Tomb of Absalom on the east side of the Kidron Valley in Jerusalem today, which dates from a much later time.

brings grief and mourning (18:33–19:4); and the conquering troops come slinking back in shame as though they had run away in a pell-mell retreat (19:2-3). Everything misses its mark. Intentions are not matched with right results. A sad triumph indeed.

Practical Exposition

What useful teaching can this twisted story press upon God's people? Everything seems to end up aruck and amuck. There are only four references to Yahweh in the whole story, three in battle reports (18:19,28,31), one in an oath (19:7). The larger context can help us evaluate these. However, I want us to keep our anchor in this story, and I propose we get at its teaching through a series of observations about the characters involved.

The One Who Meets the Crudest End (Absalom; 18:9-18)

Absalom happened to find himself in front of some of David's men (v.9). He didn't intend the appearance; but scrub and forest make normal military movements torturous (v.6) and all sorts of harum-scarum surpises occur. It was an unplanned disaster, an accident our common parlance calls it. And it led to an accident, for as Absalom hurries off (to find reinforcements?) he and his mule go under a large terebinth or oak and – was he looking back? – Absalom's head is slammed into the fork of some large, low branches and only the mule keeps going (v.9b).

Who knows how severely injured he was? But he dangles safely until Joab arrives. Joab shoves three shafts or darts into Absalom's mid-section (v.14) – the wounds are surely mortal, but the *coup de grâce* is left for Joab's adjutants (v.15).[7] They 'heaved him into a deep pit in the forest and piled over him a very high heap of stones' (v.17).

There may be more than meets the eye in this note about Absalom's burial place in verse 17. McCarter's comment is to the point.

---

7. Some think Joab only used the shafts to knock Absalom out of the tree (Does one need *three* shafts for that?), after which Joab's armor-bearers do the bloody work (so McCarter). Here I prefer to follow Hertzberg (*I & II Samuel*, The Old Testament Library [Philadelphia: Westminster, 1964], 359). Conroy (*Absalom Absalom!*, 49) observes the clinical way in which Absalom's end is described: 'Absalom himself is spoken about in a completely impersonal way: no words of his are mentioned, no pleas for mercy, just the physical fact of his being caught in the tree.'

This is the burial of an accursed man. Compare: (1) Josh 7:26, where Achan, having been stoned to death for his sacrilege (Josh 7:15), is buried under 'a large pile of stones'; (2) Josh 8:29, where the king of Ai, having been hanged on a tree, is thrown into a pit (LXX) and covered with 'a large pile of stones'; (3) Josh 10:27, where five enemy kings, having been put to death and hanged from trees, are thrown into a cave, the mouth of which is then covered with large stones. Abishalom [sic] is accursed as a fratricide and rebel, and he too was hanged on a tree (cf. Deut 21:23).[8]

This is the end of Absalom, the darling of the media (14:25-27), the rising prince who could work the crowds with such finesse and flair (15:1-6) and who, with disdain and arrogance, let his glands do the talking before all Israel (16:20-22). This is the end of the one who would destroy Yahweh's chosen king.

We have seen this pattern before, this plunge of the wicked from the pinnacle to the pit. On Hitler's birthday, April 20, 1945, Reichsmarschall Hermann Goering stood outside his castle and estate fifty miles northwest of Berlin. This was Karinhall (in nostalgic memory of Goering's first wife Karin), the repository of Goering's unquenchable appetite for opulence and luxury. Anyone with eyes could see that the Third Reich was being flushed down the historical drain. So Goering was getting out. Twenty-four Luftwaffe trucks lined the road outside Karinhall; they were stuffed with the antiques, paintings, and silver Goering hoped to salvage. The convoy was making a break for the south. Goering swept a last view over the wings and buttresses of his huge castle. An engineering officer indicated all was ready. Goering walked across the road, grabbed the handle of a detonator, and pushed the plunger. Karinhall exploded into a mass of rubble.[9] That is where all the pride, arrogance, swaggering, and greed ends – at the plunger of a detonator. Or in a pit in the Forest of Ephraim.

We must see that Absalom's end is a microcosm. His death as a man under the curse is typical of what will be the lot of all who at any time set themselves against God's kingdom, his chosen King, and/or his people. This is a somber truth, but Yahweh's true subjects have no hope unless it *is* true.

---

8. McCarter, *II Samuel,* 407. Cf. my discussion of Joshua 8:29 in *No Falling Words: Expositions of the Book of Joshua* (Grand Rapids: Baker, 1988), 68-69.
9. Cornelius Ryan, *The Last Battle* (New York: Simon and Schuster, 1966), 402-3.

> Yahweh, happy the man whom you instruct,
> the man whom you teach through your law;
> his mind is at peace though times are bad,
> while a pit is being dug for the wicked.
>
> (Ps. 94:12-13, JB).

The One Who Acts with the Clearest Realism (Joab; 18:11-16; 19:1-8)

'Deal gently with my boy Absalom, for my sake' (18:5, NJPS). Those orders would make sense if Absalom was about to enter therapy rather than war. The orders were clear, public, memorable, even moving – but hardly wise. As Adar points out, David's order

> shows that even before the battle David was willing to abandon military and moral considerations in view of his personal feelings. On the one hand he is sending out the people to risk their lives for him and his throne, while on the other hand he is prepared to ask expressly that his son, who is the root of all the evil, shall not be killed.[10]

One would think, however, that in the usual dash and bash of battle there would be no opportunity to exercise leniency toward Absalom. But, oddly enough, when Absalom found the tree and lost the mule (18:9), such a possibility occurred. One soldier reported the situation to Joab, who could not believe the man refrained from applying the finishing touch to Absalom (18:11). But the soldier's memory of David's words would not permit him, and his knowledge of Joab's character could not tempt him, to execute Absalom (18:12-13). Joab suffered from no such compunctions; he ignored the king's order and liquidated Absalom (18:14-15)

The narrative, typically, reports but does not evaluate Joab's action. His act was both rebellious and rational: rebellious, in light of David's order; rational, for the welfare of David's regime. At least this was likely Joab's thinking.

> He liquidates Absalom because it is politically necessary and there is no alternative for the arch-rebel. What option connected with sparing the prince's life is still viable? To return Absalom to Jerusalem in custody would be equivalent to taking half-measures. Joab has every

---

10. Zvi Adar, *The Biblical Narrative* (Jerusalem, 1959), 171.

reason to fear that David will again deny that this desperate case needs desperate remedies. His political assessment is that the Davidic State can be sound only by radically cutting out the growth. By the final elimination of the incorrigible prince he consciously assumes a king's responsibility for the State, which in his opinion David neglects or, as a sentimental father, is unable to bear.[11]

David would treat cancer with candy. Joab knew it required surgery – and he nominated himself as surgeon.

Joab's realism appears also in his speech to David following the victory. Joab gets the report: 'The king is weeping and in mourning over Absalom' (19:1). And David's grief had cast a pall of shame over the army (19:2-3). Many of the troops could probably hear David's cries and sobs (19:4) – it sounded like Absalom was the center of the universe. No parties in Mahanaim tonight.

Joab decides David needs reality therapy; he barges in and delivers it in a blistering barrage (19:5-7):[12]

5. Today you have covered the faces of all your servants with shame – your servants who delivered your life today, and the life of your sons and daughters, the life of your wives, and the life of your concubines;

6. You've put them to shame by loving those who hate you and by hating those who love you, for you have declared today that leaders and servants are nothing to you. In fact I know that if Absalom were alive today and all of us dead today – then you'd be pleased!

7. And now! Get up, go out, and speak to the heart of your servants, for I swear by Yahweh that if you do not go out not a man will stay the night with you, and this will be a far greater disaster than all that has hit you from your youth until now.[13]

---

11. J.P. Fokkelman, *Narrative Art and Poetry in the Books of Samuel*, vol. 1, *King David (II Sam 9-20 & I Kings 1-2)* (Assen: Van Gorcum, 1981), 246.

12. Cf. Fokkelman, *King David*, 271: 'Joab's great speech contains 75 words [Hebrew text]. The first "half" is a damning accusation (46 words)...Right from the beginning Joab overwhelms David...with an extremely long sentence of 24 words. It is the longest sentence of the spoken word in I/II Sam! Thus he machine-guns the king with words.'

13. There is a moving poignancy about this last clause – even others recognize that practically David's whole life has been a series of one trouble after another.

Joab is throwing some bare-fisted punches. He is harsh and sarcastic and doubtless exaggerates (e.g., v. 6b). But Joab is desperate. He must awaken David to his own folly: he may win the battle and still lose the kingdom. He can have his pity party later; right now he'd better grab some Kleenex, wipe his eyes, and get out to thank the troops.

Joab is an enigma. Here in 19:1-8 Joab seems to be right, yet in 18:14-15 he is insubordinate. Joab was wrong to defy the king's order, yet he clearly divined what disaster David's incessant grief would bring. Thus Joab is wrong and right; he is rebellious and reasonable. He lacks subordination but not sense.

The biblical writer allows Joab to remain an enigma. The writer reports what Joab did and said yet neither critiques nor commends him explicitly. At one point, however, he lets the veil slip. Usually he tells his story by objectively describing what occurred or by providing us with the conversation of the characters. However, as he gives us the data of 19:2-3 he seems to pass beyond description to evaluation:

> So the victory [or: salvation] that day turned into mourning for all the troops, for the troops heard that day, 'The king is grieving over his son.' So the troops came sneaking back that day into the city, like troops sneak who are ashamed because they ran away in battle.

Granted, I am making a judgment call. Yet it seems to me that here the writer has gone beyond bare description; he thinks we have a troubling state of affairs on our hands. The writer may sympathize with David's condition but he agrees with Joab's mind. Hence Joab's speech is nasty but necessary.

God's people sometimes need a strong dose of realism. In the early 1800s Asahel Nettleton had been laboring in a pastorless Congregational Church in Bridgewater, Connecticut. The church was riddled with strife and animosity, quarrels and bickering. Nettleton pointedly attacked the problem in preaching and discussions. They could expect no revival, he told them, until they settled their disputes and harmony prevailed. But the congregation suffered from convenient deafness. Now as was customary in those days, so in the spring of 1816 the state government proclaimed a certain day as the Annual State Fast. This was a high day – prayer, fasting, and special services. So it was to be at Bridgewater: the occasion was to include a sermon by their celebrated interim evangelist-pastor, Asahel Nettleton. All was well planned. Meeting time came. No preacher. They waited. No preacher. Disappointed, they at last went home. Nettleton had decided something drastic must be done: He would be a 'no show' on the special fast day. He had left the community. It worked; Nettleton's invisibility made people see the point. They organised a real day of prayer and confession, dealt with their festering wounds, and peace began to rule.[14] It required not ideal but drastic measures.[15]

The One Who Speaks the Most Truth (the Cushite; 18:19-32)

Ahimaaz was in Joab's face nominating himself for messenger to carry the news of victory to David (18:19).[16] Joab refuses and designates a Cushite (a Nubian or Sudanese) instead (v.21). Ahimaaz kept badgering Joab to let him be an 'also ran', and Joab, perhaps to get the exasperating Ahimaaz off his back, permitted him to go (vv. 22-23a). One can understand Ahimaaz' intensity – he had been part of the thrill and danger of supporting David from the first (15:27-28; 17:17-22). Once he had had to alert David (17:21-22), now he longed to relieve him. Risking his life for the king had given Ahimaaz a vested interest in the whole scenario. It was dessert time and Ahimaaz wanted to enjoy it.

We cannot precisely trace the route Ahimaaz took as he outran the Cushite (v.23b) – something he surely had in mind as he pummelled Joab for permission. But it does not matter; Ahimaaz knew where he was going. *The Macmillan Bible Atlas* proposes a very plausible explanation:

---

14. J.F. Thornbury, *God Sent Revival: The Story of Asahel Nettleton and the Second Great Awakening* (Durham: Evangelical Press, 1988), 73-74.

15. Christian parents can face this dilemma when they must expel an incorrigible teenage son or daughter from the home. See the excellent discussion in John White, *Parents in Pain* (Downers Grove: InterVarsity, 1979), 200-207.

16. The root *bāśar* (as a verb = to announce [good] news) appears 30 times in the Old Testament. Our passage (18:19-32) contains nine of them (vv. 19,20 [3 times], 22,25,26,27,31). The term (verb or noun) usually connotes good news or joyful tidings. See discussion in TDOT, 2:313-316.

The location of Mahanaim, in the deep canyon of the Jabbok, serves
to explain how Ahimaaz the son of Zadok outran the Cushite: the
Cushite took the more direct route, through the difficult terrain of the
'Forest of Ephraim.' Ahimaaz ran by a longer but much easier trail
along the Jordan Plain and up the course of the Jabbok.[17]

Meanwhile David anxiously waits at Mahanaim, convincing
himself that the spotted runners bring good news (vv. 24-27), which,
for David, must involve more than victory in battle. The race appears
close, Ahimaaz arriving only a bit before the Cushite. Down the
stretch Ahimaaz hollers 'All is well!' (NJPS; shālôm) to David.
When he arrives, he falls on his face in front of the king, exclaiming,
'How blessed is Yahweh your God, who has delivered up the men
who lifted up their hands against my lord the king' (v.28). But all
is not well for David unless Absalom is well, the top item on David's
agenda. When David inquires about his 'boy', Ahimaaz hedges;
he saw, he says, a great commotion about the time he was being
sent off, but he didn't know what it was all about (v.29). Here
Ahimaaz stories; Joab had clearly told him that the king's son was
dead (v. 20).[18] Ahimaaz couldn't bring himself to tell David the
bad news. In verse 28 he told David the truth, but he didn't tell him
the whole truth.

The Cushite tells the whole truth; hence, for this narrative, the
major truth comes from a minor character. 'Today Yahweh has
vindicated your cause, by ridding you of all who had risen up against
you' (v.31b, NJB). That was David's battle, but what about David's
boy? ' "May the enemies of my lord the king," the Cushite answered,
"and all who rebelled against you to your hurt, share the lot of that
young man" '(v. 32, JB). There it was. All of it. The good news
and the bad news. The whole truth.

We knew it all along. Not the details but the result. For 17:14b
is the theological control that governs our view of all 18:1–19:8.
That's what troubled us at 18:5. How can David's men 'deal gently'

---

17. Yohanan Aharoni and Michael Avi-Yonah, *The Macmillan Bible Atlas*,
3rd ed. (New York: Macmillan, 1993), 84. Note their reconstruction on map
110.

18. McCarter (*II Samuel*, 408) argues that the last clause of verse 20 is the
narrator's parenthetical comment rather than part of Joab's words. Then
Ahimaaz is innocent of prevaricating. However, McCarter's proposal is not
the more natural way of reading the text.

with David's boy when Yahweh intends disaster for the rebel? Whose will will carry the day? Yahweh's sovereignty or David's sentimentality? The Cushite has told us: Deliverance for David also involves disaster for Absalom.

When the famous Scots preacher Alexander Whyte was a boy he caught his arm in a threshing machine. Everyone thought there was no hope of salvaging the arm. But a neighbor who was wise in down-home treatment wouldn't allow them to take the lad for such surgery. The pain became severe and Whyte's mother called for the neighbor to come again. She examined the arm and said, 'I like the pain. I like the pain.' She was correct. The arm healed. The pain was a component of the healing.[19] The two went together.

That is the way it is in our text. If the kingdom of God under God's chosen king is to be saved then the enemy who assaults that kingdom must be destroyed. God gives no secure salvation to his church unless he brings decisive judgment on her enemies. We must stop praying, 'Deliver us from evil' unless we yearn for its destruction (cf. 1 John 3:8). Otherwise we are like a patient ready to undergo cancer surgery who pleads with his doctor to 'deal gently with my cancer', who urges the surgeon to get most of it but definitely to leave a tad, since 'it *is* a part of me and I would hate to lose all of it'. There will always be those, I suppose, who think it strange that there cannot be ecumenicity between Christ and Antichrist. But God's people know the Cushite is right: the preserving of God's kingdom (v. 31) involves the perishing of its enemies (v.32).

The One Who Carries the Heaviest Anguish (David; 18:33–19:8)
The writer placed us inside David's head almost from the start. His instructions to his corps commanders (18:5) reflect his worries over their very possible victory. And his anxieties are on his sleeve as he waits in the gate at Mahanaim, talking himself into hearing a completely ideal report (18:24-32). When the truth is finally out, David is devastated:

> The king shuddered. He went up to the room over the gate and burst into tears;…he kept saying, 'Oh, my son Absalom! My son! My son Absalom! If only I had died instead of you! Oh, Absalom my son, my son!' (18:33, NJB).

---

19. Warren W. Wiersbe, *Living With the Giants* (Grand Rapids: Baker, 1993) 125.

Clearly, the writer wants us to see and hear David's anguish. Fokkelman has pointed out that a mere historian would have been far more concise, with something like: 'Joab sent the king news of the battle. When David learned that Absalom had perished, he went into deep mourning.' But the text (18:19, 24-33) is twenty times longer than this. It is 'concerned with describing David's state of mind from within, gradually building up to David's nadir of mourning'.[20] And so now we hear David's pitiful and helpless wail, and the writer wants us to hear it.

At the risk of seeming clinical, I want to ask about the reason behind David's eruption. I do not doubt that deep natural affection plays its part (though David had shown that affection could have limits, 14:21-24). Is that the only explanation for a grief that refuses to be curbed except by the dire threat of Joab's 'Dutch uncle' speech (19:5-8)?

I suggest there is a deeper dimension to David's grief. As we must use 17:14b to control our overall view of 18:1–19:8, so we must allow 12:10-12 to illumine David's sorrow. How Nathan's words in this latter text must have echoed in David's conscience. 'The sword will not depart from your house forever' (12:10).[21] It is David's guilt that inflames his grief. Nathan had assured David that he would not die but that David's infant son would die (12:14). And he did (12:19). Then Amnon was murdered (ch.13), and now Absalom has perished. David knew that his sin had set the sword loose in his household. 'If only I had died instead of you!' David was the guilty one yet Absalom suffers the consequences of David's guilt. (This does not negate Absalom's own guilt.) There was that time when unlike his *ḥesed*-ways with Mephibosheth (ch. 9) and Hanun (ch.10), David acted as the king without *ḥesed* and pity (12:6) because he wanted to writhe and thrive with Bathsheba and didn't blink at having hired butchers dispense with husband Uriah. Perhaps David wished he had died instead of Absalom because he knew he deserved to die. Guilt has aggravated grief. So we end

---

20. Fokkelman, *King David,* 265.
21. On 12:10 see C.F. Keil, *Biblical Commentary on the Books of Samuel* (1875; reprint ed., Grand Rapids: Eerdmans, 1950), 390. On the link between David's previous guilt and current grief, see the useful homiletical remarks of C. Chapman, *II. Samuel,* The Pulpit Commentary (London: Funk and Wagnalls, n.d.), 470-471.

with a paradox: a safe kingdom, a sad king. Maybe there's a reason why, at the last, God himself must wipe away every tear from our eyes (cf. Isa. 25:8, Rev. 21:4).

First and Second Samuel clearly show us that as the anointed king David is a suffering king. Here, however, he sheds tears for his own griefs and over his own guilt. We will have to wait for his Descendant, the man of sorrows, who will bear *our* griefs and carry *our* sorrows (Isa. 53:4).

21. Welcome Home – Maybe
2 Samuel 19:9-43

It was good to be home. I had been gone a week helping at a church camp; my wife had been, as I recall, visiting her parents. But now we had returned to the Presbyterian manse that was home in a delightful small town in Northeastern Kansas. We walked in and whiffed a musty smell. We walked further and discovered water dripping from dining room and family room ceilings – ceilings ruined, floors and furniture wet, books soaked. There was a crack in the toilet tank on the second floor (one theory attributes it to lightning); hence the tank kept leaking, the water kept pumping but never shut off because the tank never filled up. Tired bones were in for hours of work, and one set of those bones was seven months pregnant. Photo albums and all manner of yuck were spread on the picnic table to dry; there were other futile attempts to control the disaster. We almost wished we hadn't come back. That is nearly the impression 2 Samuel 19 gives us of King David's return from exile; it ends up becoming one of those 'welcome home – maybe' situations. He returns home as king, but the kingdom seems to crumble in his hands.

The narrative follows an orderly pattern. The following scheme should summarize it adequately:

Israel and Judah: deciding about bringing back the king, vv. 9-15
        Confession and sparing of Shimei, vv. 16-23
        Clarification and truth about Mephibosheth, vv. 24-30
        Faithfulness and refusal of Barzillai, vv. 31-39
Judah and Israel: disputing about bringing back the king, vv. 40-43

The Strife in the Kingdom (19:9-15, 40-43)

Let us look first at the two end-pieces of our story where we can overhear the furore that arose among the tribes over David's return to the throne.

All Israel was in a dilemma. And (as often happens with people in dilemmas) they began bickering among themselves (v. 9a). The writer allows the people to describe their own political pickle:

> *The king* has delivered us from the grip of our enemies,
> and *he* has rescued us from the grip of the Philistines,
> yet now he has fled from the land because of Absalom;
> but *Absalom*, whom we anointed over us, has died in battle;
> and now – why are you keeping silent about bringing back
> the king? (vv. 9b-10; emphasis in Hebrew)

David got wind of this sentiment.[1] He fired off a message to the elders of Judah, his own tribe, via his priestly friends Zadok and Abiathar. He appealed to their *pride:* why should they lag behind the rest of the tribes in restoring the king? (v. 11b); he appealed to their *relationship:* David himself was from Judah; they were his 'bone and flesh' (v. 12a); and he appealed to their *anxieties:* he swore to appoint Amasa, commander of Absalom's army, over his army in place of Joab (v.13).[2] This last was a signal that those in Judah who had supported Absalom need fear no retribution from a neo-Davidic regime. David still had the old magic: 'He won over the hearts of all the men of Judah as though they were one man' (v.14, NIV).

There are some who charge David with a first-class political blunder here.[3] By making this pitch to his own tribe he polarizes rather than unifies Israel and simply provides the props for the animosity and divisiveness of verses 40-43. I find that view naïve.

---

1. This is explicit in LXX, which has 'And the word of all Israel came to the king' at the end of verse 10. In any case, we know David picked up the political scuttlebutt because he asked the elders of Judah why they were going to be the last ones (v.11) to bring back the king.

2. Amasa was a nephew of David, as was Joab (see 2 Sam. 17:25 and 1 Chron. 2:13-17). On the complications the former text raises, see Nola J. Opperwall, 'Zeruiah', ISBE, 4:1194.

3. E.g., J.P. Fokkelman, *Narrative Art and Poetry in the Books of Samuel*, vol.1, *King David (II Sam. 9–20 & I Kings 1–2)* (Assen: Van Gorcum, 1981), 290-92.

What else could David have done? He had to have some assurances from Judah. He could hardly go back without confirmation of Judah's support. True, Judah was David's own tribe and any overture might appear to smack of favoritism. But Absalom's revolt had erupted in the heart of Judah – in Hebron (15:7-10). That couldn't have happened without some Judean support. Moreover, Ahithophel, David's turn-coat counselor, was from Judah (15:12), as was Amasa, whom Absalom appointed general (17:25). Absalom had apparently won significant support within Judah. Hence this tribe had every reason to expect that if David returned life might not be all games and interviews for them. There may have been a guilt-ridden reason why no word had reached David from Judah. Many of them likely feared David would return with an axe rather than a sceptre. Hence David's appeal and reassurance was precisely what was needed.

One could with more reason place the blame for the strife on the northern tribes. 'All the people of Judah, along with half the people of Israel, brought the king over' the Jordan (v. 40b). But then 'all the men of Israel' (perhaps additional arrivals from the northern tribes) came to David: 'Why have our brothers, the men of Judah, stolen you, and brought the king and his household over the Jordan?' (v.41). The men of Judah appeal to their relationship to the king ('closely related to us') and to the fact that they have not abused that relationship ('Have we eaten anything from the king's holdings or has he ever lifted away tax obligations for us?' v. 42).[4] No one can whitewash the men of Judah, for, at the last their words were 'even more intemperate' (v. 43b, NJB) than Israel's. Yet not without some justification, for Israel's rhetoric did not inquire but incited ('Why have...the men of Judah *stolen* you?' v.41), and her pride was peeved because her precedence in numbers ('We have ten shares in the king...') and initiative ('Were we not the first to suggest bringing back our king?' v.43, NJB) carried no clout. Israel may have suffered from corporate hyper-sensitivity ('Why have you despised me?'). It was not the first time the north had tried to throw her weight around (Judg.8:1-3; 12:1-6). But Judah could trash-talk too – and they did (v. 43b).

---

4. The latter is the rendering of Bruce K. Waltke and M. O'Connor, *An Introduction to Biblical Hebrew Syntax* (Winona Lake, Ind.: Eisenbrauns, 1990), 587.

This fiasco was not the fault of David's politics but of the reaction of Israel to the manner of his return and of Judah's reaction to Israel's reaction. The impression is clear: 'it seems as if political life is full of nothing but quarrels, either through opposition to the king or because of devotion to him'.[5] The rightful king has returned but there is no peace in the kingdom. The animosity and envy among his subjects threaten the stability of his kingdom. This negative situation, however, carries a positive witness: this kingdom must truly be the kingdom *of God* or it would have self-destructed long ago.

Most pastors get more than a taste of this point. How often on any given week I used to marvel that a congregation ever survived between petty bickering and flagrant sins, between hurt feelings and asinine stubbornness, between trivial priorities and tragic apathies. Yet it seemed that the fragmenting tendencies of human folly were always overcome by the glue of divine grace. Surely Jesus is building his church or it would have vanished long ago. And just as surely the kingdom is the Lord's or it would have been swept away in the sewage line of history before David's greater Son ever appeared in the flesh.

The Subjects of the Kingdom (19:16-39)
The writer has already related a series of encounters during David's exodus from Jerusalem (15:13–16:14, with Ittai, Zadok, Hushai, Ziba, and Shimei); now he rehearses a corresponding set of encounters on David's return, with Shimei (19:16-23), Mephibosheth (19:24-30), and Barzillai (19:31-39). We get to listen to them, for all of them make speeches (vv. 19-20; 26-28, 30; 34-37). As readers we welcome the clips on Shimei and Mephibosheth since we have been wondering since chapter 16 just what might happen to them. Now David is in the process of being restored to his kingdom and the writer provides us with these three cameos of his subjects.

Policy, the Strategy of Shimei (19:16-23)
Shimei has spoken before (16:5-8) and now as he speaks again one forms the distinct impression that he is a snake. Yet even snakes want to live.

The general picture of the text is clear in spite of problems in details. Shimei is an early worm, arriving with the men of Judah at

---

5. Zvi Adar, *The Biblical Narrative* (Jerusalem, 1959), 182-83.

the Jordan (v.16); apparently he crosses the Jordan, perhaps with
Ziba's clan, and falls before David as the king is preparing to cross
the river (v.18, NASB), and proceeds to eat crow:

> Let not my lord hold me guilty. Do not remember the wrong your
> servant did, the day my lord the king left Jerusalem. Put it out of your
> mind. For your servant admits that he has sinned, and here I am today,
> first of all the House of Joseph to come down and meet my lord the
> king (vv. 19-20, JB).

Shimei candidly admits his wrong (What else could he do?),
but he also comes with his arguments. He is, after all, the first of
all the house of Joseph (the northern tribes) to come down to meet
the king. Perhaps that should count for something. However, his
visible argument may have weighed more than the verbal one:
Shimei had brought a thousand other Benjaminites with him (v.
17; either a literal number or a military contingent). He had
persuaded a good number of his fellow tribesmen to jump back on
the Davidic bandwagon. Abishai nevertheless wanted to defend
David's position and dish out to Shimei his just deserts (v.21). But
David did not want that kind of assistance just now (cf. 1 Kings
2:8-9). Abishai was right: Shimei's head should be carried off in a
bucket. But he was not sharp (cf.v. 23). If David axed Shimei, the
other Benjaminites and northern tribes might wonder if a purge
were coming. Would more heads start rolling? So David met Shimei
with clemency (v. 23).

There is no reason to hold that Shimei had undergone any
massive change of heart. He had committed a tactical error called
treason and now he must save his skin, if he can. He does not submit
to David out of love but out of policy. He recognizes the realities
of power and politics and adapts himself accordingly. He is like
the senator who went off on an overseas vacation, enjoying fun
and girls on a yacht while his wife was home near to giving birth.
Several days after the stillborn child was delivered, he returned
home, not out of urgent concern for his wife but because his
associate convinced him that a shattered marriage would destroy
his political career. Not a matter of love, nor even loyalty, but of
policy.

One can bump into a Shimei in the church, someone who aligns
himself/herself with Christ's people out of self-interest. There is

some advantage to be gained. Perhaps it mollifies ageing parents or pacifies a spouse. It is a token submission to Christ; not a matter of conviction but simply of policy.

Sincerity, the Mark of Mephibosheth (19:24-30)

We have not heard of Mephibosheth since 16:1-4, and there we only heard *about* him. It was not good: Mephibosheth, Ziba alleged, stayed in Jerusalem because he somehow fancied Absalom's revolt would dump royal power into his lap (16:3). The helpless cripple was a treacherous conniver. Now, however, Mephibosheth gets to speak for himself, for he 'came down to meet the king' (v. 24a), presumably at the Jordan.[6]

David, perhaps with more than a little suspicion, asked Mephibosheth why he had not shared his exile (v.25b). Mephibosheth's apologetic consisted of a sign and a speech. One look at Mephibosheth told where his heart was: he 'had not pared his toenails, or trimmed his moustache, or washed his clothes from the day that the king left until the day he returned safe' (v.24b, NJPS). He had 'let himself go'. He made no secret of his loyalty (risky, with Absalom in town), of his grief over David's exodus. Indeed, his disheveled appearance showed that he had forced himself to share David's exile in spirit.

Mephibosheth's speech (vv. 26-28), however, explains the sign but especially his absence from David's exit party. 'My servant deceived me' (v. 26).[7] Mephibosheth had called for a donkey to be saddled so he could ride and go with the king. His little aside, 'for your servant is lame' (v.26c), was meant to remind David that he was incessantly dependent upon others for all sorts of assistance. In his case, where there was a will there was not necessarily a way. But his servant (Ziba) not only deceived Mephibosheth but also slandered him to the king (v. 27a). Those are the facts. Ziba had lied through his teeth. But Mephibosheth cuts short his defense: let David do what he wants (v. 27b); Mephibosheth, as a member of

---

6. Verse 25a actually says, 'When he (Mephibosheth) came to Jerusalem to meet the king,' but most translators assume on the basis of verse 24a that 25a intends to say 'from Jerusalem'. See P. Kyle McCarter, Jr., *II Samuel,* The Anchor Bible (New York: Doubleday, 1984), 431, for a cogent explanation of the text as it stands.

7. The Hebrew text places emphasis on the subject, 'my servant'.

the former opposing regime had no right to expect anything but death, let alone David's kindness (v. 28; see 2 Sam. 9); all that matters is that the rightful king has come back safely (v.30).

David made a decision that was both understandable and unjust: Mephibosheth and Ziba would divide the estate. Apparently he recognizes the veracity of Mephibosheth's explanation. Hence his cavalier ruling of 16:4 must be reversed, for Ziba is nothing but a greedy liar. But he was also a helpful greedy liar (16:1-2 and 19:17). And so David only reversed his decision half-way. I suppose David did not want unnecessarily to alienate the Ziba contingent. A man with fifteen sons and twenty servants (v.17) was someone to be reckoned with. He had clout. And since David needed to win all the support he could for the restored regime he could ill afford to bite the dirty, lying hand that had fed him. If David acted with clemency in Shimei's case, in Mephibosheth's he acted with expediency. Pragmatism rather than justice prevailed.[8]

Mephibosheth was lame; his servant had given him the shaft; yet his feet and whiskers and smelly clothes testified of his loyalty to the true king. Jesus' words come to mind about the woman who poured her expensive ointment on him: 'She has done what she could' (Mark 14:8). It was the same with Orop, a boy who lived near the Akobo (Sudan) mission station. Missionary Don McClure tells how Orop loved to come to school. But he couldn't learn anything; he couldn't even write the letters of his own name in the right order. So he had to give up his place in school for another child. He would still come, however, and sit outside the school window to listen to the Bible stories. Then he would round up a group of boys and retell the Bible stories. But he'd get them all mixed up; so McClure had to forbid Orop to tell stories about Jesus! But then Orop received his call. Dr. McClure told him that when he went out to a village to preach Orop could carry God's Book (McClure's Bible) for him. So every day as the sun came up Orop would be waiting for McClure and carry God's Book to the village du jour. He did what he could. One day a bunch of small boys were playing in the river when a crocodile latched on to one of them. All ran. But Orop jumped in to fight the croc. He succeeded in freeing

8. Joyce G. Baldwin *(1 & 2 Samuel,,* Tyndale Old Testament Commentaries [Leicester: InterVarsity, 1988], 277) gives an accurate and sensitive assessment of David's treatment of Mephibosheth.

the boy but the crocodile grabbed Orop instead. They only recovered one arm and one leg to bury. He did what he could. Orop had told his mother that he was not afraid to die, because Jesus would come to take him by the hand and lead him home. After his death this testimony stirred his mother to seek Jesus.[9] He had done what he could.

That was Mephibosheth. He was lame and limited but loyal. And his loyalty was not driven by survival (Shimei) or greed (Ziba). He could not sustain David with abundant provisions like the wealthy farmer Barzillai (17:27-29; 19:31-32). Oddly enough, toenails and facial hair and dirty clothes were the sacraments of his faithfulness. He did what he could.

Contentment, the Blessing of Barzillai (19:31-39)

We have already met Barzillai in 17:27-29 (see exposition there). He is the elderly and wealthy Gileadite farmer who 'had sustained the king' (v. 32) while the latter had stayed in exile at Mahanaim. Now Barzillai comes down from Rogelim to bid the returning David farewell. We cannot be sure whether Barzillai accompanied David across the Jordan a little ways (see, e.g., vv. 31,36 in NIV and NKJV) or whether he simply said his goodbyes on the east side (see NJPS).[10] In any case, David expresses his gratitude by inviting Barzillai to live at court: as Barzillai had sustained David, so now David will sustain his old friend (v. 33). But Barzillai respectfully declines in a speech that runs to four verses.

Barzillai pleads his age (vv. 34-35a) and the ravages of age (v. 35b) as the basis of his refusal. He can no longer enjoy either common pleasures (e.g., tasting food or drink) or exceptional entertainment (e.g., male and female singers). He would be glad, however, if David wanted to take Chimham (v. 37b; a son of Barzillai?) along as his surrogate and lavish his royal care upon him. But as for himself Barzillai pleads: 'Please let your servant

---

9. Charles Partee, *Adventure in Africa: The Story of Don McClure* (Grand Rapids: Zondervan, 1990), 209-210.

10. NJPS renders verse 31, 'Barzillai the Gileadite had come down from Rogelim and passed on to the Jordan with the king, to see him off at the Jordan,' and verse 36, 'Your servant could barely cross the Jordan with your Majesty!' The text is difficult, especially in verse 31, but NJPS is a plausible way of taking it.

return and let me die in my own town, near the grave of my father and my mother' (v.37a). That is all Barzillai asks. That is enough.

I confess that I am a little skeptical about stressing Barzillai's contentment in these verses. The big truth about Barzillai is his fidelity to Yahweh's appointed king (17:27-29).[11] He had used his wealth well (cf. Luke 16:9). And yet Barzillai's farewell request does breathe an air of contentment (not simply resignation). He was eighty years old when he performed what was arguably his most important service for the kingdom of God. Barzillai had been faithful to Yahweh's covenant king. Besides that, what else matters? What ever could one want beyond that? A man like that is free – content to go back to his hometown and finish out his days.

22. No Surprises
2 Samuel 20

During college years I worked two summers at a Pennsylvania state park. I worked mostly evening hours at the park office issuing overnight camping permits to tent and trailer types. Pets were prohibited, and the first question I was to ask all prospective campers was: 'Do you have any pets?' Should they give the right answer I was to write 'NP' at the top of the receipt. Some men, however, would wax cute and answer, 'Only my wife!' They usually said this with a smirk, amused at their clever retort. Perhaps my non-response perplexed them. What they didn't realize was that I had already heard the remark twenty-seven or forty-two times before – and somehow repetition had dulled the hilarity of it all. Hearing it only confirmed a certain weariness.

Now 2 Samuel 20 is like that. Not that the story isn't interesting; but as we read through the chapter we know we have heard this before. There are no surprises – only more rebellion, more tragedy, and so on. Aside from the woman's reference to the 'inheritance of Yahweh' in verse 19 there is no reference to God nor any overt

---

11. Fokkelman notices how Barzillai's request in 19:37a forms a contrast to Ahithophel's end in 17:23. 'The contrast is plain. David's adversary is defeated, his last journey is solitary and his death violent. The king's friend gives and receives warmth, his death will be natural and peaceful, in an atmosphere of harmony and fulfilment' (*King David*, 308).

indication of how he is at work. The whole story seems to consist of bump-a-long human activity. In one sense the human actors function as the focal points of the story:[1]

> The new rebel, vv. 1-2
> The sad women, v.3
> The old butcher, vv. 4-13
> The wise woman, vv. 14-22

Human Rebellion (20:1-2)

Almost all of 2 Samuel 20 is about Sheba: introducing Sheba (vv. 1-2), pursuing Sheba (vv. 4-13; note the four occurrences of *rādap*, to pursue, in vv. 6,7,10,13), and eliminating Sheba (vv. 14-22). Sheba was from Benjamin, King Saul's tribe, and probably had affinities toward the old regime.[2] His rebellion, at least initially, is more secession than revolt.[3] But the writer leaves no doubt about how you are to regard Sheba: he is a 'scoundrel' (v.1; lit., 'a man of Belial'). That takes some guesswork out of interpretation.

But why is this scoundrel such a scoundrel? Because he is rejecting Yahweh's chosen. He is rebelling – and calling the northern tribes to rebel – against Yahweh's anointed king (1 Sam. 16:1-13) and breaking the covenant that bound the king and the northern tribes in mutual loyalty (2 Sam. 3:21; 5:3).[4] Perhaps Sheba could whitewash his deed alleging that Judah's nasty words (19:43b) had caused him emotional distress or that David's politiking (19:11-15) smacked of gross favoritism. All of which would not alter his

---

1. Verses 1 and 22 place a literary wrapper around the story: Sheba and Joab both 'blew on the horn' and the people are either called to or going 'each man to his tent' (lit.); see Ronald F. Youngblood, '1, 2 Samuel,' *The Expositor's Bible Commentary*, 12 vols. (Grand Rapids: Zondervan, 1992), 3:1042.

2. The text always refers (eight times) to Sheba as the 'son of Bichri' (Hans Wilhelm Hertzberg, *I & II Samuel*, The Old Testament Library [Philadelphia: Westminster, 1964], 370-371). If there is a link between Bichri here and the Becorath of 1 Sam. 9:1 (Saul's ancestry), then Sheba might have been of Saul's family.

3. J.P. Fokkelman, *Narrative Art and Poetry in the Books of Samuel*, vol. 1, *King David (II Sam. 9–20 & I Kings 1–2)* (Assen: Van Gorcum, 1981), 319.

4. Cf. T.N.D. Mettinger, *King and Messiah*, Coniectanea Biblica (Lund: CWK Gleerup, 1976), 138-39, 227-29, and Gerard Van Groningen, *Messianic Revelation in the Old Testament* (Grand Rapids: Baker, 1990), 26-28.

crime: rebelling against covenant kingship and, in so doing, rebelling against Yahweh.

Which is somewhat tiring to the reader of 2 Samuel. We've been through chapters of this already with Absalom (2 Sam. 15–18). And the same revolt in principle goes on and on in the so-called evangelical church. There people are perfectly happy to be in a church that has a 'high view' of the authority of the Bible. But let a married woman find another man she prefers to her husband, or a husband who has gotten close to another woman at work and wants to ditch his wife, and somehow the authority of the Bible doesn't matter. Or someone has been wronged by another. It was too much, the wound too deep, the offense too vicious – the one could never be reconciled to the other, even though the offender is repentant and seeks forgiveness. No – impossible. Point out to the offended that he'd better never pray the Lord's Prayer again (Matt. 6:12) and that Jesus gives no option but to reconcile (e.g., Matt. 6:14-15; Luke 17:3-4). Too bad for the Lord's Prayer and too bad for Jesus. His rage is too precious to him. Rightful authority can simply go down the tube. There are Shebas in the church; some of them are evangelicals of the stricter sort. They rebel against rightful authority; they are determined to go their own way, to call their own shots; they lift up their hand against the King.

Human Sadness (20:3)

Our writer puts Sheba on hold:

> When David arrived at his palace in Jerusalem, he took the ten concubines he had left to take care of the palace, and put them under guard. He provided for their needs, but did not have intercourse with them. They were kept confined for the rest of their lives, living like widows (v.3, TEV).

And one might be tempted to think this information about the concubines is merely that, simply filler to provide us with the whole story. That would be a mistake, for this is the very first item the writer reports to us about David's activities upon his re-entry of Jerusalem. The prominence the writer gives this matter implies that he sees a definite importance about it. Had he only wanted to provide data he could easily have inserted the contents of verse 3 after verse 22 with the lead-in, 'Now when David had returned to

Jerusalem, he....' Instead, he places it front and center where we run smack into it.

Understandably so. We cannot read this little note without 12:11-12, 15:16, and 16:20-22 coming to mind. The same must have been true for David. He was informed of Absalom's afternoon with these concubines (16:20-22). And as he began to make arrangements for them, the unceasing echo of Yahweh's threat must have reverberated through his head: 'I shall take your wives before your eyes and I shall give them to your companion, and he shall lie with your wives...' (12:11). The misery of these women was occasioned by David's sin in the Bathsheba-Uriah affair. No, they were not homeless; David situated them in secluded quarters. Nor were they starving or destitute, for David provided for them. But he would have nothing more to do with them. They were confined, isolated, and alone. They passed the days of their bland existence as de facto widows. W.G. Blaikie catches the mood:

> The only way of disposing of them was to put them in ward, to shut them up in confinement, to wear out the rest of their lives in a dreary, joyless widowhood. All joy and brightness was thus taken out of their lives, and personal freedom was denied them. They were doomed, for no fault of theirs, to the weary lot of captives, cursing the day, probably, when their beauty had brought them to the palace, and wishing that they could exchange lots with the humblest of their sisters that breathed the air of freedom.[5]

There is simply something intensely, irretrievably sad about verse 3.

Yet this is no surprise. We have seen it before – in the tragedy of Tamar (2 Sam. 13).[6] Amnon had craved her (13:1-11) and violated her (v. 14), then despised her (v. 15) and threw her out like human refuse (vv. 17-19). He had 'laid her' (13:14) and she was 'laid waste' (13:20), desolate the rest of her days. Amnon sinned and Tamar suffered. His glands ensured her gloom.

We continue to meet this radical sadness in the kingdom of

---

5. W. G. Blaikie, *The Second Book of Samuel,* The Expositor's Bible (Cincinnati: Jennings & Graham, n.d.), 319. Blaikie goes on to add: 'Strange that, with all his spiritual instincts, David could not see that a system which led to such miserable results must lie under the curse of God!'

6. Karl Gutbrod, *Das Buch vom Reich,* Die Botschaft des Alten Testaments, 2nd ed. (Stuttgart: Calwer, 1973), 231.

God.[7] Scores of Christ's people know what it is to have their lives
turned to gray because of the sins of others. And when all is said
and done, there is no help for it, except in the One sent to 'bind up
the broken-hearted' (Isa. 61:1) and in the hand that promises to
wipe away the tears from all faces (Isa. 25:8).

Human Treachery (20:4-14)
David would not allow Sheba's revolt to mushroom. He ordered
his newly-appointed military chief to call out the Judah militia
within three days (v.4). Amasa either had the slows or simply
couldn't accomplish the call-up within the time allotted (v.5). David
then orders Abishai to take the king's own crack troops to dispense
with Sheba (v. 6); the less time Sheba has the less havoc he will
cause.[8] Verse 7 begins: 'So the men of Joab went out after him,'
that is, after Abishai. David still passes over Joab; he appoints
Abishai commander *pro tem*. But, significantly, the troops are called
the 'men of Joab'.

The late Amasa (soon to be late in more ways than one) catches
up with Abishai's troops at Gibeon, six miles northwest of Jerusalem
(v.8), where Joab moves to the fore again. Verses 7-10 relate the
Amasa-Joab encounter in close detail, a brutal and fascinating scene.
We may outline it this way:

> Pursuing after Sheba son of Bichri, v.7
> > Amasa appears, v.8a
> > > Joab's wardrobe, v.8b
> > > > Little detail about sword, v.8c
> > > Joab's greeting, v.9
> > > > Little detail about sword, v.10a
> > > Joab's blow, v.10b
> > Amasa dies, v.10c
> Pursuing after Sheba son of Bichri, v.10d

---

7. For a poignant example, see the story of Hetty Wesley (one of Charles and
John's sisters) in Arnold A. Dallimore, *A Heart Set Free: The Life of Charles
Wesley* (Westchester, Ill.: Crossway, 1988), 175-82.

8. The meaning of the last clause of verse 6 is disputed. Literally, it may be
read: 'And he shall tear out our eyes,' i.e., do us much more harm. See
Youngblood, *Expositor's Bible Commentary*, 3:1044. However, it may also
be construed as 'cause to remove our eye (from him),' i.e., he will escape us;
see TWOT, 2:594.

The writer puts his zoom lens on this encounter and gives us an item-by item description.[9] There is no reason to dispute the fairly literal NRSV rendering of v.8bc: 'Now Joab was wearing a soldier's garment and over it was a belt with a sword in its sheath fastened at his waist; as he went forward it fell out.' Joab approaches Amasa both with kind words (v.9a) and apparent affection (v.9b). The writer specifies that Joab reached for Amasa's beard with his right hand.

> The specific reference…to the right hand is intentional. The right hand is the hand with which one does battle. It is empty here, and thus no threat is implied. In fact it is used to grasp the beard as part of the greeting kiss so common among kinsmen and friends.[10]

So Amasa was mentally disarmed – he gave no thought to the sword 'in Joab's hand' (v.10a). Here the writer is paying tribute to your intelligence as a reader. He assumes that you will assume that the sword is in Joab's *left* hand since he has already told you his right hand was on Amasa's beard; and he assumes that you will assume that Joab had picked up the dropped sword with that hand as he approached Amasa. Which means it's all over but the stabbing. It wasn't pretty: 'Then he struck him with it in the belly and spilled his insides on the ground' (v.10b). Joab was so brutal and thorough that a second blow was unnecessary. The writer appends the obvious in one Hebrew form: 'so he died' (v.10c). 'And Joab and Abishai his brother pursued after Sheba the son of Bichri' (v.10d). It was business as usual. No need to cry over spilled blood. It's merely a clinical matter for Joab. An obstacle has been removed and he proceeds to the next item on the agenda.[11]

Well, almost removed. Amasa is still an obstacle. Has been all chapter long. First, Amasa's delay was an obstacle to David's urgency in crushing Sheba (vv. 4-6). Then Amasa's leadership was an obstacle to Joab's designs (vv. 8-10). Now Amasa's corpse is

---

9. Such data must come from an eyewitness; this kind of detail is not easily invented.

10. Edward A. Neiderhiser, '2 Samuel 20:8-10: a Note for a Commentary,' *Journal of the Evangelical Theological Society* 24 (1981): 210.

11. Cf. Walter Brueggemann, (*First and Second Samuel*, Interpretation [Louisville: John Knox, 1990], 331): 'Joab has not uttered a word. He never blinks, never misses a step. He proceeds immediately to the northern campaign. Swiftly, silently, and mercilessly, Joab has eliminated his rival.'

an obstacle to rousing the troops after Joab (v. 11-13). 'Amasa was
wallowing in his blood in the middle of the road' (v.12a) and every
Judean stopped in his tracks when he saw him. Joab's henchman
figured it out, dragged Amasa's remains from the road into the
field, threw a cover over him, and got the military traffic flowing
again.

We are not surprised. Sadly, we've seen it all before. Joab
butchered Abner (3:27) and Absalom (18:14-15). Now Amasa. Joab
specializes in treachery and blood. And succeeds. He 'returned to
Jerusalem to the king' (v.22b) and apparently faced no retribution.

> No doubt he trusted to the principle that 'success succeeds,' and
> believed firmly that if he were able entirely to suppress Sheba's
> insurrection and return to Jerusalem with the news that every trace of
> the movement was obliterated, David would say nothing of the past,
> and silently restore the general who, with all his faults, did so well in
> the field.[12]

Joab gambled and won.[13] 'David can hardly have welcomed
him with open arms, and yet he had saved the kingdom.'[14] Joab is
both intensely loyal and completely uncontrollable. He does not
raise the standard of revolt against David like Sheba, nor does he
seek David's throne like Absalom. Joab is faithful to David. He
does not try to become king and yet he acts as his own king. He is
extremely loyal to David but essentially unsubmissive to David.

Could it be that 2 Samuel 20 depicts a double rebellion? There
is Sheba who wants to leave the Davidic kingdom behind; and then
there is Joab who will not be controlled within the kingdom but is
ever hacking and slicing away to keep his own position unrivalled.
There is a spillover in principle. 'Not everyone who says to me
"Lord, Lord," will enter the kingdom of heaven, but only the one
who does the will of my Father who is in heaven' (Matt. 7:21).
There is such a thing as acknowledging the king's sovereignty and
disregarding his will. Such folk will have no place in the kingdom

---

12. W.G. Blaikie, *The Second Book of Samuel*, 321.

13. Still we may wonder why David did not bring him to justice long before
his death-bed advice to Solomon (I Kings 2:5-6). Did David think Joab packed
too much clout among the royal troops to risk a move against him?

14. Joyce G. Baldwin, *1 & 2 Samuel*, Tyndale Old Testament Commentaries
(Leicester: InterVarsity, 1988), 281.

at the last. There are scores of Joabs on our church membership rolls.

Human Cleverness (20:15-22)

The future is beginning to look bleak for Sheba. He 'passed through all the tribes of Israel to Abel of Beth-maacah; and all the Bichrites assembled, and followed him inside (v.14, NRSV).[15] Abel Beth-maacah was in the far north of Israel, about twenty-five miles north of the Sea of Galilee (or Chinnereth) and several miles west of Dan. The fact that Sheba had gone so far north shows he had gathered little support for himself or his secession movement.[16] His advocates seem to have consisted of his own clan. Joab & Co. promptly began siege operations. The picture in verse 15 is not crystal clear: it looks like Joab's men built up a siege mound in order to negotiate the glacis (perhaps = Heb. $\hbar\bar{e}l$) outside the main wall ($\hbar\hat{o}m\bar{a}h$) and then were battering or undermining the main wall[17] – when a female voice pierced the air.

The woman wanted words with Joab. The interview has its amusing side. Every little piece of introductory conversation is recorded (v.17). The woman sports local pride in her town's reputation. One could almost hear her ask, 'Have you never seen our Chamber of Commerce brochure, Joab?' She accuses Joab of seeking to wipe out a mother-city in Israel, of wanting to 'swallow up the inheritance of Yahweh' (v.19). Joab defends himself with 'Far be it from me that I should swallow up or destroy!' (v.20). (Supreme irony in those words!) Joab explains: 'That's not the case, but a man from the hill country of Ephraim – his name is Sheba son of Bichri – has lifted up his hand against the king, against David; hand only him over and I'll leave the town' (v.21). The woman makes a heady promise (v.21b) and goes back to propagandize her fellow citizens (v.22a). They agree with her and

---

15. The text of verse 14 is difficult; NRSV is a reasonable rendering with minimal emendation. For discussion see S.R. Driver, *Notes on the Hebrew Text and the Topography of the Books of Samuel,* 2nd ed. (1913; reprint ed., Winona Lake, Ind.: Alpha, 1984), 344-45.

16. Gutbrod, *Das Buch vom Reich,* 232-33.

17. See K.N. Schoville, 'Fortification', ISBE, 2:347-49; for more extended discussion, cf. Amihai Mazar, 'The Fortification of Cities in the Ancient Near East', *Civilizations of the Ancient Near East,* 4 vols. (New York: Charles Scribner's Sons, 1995), 3:1523-37.

it isn't long before Sheba loses his head over the matter, and Joab goes south (v.22b).

The episode emphasizes human cleverness. The deliveress at Abel is called a 'wise woman' (v.16), who goes to her townsfolk 'in her wisdom' (v.22). She is sharp, clever, insightful. And her sharp thinking saves her city (cf. Ecc. 9:13-16).

Yet – no surprise – we've seen it all before. In fact we've seen so much 'wisdom' in 2 Samuel that we're wary of it. Naturally the 'wise woman' of chapter 14 (see 14:2) comes to mind. But 2 Samuel pummels us with wisdom, with or without the specific terminology – with David's double scheme to cover up his affair with Bathsheba and to liquidate Uriah (ch. 11); Nathan's artless approach with the ewe anecdote (12:1-7a); Jonadab's damnable skill in getting female flesh (13:1-22); and Absalom's in neatly packaging Amnon for murder (13:23-39); his clever ruse in gaining Joab's attention (14:28-33); his blatant charm in duping the men of Israel to his side (15:1-6); David's skill in enlisting Zadok, Abiathar, and Hushai as his fifth column in Absalom's city (15:24-37); Ziba's conspiracy against Mephibosheth to fatten his holdings (16:1-4); the 'divine' wisdom of Ahithophel in the service of Absalom (16:20–17:4); the deceptively reasonable advice of Hushai that sabotages all Ahithophel's and Absalom's dreams (17:5-14). An easy dozen. Some legitimate, some corrupt. At Abel Beth-maacah I suppose the woman's skill in turning opinion against Sheba was a plus. Likely, she saved many lives, not to mention a town.

Yet we're rightly wary of wisdom, for in a neutral sense wisdom is simply the skill to know how to be successful. That skill can be used for good or ill. Wisdom that is not mixed with sanctification is lethal. Here in chapter 20 wisdom is beneficial; but it is not always so. We know. We've seen it before.

We shan't take space to discuss the list of cabinet posts (vv. 23-26) with which our chapter closes. Predictably, Joab is in command of the army. This section forms the conclusion for all of 2 Samuel 9– 20 (just as 8:15-18 wrapped up 1 Sam. 15–2 Sam.8).[18] In their own way these verses quietly say that the kingdom of David is still intact. The kingdom is fragile because of the sinfulness of the king

18. See the Introduction to this commentary for the structural divisions of the Samuel materials.

and because of the rebellions of Absalom and Sheba. Yet in spite of all the corruption from within and attacks from without, the kingdom is still standing. Its administrators are all at work.

That is the way it is with the kingdom of David's Son. Apparently fragile but always standing. Just last evening I was with a brother and his congregation in western Tennessee for a Reformation Day service. As often at such services, we sang Luther's 'Mighty Fortress'. The last four words of that hymn always seem to strike me. Last night was no exception. We closed the service with the unchangeable fact: 'His kingdom is forever.'

Part 3

A Kingdom in God's Hands

2 Samuel 21–24

23. The Cost of Covenant-breaking
2 Samuel 21:1-14

Scottish pastor Kenneth MacRae was puzzled over his congregation at Kilmuir. Presently, in the mid 1920s, two other congregations he served seemed to show signs of revival. But not Kilmuir. MacRae knew that revival comes at God's pleasure, but he also saw a very human obstacle. Kilmuir did not expect revival; indeed, the folks did not think it could occur at that time. The reason? Over a hundred years before one of their leaders thought to have prophetic powers had indicated there would be no revival until a wave of bloody persecution came. In 1924 there was no persecution; obviously, there could be no revival.[1] Something someone did or said years before carried a deadening effect in the current generation.

That is the situation in 2 Samuel 21:1-14. Something Saul had done years ago placed David's Israel under a curse. Before we work through the text, however, let us tend to some housekeeping chores. We have now entered another major division of the 1–2 Samuel materials; we should get oriented to this section in general and to our passage in particular.

Preliminaries

These chapters (2 Sam. 21–24) are often dubbed the 'appendices' of 1-2 Samuel or 'diverse supplements to the Davidic tradition'.[2] Some scholars hold that 2 Samuel 9–20 and 1 Kings 1–2 constitute a Succession Narrative, a story of how Solomon came to follow David as king. For them 2 Samuel 21–24 are an intrusion in the nice flow of the Succession Narrative.[3] Why did the writer or editors have to reach into the miscellaneous file and tack on these fragments before a perfectly fine story could reach its climax? For a while at least the hypothesis of the Succession Narrative seemed to have a sort of sacred-cow status. Perhaps that's why chapters 21–24 seem

---

1. Iain H. Murray ed., *Diary of Kenneth A. MacRae* (Edinburgh: Banner of Truth, 1980), 194-95, 220.
2. John H. Hayes, *An Introduction to Old Testament Study* (Nashville: Abingdon, 1979), 230.
3. The reader who may be interested in the origin and combination of the various sections in 2 Samuel 21–24 can consult the massive piece of guesswork in Otto Eissfeldt, *The Old Testament: An Introduction* (New York: Harper and Row, 1965), 277-79.

to be under-appreciated: they jostle the place of the holy heifer! Sometimes, however, an hypothesis can be so dominant, so taken for granted, that it stifles thinking. What if 1 Kings 1–2 belong to a different section of narrative? What if the writer placed chapters 21–24 here because they constituted the climax of his argument instead of an inconvenience to someone's theory? Why can't someone consider that the writer wants to provide us with a final perspective on the kingdom of God as it is currently extant in the kingdom of David?[4] I hold that these chapters are not an appendix or intrusion but the intended wrap-up for all 1–2 Samuel; in them the writer wants to show us how we are to regard God's kingdom as it is ordered under David.

Though these chapters are sometimes viewed as a collection of fragments, it has long been recognized that they are a carefully organized collection of fragments. The six sections have been arranged in an obviously deliberate structure (which ought to suggest, by the way, that the writer had a definite purpose in mind in including them). Note the following lay-out, which is Gottwald's, with slight additions:[5]

A. Narrative of expiation of Saul's murder of Gibeonites,
        21:1-14 [sin of Saul]
  B. Annalistic report of battles of David's heroes
        with Philistines, 21:15-22

    C. Song of David, 22:1-51 [Retrospect]

    C¹ Last Words of David, 23:1-7 [Prospect]

  B¹ Annalistic report of battles with Philistines and
        list of David's heroes, 23:8-39
A¹ Narrative of expiation of David's census-taking, 24:1-25
        [sin of David]

---

4. See the fine summary in B.S. Childs, *Introduction to the Old Testament as Scripture* (Philadelphia: Fortress, 1979), 273-75.

5. Norman K. Gottwald, *Encyclopedia Judaica,* 14:796. I do not know who first recognized this literary pattern but both Erdmann (1873) and Keil (1875) knew of it long ago. Note the former in C.F.D. Erdmann, *The Books of Samuel,* Lange's Commentary on the Holy Scriptures, in vol. 3, *Samuel-Kings* (1877; reprint ed., Grand Rapids: Zondervan, 1960), 21-24.

These chapters are not a hodge-podge but constitute a careful piece of work. Hopefully this literary pattern will help readers to track their way through the text.

In addition to these scintillating critical and literary remarks, let me add one additional note about chronology. Here I refer only to the focus for this chapter, 21:1-14.

Our passage begins by reporting a famine 'in the days of David' (v.1) – sometime during David's reign. By this very general time reference the writer keeps us from assuming that the episode of 21:1-14 followed chronologically the events of 2 Samuel 20. He does not place the famine in any tight time sequence; the famine, he says, happened sometime during David's reign.

The writer does drop one hint. Verse 7 suggests that David had already brought Mephibosheth, Jonathan's son, to Jerusalem before the famine and/or executions reported here. Hence 21:1-14 takes place after 2 Samuel 9. Those wanting to scour the depths of this matter may search elsewhere.[6] We must press on to make sense of this strange text.

Exposition
I see four teaching points arising from this text. The first is easily overlooked. The passage begins with the mercy of God.

The Mercy of Clarity (21:1-2)
Something is clearly wrong. This was no ordinary famine (if there is such a thing). This was a famine of three years running. This famine might mean that Israel is suffering the covenant curses (see Lev. 26:19-20; Deut. 28:23-24) for some infidelity. But who knows? David was in the dark, so he began to seek the face of Yahweh (v.1b), which always brings light. Yahweh answers: 'There is bloodguilt on Saul and on his house, because he put the Gibeonites to death' (v.1c, NRSV).

Gibeonites? Who are they? In case we've forgotten the writer inserts a little footnote (v.2b), as if to say: you remember that story

---

6. See the lucid discussion in Eugene H. Merrill, *Kingdom of Priests* (Grand Rapids: Baker, 1987), 252-54; also M.H. Segal, *The Pentateuch: Its Composition and Authorship and Other Biblical Studies* (Jerusalem: Magnes, 1967), 193-94. For a differing view, cf. R.A. Carlson, *David, the Chosen King* (Stockholm: Almquist & Wiksell, 1964), 199-200.

in Joshua 9; the Gibeonites were that pagan enclave in the land who flattered and tricked Israel's leaders into going on oath to spare their lives; though they deceived Israel about their domicile the leaders of Israel did swear in Yahweh's name to preserve them and so had no choice but to grant Gibeon immunity.[7]

But, our writer adds, Saul in his pro-Israel fervor had tried to wipe out the Gibeonites. He had violated Israel's oath. Swearing an oath in Yahweh's name and violating it discredits Yahweh's reputation. It says that Yahweh cannot be depended upon, that his name guarantees nothing. It is 'taking his name in vain' (Exod. 20:7); it makes Yahweh's name mud. Swearing an oath in Yahweh's name also means that the swearers ask that Yahweh bring the curses of the covenant upon them should they fail to keep their covenant word. That is what is happening here: Saul's fervor violated the covenant; Yahweh's famine inflicts the curse for the violation. 'The issue in II Samuel 21, then, is not just blood revenge; the Lord's name had been desecrated, and therefore there was a curse on Saul's descendants.'[8]

Certainly we are in for a brutal story, but don't you see how Yahweh spills his mercy all over the page right from the start? He does not keep David in the dark. When David seeks him, he plainly tells him what is wrong. He is not cruel: he does not keep David in a perpetual dither, stewing about what could be at the bottom of it all. He reveals guilt. Guilt can then be faced, hopefully atoned for. Mercy makes guilt clear.

I doubt most believers appreciate the God of the Bible in this regard. In J.B. Pritchard's *Ancient Near Eastern Texts* there is a moving and pathetic piece from the late Babylonian period. The translator has called it 'Prayer to Every God'.[9] The worshiper prays to all the gods and goddesses, the ones he knows and those he doesn't know. Some god or goddess has inflicted illness and suffering upon him. He does not know which god or goddess he has offended; he does not know what his offence has been; indeed,

---

7. For additional exposition see my *No Falling Words: Expositions of the Book of Joshua* (Grand Rapids: Baker, 1988), 75-80.

8. S.G. DeGraaf, *Promise and Deliverance*, 4 vols. (St. Catharines: Paideia, 1978), 2:182.

9. Ferris J. Stephans in James B. Pritchard, *Ancient Near Eastern Texts*, 3rd ed. (Princeton: Princeton University, 1969), 391-92.

he alleges, this miserable agnosticism plagues mankind as a whole
– no one knows whether he's committing sin or doing good as he
lives out his life. That is paganism – nebulous, hopeless, cruel.[10]
But Yahweh is kind: he declares our guilt to us. That is the mercy
of clarity.

The Gore of Atonement (21:3-9)

The problem is clear. But what must be done about it? That's what
David asks the Gibeonites at the start of the interview: 'What can I
do for you and how can I make atonement that you may bless
Yahweh's possession?' (v.3b). The Gibeonites' reply (v.4) can be
construed several ways. I understand them to say that this is not a
case to settle 'out of court' with payment for damages, and yet
they do not have the authority to put anyone to death in Israel.[11]
That was a clear hint, but they weren't explicit. So David asks
them to get to the point (v.4c). They do:

> The man who finished us off and who schemed (this) against us
> – we have been annihilated (and) have no place in all the territory
> of Israel – let seven men of his sons be given to us, and we shall
> impale them before Yahweh in Gibeah of Saul, Yahweh's chosen
> (vv. 5-6).[12]

---

10. Note this same contrast in the area of law: 'Biblical law was public law,
and this was another important difference from the pagan laws of the Near East.
In many nations of the ancient Near East, the king carried the laws in his head,
as they were his personal possession. He did not publish them until he was
ready to give up his throne. Thus a person could be arrested for breaking a law
he had never known. The laws were kept secret, even when a person was put on
trial for breaking them. (There are few instances in which anyone cited the royal
codes in a court case.)' James I. Packer *et al.*, *The Bible Almanac* (Nashville:
Thomas Nelson, 1980), 382. Cf. also Joe M. Sprinkle, 'Law', *Evangelical
Dictionary of Biblical Theology* (Grand Rapids: Baker, 1996), 468.

11. In verse 4a ('It is not a matter of silver and gold for us with Saul and with
his house') note their significant mention of Saul's house. This may give a
hint of what they have in mind.

12. On the difficult text of verse 5, see J.P. Fokkelman, *Narrative Art and
Poetry in the Books of Samuel*, vol. 3, *Throne and City (II Sam. 2-8 & 21-24)*
(Assen/Maastricht: Van Gorcum, 1990), 279. The verb I have translated
'impale' is a causative form of *yāqa‘* (three times here, vv. 6,9,13,and Num.
25:4). This action was not the means of death but its aftermath. By analogy
with Deuteronomy 21:22-23, the men were first put to death and then impaled,

The king consents (v.6c), selects the candidates (v.8), and hands them over (v.9).[13] The Gibeonites carried out their gruesome task – they 'impaled them on the hill before Yahweh' (v.9b).

All this puzzles the contemporary western mind. Our thinking is like that congressman who asked why Arabs and Jews couldn't settle their differences like good Christians! That is our mind-set: Now why couldn't someone have entered into long, tedious, wearying political discussions with these Gibeonites, pressuring, cajoling, and edging them toward a palatable compromise in this matter? Maybe a neutral party, say an Edomite of good will, could head up the negotiating team. The problem with that proposal is that there were no Edomites of good will! But beyond that, there are two reasons a tidy solution was impossible: blood and wrath.

First, Saul's butchery of the Gibeonites polluted the land with their blood, 'and atonement cannot be made for the land on which blood has been shed, except by the blood of the one who shed it' (Num 35:33, NIV). Secondly, Saul's offense had violated a covenant oath. According to custom, when Israel's leaders had sworn that oath they had asked Yahweh to bring wrath upon them should they ever break their word (cf. Josh. 9:15,19). That wrath would be lethal. Joshua 9 informs us that Israel 'cut' (kārat) a covenant (vv. 15,16; also vv. 6,11) with Gibeon. An animal was cut, its pieces put opposite one another, and those taking the covenant obligation upon themselves would walk between the pieces. By this they were saying, 'As this animal is cut in pieces, so may we be cut up if we do not keep this oath.'[14] Now the Gibeonites demand that this curse be carried out. God's wrath, however, stands behind Gibeon's request. Yahweh has already mercifully signaled this in the famine (v.1). Yahweh's wrath then must be appeased, satisfied, or – to use

---

put up on stakes and exposed. See Jacob Milgrom, *Numbers*, The JPS Torah Commentary (Philadelphia: Jewish Publication Society, 1990), 213,478. Others, however, prefer to translate 'dismembered' (so NJB).

13. The victims were two sons of Saul by Rizpah, his concubine (2 Sam. 3:7), and five grandsons, children of his older daughter Merab. Most manuscripts read 'Michal' in verse 8, but a comparison with 1 Sam. 18:19 shows Merab is surely meant.

14. See the instance in Jeremiah 34:8-20 (note esp. vv. 18-20). For discussion, O. Palmer Robertson, *The Christ of the Covenants* (Phillipsburg, NJ: Presbyterian and Reformed, 1980), 7-10; J. Arthur Thompson, 'Covenant (OT)', ISBE, 1:790-91.

the old word – propitiated.[15] The curse of the covenant must be carried out.

Now, however, the questions fly. How can Yahweh permit this? Doesn't it run against Deuteronomy 24:16: 'Fathers shall not be put to death for their children, nor children put to death for their fathers; each is to die for his own sin' (NIV)? Is this justice or injustice? How are we to deal with this?

Walter Brueggemann deals with it by rewriting the text. He denies that there ever was any revelation of Yahweh to David as stated in verse 1; nor did Saul ever wipe out Gibeonites. Verse 1 is 'a piece of Davidic fabrication', giving David the rationale he desired for eliminating some of Saul's descendants.[16] That is one way of handling the problem: simply deny the historical-theological truth claims of the text. Brueggemann's reductionism gives us no help with our text. It gives us the gospel according to Walter, but that is hardly good news.

Others suggest we may stomach the text by realizing that though the Gibeonites had been included among the covenant people, their seven-sons demand clearly shows that they had not given up their original pagan way of thinking. Perhaps there are overtones of human sacrifice as a means of guaranteeing the fruitfulness of the soil.[17] If the episode is laced with shreds of a pagan mind-set, then we hardly need worry about appropriating its truth for its truth is a mixed bag.

---

15. P. Kyle McCarter, Jr., *II Samuel,* The Anchor Bible (New York: Doubleday, 1984), 444. The plague prayers of Mursilis II, the Hittite king (ca. 1340-1310 B.C.), indicate that he had faced a sort of 'Davidic situation'. His land had suffered years of plagues. Mursilis discovered the scourge came because his father had attacked Egyptian territory in violation of his sworn treaty with Egypt. For details, A. Malamat, 'Doctrines of causality in Hittite and Biblical Historiography: A Parallel, '*Vestus Testamentum* 5 (1955): 1-12; more briefly, Johan De Roos, 'Hittite Prayers', *Civilizations of the Ancient Near East,* 4 vols. (New York: Charles Scribner's Sons, 1995), 3:2003.

16. Walter Brueggemann, *First and Second Samuel,* Interpretation (Louisville: John Knox, 1990), 336-37. I only allude to Brueggemann's approach but do not analyze his argumentation. There are holes in it; the perceptive reader will note them.

17. So Karl Gutbrod, *Das Buch vom Reich,* Die Botschaft des Alten Testaments, 2nd ed. (Stuttgart: Calwer, 1973), 243-44, drawing upon Gressmann for the latter point. The deaths in the text, however, were not human sacrifices but judicial executions.

The problem with this view is that the text knows nothing of it – it must be assumed or read between the lines. Indeed, the Gibeonites themselves only talk in terms of Yahweh's involvement: 'We shall impale them before Yahweh' (v.6; see also v.9). If we are skeptical of their testimony, we must still face verse 14b, which, with verse 1, forms the theological frame around the whole episode: 'After that, God answered prayer in behalf of the land' (NIV). This bottom line imports that God approved – or at least accepted – the measures taken to turn away his wrath for covenant-breaking. Now Israel could move from famine to favor. I see no way around taking it straight.

Does the seven-man execution here violate the principle of justice laid down in Deuteronomy 24:16? I don't think so. That law regulated individual criminal cases. Here the situation is much broader. Saul did not trample on the Gibeonite covenant merely as an individual. He was king of Israel. In his office as king his deeds had an official character. As king the people were represented in him. Hence his offence had a *representational* as opposed to an individual character, and to that extent involved Israel in the guilt. The offence itself was *national* as opposed to individual, for the covenant with Gibeon (Josh. 9) was sworn by Israel's leaders on behalf of the whole people. Should the covenant be broken all Israel would be liable for it, even if only one man (Saul) was the primary instigator. 'The few instances where punishment of children was legally sanctioned were not criminal cases but those involving offences against God, such as violation of...national oaths.[18]

No one can evade the raw horror of this scene. We can only try to understand (up to a point) what is happening. King Saul violated the covenant with Gibeon. He is off the scene and cannot personally suffer the curses of the covenant-breaker. Hence, per Gibeon's request, those who belong to Saul stand as surrogates. They become, as it were, the covenant-breakers who stand in the place of Saul – and Israel.[19]

Having written all this, I still have questions about this passage.

---

18. Jeffrey H. Tigay, *Deuteronomy*, The JPS Torah Commentary, (Philadelphia: Jewish Publication Society, 1996), 227.

19. On this whole passage in general and corporate solidarity in particular, see Walter C. Kaiser, Jr., *More Hard Sayings of the Old Testament* (Downers Grove: InterVarsity, 1992), 174-78.

I have not worked out all its implications. Most readers, however, are simply aghast at the sheer horror of the episode. That, I suggest, points us to its primary application. Readers should be aghast. The text says atonement *is* horrible, it *is* gory. Atonement is never nice but always gruesome. We need to see this for we easily fall into the trap of regarding atonement as merely a doctrine, a concept, an abstraction to be explained, a bit of theology to be analyzed. Or, little better, to view it as a moving story to be re-played during Passion Week. But we should know better. Surely the Israelite worshiper realized this when he towed a young bull to the tabernacle and had to slit its throat, skin it, cut it in pieces, and wash the insides and legs (Lev. 1:3-9). It was all mess and gore. From slicing the bull's throat in Leviticus 1 all the way to Calvary God has always said atonement is nasty and repulsive. Christians must beware of becoming too refined, longing for a kinder, gentler faith. If we've grown too used to Golgotha perhaps Gibeah (v.6) can shock us back into truth: atonement is a drippy, bloody, smelly business. The stench of death hangs heavy wherever the wrath of God has been quenched.

The Safety of Covenant (21:7)
Verse 7 is almost an aside, a parenthesis. David must hand over seven of Saul's descendants to the Gibeonites (v.6) and does so (v.8), but in the midst of it all our writer assures us that

> The king spared Mephibosheth, son of Jonathan son of Saul, because of the oath of Yahweh which was between them, between David and Jonathan, the son of Saul (v.7).[20]

The 'oath of Yahweh' takes us back to 2 Samuel 9 and 1 Samuel 20; it refers to the covenant between David and Jonathan in which David promised to show devoted love to Jonathan's house (1 Sam. 20:15). David was faithful to that promise in 2 Samuel 9, and here he continues to be faithful by exempting Jonathan's son from the Gibeonites' demand.

In spite of its semi-parenthetical nature verse 7 is important for our writer. He means to draw a contrast. Note his allusion to the

---

20. Thus Mephibosheth, Jonathan's son, is clearly distinguished from the other Mephibosheth, son of Rizpah (v.8), who was one of the victims.

'oath of Yahweh' here which David and Jonathan had sworn. Then note his reference in verse 2 to the fact that 'the sons of Israel had gone on oath' to the Gibeonites in Joshua 9. Saul, however, had violated that covenant (v.2); yet David had remained faithful to the covenant of verse 7. Over against Saul the covenant-breaker our writer places David the covenant-keeper. Though the passage focuses major attention on an instance of covenant-breaking and its tragic fallout, it also includes this exhibit of covenant-keeping in David's treatment of Jonathan's son. As if to say, There *is* a king who keeps covenant. Mephibosheth was liable to hideous suffering, but David had committed himself to his safety.

This Mephibosheth note reminds me of the resourcefulness of Gerd Buchwald, a German teacher. Russian troops, whose forte was pillage and rape, were overrunning his district of Berlin in 1945. One evening several drunk Russians appeared at Buchwald's apartment shouting, 'Frau! Frau!' With mussed hair and two-day stubble Buchwald managed a friendly smile and with a gesture of resignation declared, 'Frau kaput.' They seemed to savvy: his wife was dead. But that's no reason not to ransack his apartment (which had already been rifled by women soldiers of the Red Army). Buchwald stretched out on the sofa while they looked around. They made off with a pair of his suspenders and disappeared. After their exit Buchwald bolted the door, then, moving the sofa, helped Elsa, his wife, from the three-by-three-foot hole he had dug in the concrete floor.[21] She had a refuge because he had – obviously – committed himself to her safety.

That is what David had done for Mephibosheth. David's covenant had drawn a circle of security around Jonathan's son. Yet David's commitment points beyond itself to the flaming fidelity of the final Davidic Monarch, who is charged to lose none of all those his Father has given him (John 6:39), whose holy anxiety rests upon the protection of his people from the evil one (John 17:11-12, 15), and who dogmatically vows that no one can snatch his sheep out of his hand (John 10:28). The Davidic King has committed himself to our safety.

---

21. Cornelius Ryan, *The Last Battle* (New York: Simon and Schuster, 1966), 486.

The Pathos of Love (21:10-14)

The Gibeonites carry out their work; the executions occur, the bodies set up on stakes. All this at the beginning of what would normally be barley harvest (v.9).

Now we catch a scene both heartening and heart-rending. Rizpah comes trudging out of Gibeah to the place of death carrying her bolt of sackcloth. She is going to camp out there and keep both vultures of the sky and predators of the earth from picking and consuming the bodies (v.10). She acts out of mother love (for two of the victims are her boys) and out of loyalty toward Saul's whole family. She could not prevent the executions nor the exposure. There was so much she was helpless to change; but she will do what she can. With vigilance by day and sleeplessness by night she can guard and defend the rotting flesh of her dear ones.

> The moment we allow our imagination to dwell on the details of her situation, we recoil: the bodies just hang there, exposed to the elements. The stench and the sight of decay can hardly be borne by an outsider let alone a relative – and Rizpah is a mother who, day in day out, week in week out, is forced to experience this with her own children! The horror defies description, and the narrator does not describe it either.[22]

No one knows how long Rizpah's tireless vigil went on.[23] In any case the day came when 'waters were poured out upon them from heaven' (v.10a) signaling the end of the famine on the land and of the wrath of the Lord. Someone reports to David the gripping tale of Rizpah's devotion (v.11). Apparently moved by this, David, as an act of tribute, gathers the bones of Saul and Jonathan from Jabesh-gilead, along with those Rizpah had protected, and gave them all an honorable burial in their home territory of Benjamin (vv. 12-14).

---

22. J.P. Fokkelman, *Throne and City,* 285-86. The law in Deut. 21:22-23 stipulated that the exposed body of an executed criminal was to be taken down and buried before day's end. If we date Deuteronomy to Moses' time, why was this stipulation not followed in 2 Samuel 21? The best answer is probably to say (with Matthew Henry) that this was an extraordinary case.

23. Some are convinced the ordeal lasted from mid-April (barley harvest time) until the early rain of October/November (e.g., Fokkelman), while others argue for an extra rain during the harvest period, which occasionally occurs (e.g., Hertzberg). Certainty eludes us here.

I suppose our writer could have told us this story minus the
Rizpah notes. Surely he could have revised his story and dropped
her from the text. But he didn't. Why then these wrenching lines
showing this woman's tender affections, tenacious will, and
horrendous perseverance?

Perhaps our immediate impulse is to insist we must 'get
something out of' this text. We want to find some application from
it. Hence we may be tempted to tell believers: You too can have a
Rizpah-ministry, seeking to show kindness to those who are victims
of other people's sins. But would that not trivialize the text?

Admittedly, I cannot psychoanalyze the writer's intention. But
allow me a suggestion: the writer tells you this very solemn story –
especially about Rizpah – because he wants to make you solemn.
He depicts this very sad episode because he wants you to be sad
over it and to marinate in that sadness and not to go worrying about
how to pilfer some application from it.

My first visit to Jerusalem: I remember how moving it was to
stand at the western wall – to see the Jews praying, to note the
rolled up slips of paper with prayers written on them resting in the
crevices of the wall, to think how God had allowed a Gentile like
me to piggyback on the covenant privileges of Israel. I am not
easily given to emotion, but as I stood there all of Romans 9–11
seemed to come washing over my mind. And, like many Christians
privileged to stand there, I began musing on the 'hardening in part'
that was upon Israel (Rom. 11:25) and praying for her salvation.
These were melancholy moments; they were meant to be so. There
was, for someone who worshiped a Jewish Messiah, a sadness about
it all. And I *wanted* to be sad, to be solemn, quiet, and pensive. In
an instant one of our group's leaders shattered my reverie. He was
an archaeological bug. In his usual take-charge, demanding, come-
on style he said there was an archaeological site nearby he wanted
me to see before it closed. I could have slugged him. (Sometimes
one has no difficulty moving from acts of devotion to acts of
violence, a very revealing fact, I'm afraid.) In fairness to the man
he didn't know he had just destroyed the highlight of the trip for
me. It is simply that his bossy interruption seemed so inappropriate.
It destroyed the sadness I wanted to have.

I propose the writer of our text wants you to take the Rizpah
scene (vv. 10-11) in that way. Don't fly off to figure out 'some

way I can apply this to my life'. Just stay at Gibeah. Let the sights, sounds, and smells at Rizpah's draining vigil sink into your faculties. It is passing sad. And the writer wants to leave you sad and solemn – he doesn't want you running off to practice hermeneutics or to be rushing to your next Christian activity. There is something irreducibly sad about this sight. And, as often (Ecc. 7:2-4), there is a goodness in that sadness. Here is heart-and-gut-wrenching misery. And the writer would fill your senses with it. As if to say: Look what comes from covenant-breaking (vv. 1-2). Psalm 90:11 comes to mind:

> Who considers the power of your anger?
> Who considers your fury in the way you ought to be feared?

Who ever stops to consider the wrath of God? The Psalm answers, Nearly no one. But our writer says you should. Stay at Gibeah. Let it sink into your pores. Share the tragedy. It will do you good.[24]

You may find yourself in a strangely similar situation again. You will see the darkness come over the land at midday (Mark 15:33), signifying the judgment and curse of God, and you will hear the wrenching cry of the Forsaken (Mark 15:34). Don't run off. Stay at Golgotha. Let the sadness sink in. Consider the wrath of God.

And ponder the pathos of love (1 John 4:10).

24. The Bigger They Are, The Harder They Fall
2 Samuel 21:15-22

Every year my father produced his pastor's report for the annual congregational meeting of the church he served. His reports followed a predictable form and covered routine matters: how many times he preached, number of pastoral calls, funerals, outside speaking engagements, and so on. Yet his reports were seldom dull. As I read over them I often find some aside, some addendum that leaves me either amused or aghast. In one he 'reported' that during the last year two other churches had solicited him to consider becoming their pastor but that family conditions dictated he refuse

---

24. For biblical exposition on divine wrath, see J.I. Packer, *Knowing God* (Downers Grove: InterVarsity, 1973), chapters 15 ('The Wrath of God') and 18 ('The Heart of the Gospel').

these offers, 'although they offered nice increases in salary'! He had a way of splattering a routine item with interest.

Now a reader coming on to 21:15-22 may think he has arrived in dullsville. It looks like a composite of snips taken from a military report. Names, places, weapons, results. No flowing narrative or intricate plot here. In spite of its report form, however, this text alludes to suspenseful and scary moments in the battles of David and his men and so packs its own interest. And, I would hold, bears its own witness. To hear that witness I want to approach the text from several angles, looking at what is essential, proper, accomplished, and clear.[1]

What is Essential: Preserving God's King (21:15-17)

Best we can tell, the Philistine galoot who zeroed in on David was Ishbi-benob. Verse 16 makes us guess a bit about details. Part of Ishbi-benob's weaponry weighed three hundred shekels of bronze (over seven pounds; cf. 1 Sam. 17:7). Most translations guess it was his spear or spear-head, but we can't be sure. The word (*qayin*) is only used here. And he strapped on something new for this battle. Maybe it was a sword, helmet, or armor. Translators have to guess; the text doesn't say. Anyway, he is formidably equipped. And we needn't guess about his design: Ishbi-benob sees David exhausted (v.15c), licks his chops, and moves in for the kill (v.16d).[2] Abishai, however, rushes to David's assistance, tangles with Ishbi-benob, and disposes of him (v.17a). This isn't a movie, only a report; so there is no dramatic blow-by-blow with tension-packed music. But Ishbi-benob is horizontal now, along with his souped-up weapon and spanking new equipment.

This close call sobered David's men. They passed a new war policy and imposed it on David via a solemn oath: 'You will never

---

1. On the structure and arrangement of v. 15-22, see J.P. Fokkelman, *Narrative Art and Poetry in the Books of Samuel*, vol. 3, *Throne and City (II Sam. 2-8 & 21-24)* (Assen/Maastricht: Van Gorcum, 1990), 297-98, and Ronald F. Youngblood, '1,2 Samuel', *The Expositor's Bible Commentary*, 12 vols. (Grand Rapids: Zondervan, 1992),3:1058. There is a complementary relation between 21:1-14 and 21:15-22, the former dealing with an internal threat, the latter with an external threat.

2. We have no way of dating this episode. David's exhaustion (v.15c) needn't indicate advancing age but only the rigors and drain of marching and combat.

again go out with us to battle, and you must never put out the lamp of Israel' (v.17b).[3] The stakes were too high, the risk too great. Should David's life be snuffed out in battle Israel would flounder in darkness and confusion. King David's life means light for Israel; his death would spell disaster. In one sense David *is* Israel.

So much can seem to hinge on one person. Recently, a couple of our seminary families were involved – through no fault of their own – in what could have been a fatal auto collision. All were spared. While giving thanks for this I thought of one of the students involved – an international student whose gifts, learning and leadership have been and will be so vital for the evangelical church in his country. What if his life had been snuffed out on our highways? A certain light would have gone out for the church in his native land.

It is Advent as I write this and so one naturally conjures up those crises when the lot of the people of God seems to rest on the precarious situation of one person. There never would have been a covenant seed if Isaac had been terminated (Gen.22). Israel never would have been liberated if an Egyptian princess had dropped the liberator into Davy Jones' locker (Exod. 2:1-10). Israel would have plummeted into disaster if Ishbi-benob had been allowed to run David through with his three hundred shekels of whatever (2 Sam. 21). And none of God's flock would have had salvation had not the real King of the Jews saved the Savior from the clutches of antichrist Herod (Matt. 2:13-23). Somehow the God of heaven has always been up to the challenge: he always preserves the seed or the deliverer or the king.

What Is Proper: Honoring God's Servants (21:17, 18, 19, 21)
By alluding to Abishai, Sibbecai, Elhanan, and Jonathan as God's servants I am not presuming to divine their spiritual condition. But because they fought for the covenant people and under Yahweh's king they are, at least in that regard, God's servants.

It is interesting that this military extract mentions each of these

---

3. The lamp (*nēr*) symbolizes life and prosperity (e.g., Jer. 25:10; Job 21:17 with preceding context). Here (2 Sam. 21:17) David himself is the 'lamp of Israel'. Other passages imply that the ongoing line of Davidic kings constituted a lamp (*nîr*) to David (1 Kings 11:36; 15:4; 2 Kings 8:19), while Psalm 132:17 uses *nēr* to refer to the final Davidic King.

warriors by his full name: Abishai son of Zeruiah, Sibbecai the Hushathite, Elhanan son of Jari(i),[4] and Jonathan son of Shimei, David's brother. And that is only proper, for theirs were heroic exploits undertaken at great risk against these genetic wonders of the larger order, the Raphah (on which see below). These troops gambled their lives to do these extraordinary deeds, and, even though all praise belongs to God, his instruments should nevertheless receive honorable mention.

The same principle operates in the New Testament. Think of the little catalogues of greetings and commendations that pepper the last chapters of Paul's epistles. One thinks of Paul's reference to Prisca and Aquila, 'who once risked their very necks for my life' (Rom. 16:4, Williams). Who knows what the particulars were? – but it's on the same level with facing Goliath's brother. Jesus himself honors his erratic disciples with his appreciation: 'You have stayed with me all through my trials' (Luke 22:28, TEV). Of course, many of Christ's servants can't match David's giant wranglers in terms of sheer drama and danger and yet are to be properly honored. In my pastoring days how grateful I was for elders who weathered storms by my side and for godly women who joined me in ministries of worship and intercession for hurting and erring sheep. I attempted to tell them so, for it's only proper to honor Christ's servants.

What Is Accomplished: Fulfilling God's Promise

All four of these combatants are said to be from the 'offspring of the Raphah' (see vv. 16,18, 20,22). This is explicitly expressed in the case of Ishbi-benob (v.16), Saph (v.18), and the character with twenty-four fingers and toes (v.20); but the summarizing statement

---

4. Verse 19b, where Elhanan appears, is a teaser. As it stands it reads as NASB: 'Elhanan son of Jaare-oregim the Bethlehemite killed Goliath the Gittite....' The parallel in 1 Chronicles 20:5 reads: 'Elhanan, son of Jair, killed Lahmi the brother of Goliath the Gittite.' The 2 Samuel text is likely disturbed because the term '-oregim' (weavers) appears again at the end of the verse ('like a weavers' beam'). The second occurrence seems proper but its appearance in a proper name is suspect. To avoid writing a long and interesting two-page footnote I refer the reader to the discussion of R.K. Harrison, *Introduction to the Old Testament* (Grand Rapids: Eerdmans, 1969), 704. He proposes: 'And Elhanan, the son of Jairi the Bethlehemite, slew the brother of Goliath.' See also Youngblood, *Expositor's Bible Commentary,* 3:1060-61.

(v.22) clearly includes Elhanan's victim (v.19) as well. Actually, Raphah may well be a proper name, referring to the real or supposed ancestor of these warriors. They likely belonged then to a group of the Rephaim, who lived primarily east (e.g., Gen. 14:5; Deut. 2:10-11, 20-21; 3:11) but also west (Josh. 17:15; cf. Gen. 15:20) of the Jordan in pre-Conquest times and were notorious for their humongous size (cf. vv. 16,19b, 20).[5] Are these four Rephaim serving with the Philistines viewed as the last of their lineage?[6] If so, their elimination by the audacity of David's men reinforces the reliability of Yahweh's old promise (Gen. 15:18-21).

The point about Yahweh's reliability, however, does not rest on our tracking down elusive Rephaim. It makes no difference whether these four specimens were only Philistine mercenaries or were of Philistine stock. Their demise constituted victory over the Philistines (mentioned four times, in vv. 15,17, 18,19). As noted, we cannot be sure about where in David's reign to date these episodes. But they are certainly later than David's extermination of Goliath (1 Sam.17)! Now the rest of the Philistine bullies have eaten dirt. Yahweh has done as he promised: 'By the hand of David my servant I will save my people Israel from the hand of the Philistines' (2 Sam. 3:18). What Saul's regime did not do, David's, by God's power, did.[7] Hence a brief hero report testifies that what Yahweh promises at the first he brings about at the last. It shows us that Yahweh is with David now as he was in the Valley of Elah (1 Sam. 17); all the years and all the Philistines have not changed the word of Yahweh's mouth nor the strength of his hand.

It is worth noting that what holds for kingdom history here also applies in individual history. I think of a line from one of the letters of Alexander Whyte, long the beloved and renowned pastor of Free St. George's, Edinburgh. It was October 1918, Whyte was eighty-two and writing a note to a Miss Innes, a friend and former parishioner. He indicates that the confines of this note restrict him from speaking much of his 'inward life', and then adds: '[H]ere I will only say that what I preached so long to you is now the one

---

5. On the Rephaim, see B.K. Waltke, 'Rephaim,' ZPEB, 5:64-66, and Youngblood, *Expositor's Bible Commentary,* 3:863, 1059.

6. See Karl Gutbrod, *Das Buch vom Reich,* Die Botschaft des Alten Testaments, 2ⁿᵈ ed. (Stuttgart: Calwer, 1973), 247.

7. Gutbrod, *Das Buch vom Reich,* 249-50.

stay and strength of my life.'[8] The theology is the same as in this text: God's early promises prove firm even to the end. And some of us need that assurance as we knowingly approach that end.

What Is Clear: Silencing God's Enemies (21:20-21)

I want to draw particular attention now to the fourth Raphah-episode. The writer gives us a description of this warrior but not his name. He was unusually impressive – a huge hunk with six digits on each hand and foot (v. 20). I don't think the writer is ridiculing this fellow but only describing him. When someone has six fingers on each hand and six toes on each foot people tend to notice (at least those who can count). Even in that time most folks had only five per limb. This brute's extremities are interesting, but, paradoxically, they don't count. What matters is not his anatomy but his attitude. The problem is not with his hands or feet but with his mouth, not with six of the one and a half-dozen of the other but with his one tongue. He should have known better. For being such a big boy he certainly was not brilliant. So he did it anyway. 'He derided Israel' (v.21a).

That verb in verse 21a is *ḥārap*, meaning to reproach, defy, mock, deride. It is the verb and/or root used repeatedly in 1 Samuel 17 for Goliath's derision of Israel and of Yahweh, Israel's God (see 1 Sam. 17:10,25,26 [twice], 36,45).[9] We know what happened to Goliath – he lost his head. And this dull hunk did the same thing – he derided Israel, and in deriding Israel he derided Israel's God. And he met the same end – he lost his voice. Jonathan the son of Shimei, David's brother, did the honors (v.21b). It doesn't matter if it's the celebrated David who knocks off Goliath or the relatively obscure Jonathan who cuts down Mr. Six-Digits; the point is the same: those who trash talk Yahweh and his people will be silenced.

We don't usually expect a piece of military annals to teach last things. But, in a sense, the twenty-four stiff extremities of this fellow do just that. His demise is another installment of what is to come, another assurance of what will be, another picture-along-the-way of how it will be at the end. His lifeless tongue testifies to God's

---

8. G.F. Barbour, *The Life of Alexander Whyte, D.D.* (London: Hodder and Stoughton, 1923), 605.

9. Cf. my discussion in *Looking on the Heart: Expositions of the Book of 1 Samuel*, 2 vols. (Grand Rapids: Baker, 1994), 2:37-38, 47-49.

people: 'Here is how it will be at the last – all your enemies will be silenced' (cf. Isa. 54:17). Allow him to encourage you. Believe his witness. Rephaim never lie – at least not the dead ones.

25. Through Many Dangers, Toils, and Snares
2 Samuel 22

One of our sons keeps the interior of his car in a state of proverbial messiness. Gum wrappers grace the floor or seats; various change, sundry receipts, and multiple pens are promiscuously littered about, either visible or invisible to the naked eye. All of which seems not to bother him. These are mere minutiae and have no effect on the proper functioning of an automobile. As long as the oil is changed regularly, etc., why worry about details?

Sometimes we must take his attitude toward a biblical text – like 2 Samuel 22. With its mass (51 verses) and its parallel (Psalm 18) it fairly cries out for us to clean up a legion of textual details. Should we discuss the theophanic language? Or cite Canaanite parallels? How are we to construe Hebrew verb 'tenses' in any number of lines? We could spill ink on these matters and have a much cleaner text and yet have little grasp of the psalm as a whole. So, at the risk of some precision, I want to take a broad-brush approach to David's song of thanksgiving.

David's psalm is a reflective piece, looking back over a long saga of salvation 'when Yahweh had delivered him from the clutches of all his enemies and from the clutches of Saul' (v.1, NJB).[1] This heading is the lens through which readers are to view the whole psalm. Hertzberg is right:

> David's history could have been narrated as that of a great and powerful king. *This chapter, however, is concerned that it should be understood as the action of a great and powerful God.*[2]

And so David can only give thanks.

---

1. Near the beginning of the Samuel-document Hannah's song (1 Sam. 2:1-10) takes a prospective view of the kingdom to come, while near the end David's psalm (2 Sam. 22) casts a retrospective glance over the kingdom that has come. Cf. Brevard S. Childs, *Introduction to the Old Testament as Scripture* (Philadelphia: Fortress, 1979), 272-75.
2. Hans Wilhelm Hertzberg, *I & II Samuel,* The Old Testament Library

The theological witness of 2 Samuel 22 gravitates around three focal points, and I will couch these in the first person plural lest we think we are only dealing with David.

The Intensity of Our Praise (22:2-20)

David does not begin to praise; he explodes in praise.

> Yahweh – my rock and my stronghold and my deliverer!
> My God, my rock – I take refuge in him.
> My shield, horn of my salvation, my secure height
>   and my place to flee;
> my savior – you save me from violence (vv. 2-3).

David's staccato, machine-gun exuberance arises from his utter inability to stretch his praise to match God's splendor. He can't say enough but he will say much – he will pile up plaudits in his vain quest to overcome his delicious frustration of adequately lauding Yahweh. Isaac Watts captured the same dilemma in his hymn:

> Join all the glorious names of wisdom, love, and power,
>   that ever mortal knew, that angels ever bore:
> All are too poor to speak his worth,
>   too poor to set my Savior forth.

And David's very gusto is an admission that his praise is 'too poor'.[3] Yet it is passionate, intense, and exuberant. There must be some reason, some explanation, behind such intensity.

There is. David says that if you would understand his outburst of praise you must realize *the desperate extremity of his distress*:

(Philadelphia: Westminster, 1964), 396 (emphasis his). Cf. his introductory remarks: 'Indeed, [Ps. 18/2 Sam.22] is a theological commentary on the history of David. The history of David is to be read and heard in the light of this psalm. That is the intention of the final compiler' (p. 393).

3. C.F. D. Erdmann explains the 'exuberant aggregation of terms in verses 2-4' in this way and cites Sommer: 'Here at the outset the recollection of these exceeding mercies comes over his soul with overwhelming force; he can find no satisfactory term wherewith to call on the God of his salvation, and therefore piles term on term' (*The Books of Samuel,* Lange's Commentary on the Holy Scriptures, in vol. 3 *Samuel–Kings* [1877; reprint ed., Grand Rapids: Zondervan, 1960], 579).

v.5 With Death's breakers closing in on me,
    Belial's torrents ready to swallow me,
v.6 Sheol's snares on every side of me
    Death's traps lying ahead of me,
v.7 I called to Yahweh in my anguish,
    I cried for help to my God,
    from his Temple he heard my voice,
    my cry came to his ears! (NJB).

I use the rendering of the New Jerusalem Bible here not for its precision but for its vividness; it so graphically captures David's peril.[4] His scrapes have not been with the shadow of death but with its clammy clutches. What David says here in poetry he once said to Jonathan in prose: 'There is but a step between me and death' (1 Sam. 20:3). That statement actually summarizes David's life throughout the Saul years (1 Sam. 18-31). His distress went far beyond facing gall bladder surgery or replacing a defunct automatic transmission. Death daily dogged his tracks. He was most wanted man on Saul's hit list. One might escape once or twice, but what are the ordinary chances of salvaging your skin when the king stays on a concerted, relentless campaign to make Sheol your new address? But Yahweh had done it! And as the one who's forgiven much loves much (Luke 7:47), so the one who has been delivered from much praises much.

Secondly, *the lively intervention of his God* (vv. 8-16) explains the vigor of David's praise. In his distress he cried to Yahweh, and Yahweh heard (v.7). What happened? The world came unglued:

Then the earth quaked and rocked,
the heavens' foundations shuddered,
they quaked at his blazing anger.
Smoke rose from his nostrils,
from his mouth devouring fire....
He parted the heavens and came down,
a storm-cloud underneath his feet....
He wrapped himself in darkness,
his pavilion dark waters and dense cloud....

---

4. Actually verse 5 begins with a causal particle ('For', Heb. *kî*), clearly connecting the intensity of David's praise in verses 2-4 with the extremity of his distress in verses 5-6. NJB obscures this connection.

Yahweh thundered from the heavens,
the Most High made his voice heard.
He shot his arrows and scattered them,
his lightening flashed and routed them

(vv. 8-9a, 10,12,14-15, NJB).

Not exactly what we usually expect from the sweet hour of prayer.

Yahweh both hears (v.7) and comes (vv. 8-16). And when he comes it is as if Sinai (Exod. 19:9-25) happens all over again.[5] Yahweh is irate that his servant stands in such affliction and so comes in blazing anger, shuddering majesty, and world-convulsing power to rescue him.

Now David could have 'studied brevity' here. Instead of the 69 Hebrew words or the 141 English words (NIV) in verses 8-16, he could simply have written, 'Yahweh intervened on my behalf' (five words). Why didn't he? Obviously, because it would have ruined the poetry. Not so obviously, because although such a statement would be factually true it would not be impressively true. David doesn't merely want to tell you a fact about Yahweh, he wants you to *see* Yahweh in all his saving fury. He doesn't intend merely to inform you about what God has done; he wants you to see the God who did it. In all his phosphorescent splendor.

Many of us are prosaic Philistines. We patronize the poetry. We say, 'Now we must recognize that David is speaking in poetry here and knows that he is being, well, imaginative; he is having fun depicting his Savior's response. If we want to know how it really took place, why, we have the historical narratives (in 1–2 Samuel).'

In one sense, that is true. When David eluded Saul's spear (1 Sam. 18:10-11), nothing seemed to register on the Richter scale (2 Sam. 22:8). Even when the Spirit of God held Saul in His own strait-jacket (1 Sam. 19:23) there was no smoke or devouring fire (2 Sam.22:9). When Saul had shut up David within an inch of his life, we did not hear Yahweh's thunder (2 Sam. 22:14) but only a messenger hollering about a Philistine invasion (1 Sam. 23:26-28). When David seemed doomed to commit political suicide and march with the Philistines against Israel, we saw no parted heavens or storm clouds (2 Sam. 22:10) but only heard the crabbing of the

---

5. Cf. Jeffrey J. Niehaus, *God at Sinai* (Grand Rapids: Zondervan, 1995), 302-304.

Philistine brass that on no account would David & Co. march in
the Philistine ranks (1 Sam. 29:4). But why did all these things
occur precisely when and as they did? Why all these deliverances?
The poetry provides the truth behind the facts: all these came from
Yahweh, the sky-splitting, world-shaking, enemy-bashing God!
Such a God energizes praise.

Finally, *the welcome relief of his deliverance* (vv. 17-20)
accounts for the ecstasy of David's praise. He pictures this relief in
terms of *rescue:* 'He reached from on high; he took hold of me; he
drew me out of many waters' (v.17), the many waters of a thousand
deaths (vv. 5-6). David may be hinting that God has granted him a
Moses-experience, since the verb *māšāh* (to draw out) is only used
of Moses' rescue (Exod. 2:10) and here (+Ps. 18:17). He also
describes his relief as *support.* On that dark day when his enemies
stood primed to cut him down 'Yahweh was there to support me'
(v.19b, NJB) – a truth at once assuring, majestic, and simple. And
David depicts his deliverance as *freedom:* 'Then he brought me
out to a spacious place' (v.20a), the very opposite of the cramped,
constricting confinement of danger and distress. David's relief fairly
oozes out of verses 17-20. And it is all God's doing, 'for they were
too strong for me' (v.18b). David is candid about his helplessness.

All this ink has been spilled trying to explain why David's praise
in verses 2-3 is so exuberant. Basically the explanation is simple:
if you really hear verses 4-20 you will understand David's
exuberance in verses 2-3. Words and sentences may help you
understand David's praise; they can't make you *feel* it. This dilemma
reminds me of the time someone, apparently in Philadelphia, asked
George Whitefield if he might print his sermons. Whitefield replied,
'Well, I have no inherent objection, if you like, but you will never
be able to put on the printed page the lightning and the thunder.'[6]
That is our problem. We can overhear the intensity of David's
adoration, can to some degree understand it, and yet not be caught
up in it.

If, however, we cannot rise to David's gusto, at least we must
duplicate his genuineness. The outburst of verses 2-3 is no posing
for the camera – it flows out of genuine delight in what Yahweh
has done (vv. 4-20), which is a far cry from the canned homage

6. Cited in D. Martin Lloyd-Jones, *Preaching and Preachers* (Grand Rapids:
Zondervan, 1971), 58.

given the mighty of this world. In the late 1930s the Stalin cult was going great guns (hardly a metaphor) in the Soviet Union. There was a provincial meeting where, at the mention of Stalin's name, a standing ovation began. Now the tricky part – how to stop the ovation. No one dared to be the first to sit down. At last, an old man who could stand no longer plopped onto his seat. Naturally his name was noted and he was arrested the next day.[7] Joe the Butcher could coerce praise but Yahweh inspires praise. Yahweh has all sorts of folks walking around talking about him, calling him 'my rock', 'my stronghold', 'my shield', 'my place to flee' – not because they must praise but because they can't help but praise.

The Importance of Our Righteousness (22:21-31)

David makes some readers nervous as he continues:

> Yahweh requites me as I act justly,
> as my hands are pure so he repays me (v.21, JB).

Is David in verses 21-25 dragging in a Santa Claus theology of works-righteousness? Does he claim too much for himself? Has he become blind to his sinfulness? Or do these words reflect a self-righteous attitude and a weakening of the sense of sin?[8] These verses baffle thoughtful believers: how can David who had Uriah's blood on his hands and Uriah's wife in his bed (2 Sam. 11) even dream of saying anything like verses 21-25?[9]

This whole section (vv. 21-31) breaks down into three subdivisions:

> The claim he makes (vv. 21-25)
> The God he knows (vv. 26-28)
> The help he receives (vv. 29-31)

We will focus on the first section since it poses the most difficulty. Note that verses 21 and 25 are similar. They act as a frame

---

7. Robert Conquest, *Stalin: Breaker of Nations* (New York: Viking, 1991), 212-213.

8. So Walther Eichrodt, *Theology of the Old Testament,* The Old Testament Library, 2 vols. (Philadelphia: Westminster, 1967). 2:392, 472.

9. Some (e.g., Blaikie, Kirkpatrick, and, apparently, Baldwin) feel the weight of this objection and date the psalm in pre-Bathsheba time, in the earlier part of David's reign (after the situation of 2 Sam. 7:1).

around verses 22-24. If David claims that Yahweh deals with him, literally, 'in line with my righteousness' (vv. 21, 25; JB, 'as I act justly'), what sort of 'righteousness' does David claim? I propose that verses 22-24 exegete what David means.

In verse 22 David maintains, 'I have kept the ways of Yahweh, and I have not acted wickedly in departing from my God.' That can hardly be pressed as a claim to perfection. What he does claim, especially in the second half of the verse, is a general, overall fidelity to Yahweh. He has not, after all, committed apostasy, not turned his back on Yahweh.[10] Verse 23 is another general statement: Yahweh's ordinances are 'before' David and he does not turn away from Yahweh's decrees. Then, it seems to me, in verse 24 David interprets all this. 'So I proved whole-hearted toward him' (v.24). The Hebrew *tāmîm* does not connote sinlessness but wholeness, completeness, integrity. David does not claim perfection in life's particulars but wholeheartedness in life's commitment. Then note verse 24b: 'And I kept myself from my iniquity.' He knows his nature, his tendencies. He has, however, guarded himself from giving way and giving in to the pull of his iniquity.[11] When David speaks of his righteousness and purity (vv. 21,25) he does not point to sinless perfection but life direction; he is not sporting a pharisaical pride over errorless obedience but expressing a faithful loyalty via consistent obedience.[12] All of this is important, for it is such faithful, whole-hearted (though afflicted) servants that Yahweh delights to rescue (vv. 26-28) and who can then revel in the power and safety that Yahweh has provided (vv. 29-31).

The teaching of verses 21-31 is not some strange new wrinkle on your Bible page. It's been there all along. It is mainstream doctrine. Those who faithfully follow Yahweh and esteem his word

---

10. 'Though he had sometimes *weakly* departed from his duty, he had never *wickedly* departed from his God.' So Matthew Henry, *Commentary on the Whole Bible,* 6 vols. (New York: Revell, n.d.), 2:563 (emphasis his).

11. '*My iniquity* can only mean that to which I am naturally prone and subject. We have here then a further proof that the perfection claimed in the first clause [=v.24a] is not an absolute immunity from sin, but an upright purpose and desire to serve God' (J.A. Alexander, *The Psalms, Translated and Explained,* 3 vols. [New York: Charles Scribner & Co., 1865], 1:141).

12. Derek Kidner has some fine remarks on these claims to righteousness in the Psalms; see his *Psalms 1–72,* Tyndale Old Testament Commentaries (London: InterVarsity, 1973), 58-59, 87,93.

by obeying it are those who can expect his blessing; those who don't can't (see Lev. 26 and Deut. 28). One can catch the flip side of 2 Samuel 22:21-31 in Judges 10: 6-14, Psalm 50:16-23, or Jeremiah 2:26-29. Why should those who reject Yahweh's lordship and despise his law (and therefore despise him) expect his rescue? Such folks have no ongoing commitment to Yahweh, only a temporary need for him. They want no covenant relation with Yahweh; they only crave his prostituting himself for their immediate crisis. They do not seek God but a bomb shelter.

Once in my first or second year of seminary I remember overhearing a conversation between a classmate and our professor. I couldn't help it – he caught up with the prof in the hall after class and the hall was crowded. The student, I believe, wanted to make up a test. He'd been absent on the test day. Why? Well, he wasn't in class. Why not? Well, he didn't usually come to class. Why not? He didn't think it was important. I couldn't believe he said that. To the prof no less! I could understand somewhat if the prof was boring or incompetent. This prof was neither. I remember the prof's initial comment: 'This makes me angry.' (Having an aversion to conflict I wandered off at that point). Angry? Rightly so. The student had had the gall to tell him that in his estimation what the prof did in class was not important. He clearly despised the prof and in the same breath asked for a favor to avoid flunking the course.

Now David says he did not do that (vv. 21-25). Perhaps he was thinking of episodes like 1 Samuel 24 and 26, when Saul was as defenseless before him as a slug before a heavy human foot. Yet David refused the short cut to kingship. We don't know what particulars David had in mind; he has, however, told us generally what he means (vv. 22-24). And the spillover for God's people is this: It *does* matter how you live in your difficulties. You dare not use your multi-colored afflictions and pressures as excuses for turning away from your God or breaking loose from his decrees. Your call is: 'Put your hope in Yahweh, keep to his path' (Ps. 37:34a, NJB).

The Invincibility of Our Kingdom (22:32-51)

This section corresponds in bulk to verses 2-20, although the emphasis here is not on the king's deliverance but on his dominion. Verses 32-51 trace how Yahweh gives his king victory and how the surrounding nations submit to his kingship.

In his praise David celebrates *the power that establishes the kingdom* (vv. 32-43). David highlights Yahweh's activity, either in third-person description ('He') or the second-person address ('You'), as in verses 34-37 (NKJV):

34. He makes my feet like the feet of deer,
    And sets me on my high places.

35. He teaches my hands to make war,
    So that my arms can bend a bow of bronze.

36. You have also given me the shield of your salvation,
    And your gentleness has made me great.

37. You enlarged my path under me;
    So my feet would not slip.

In verses 38-43 David speaks in the first person of what 'I' have been able to accomplish:

I pursued my enemies and annihilated them
– I did not turn back until they were finished off.
So I finished them off and shattered them
– they will never rise....
I pulverized them like the dust of the earth;
like street dirt I crushed them, I pounded them   (vv. 38-39a, 43).

Clearly, these I-statements rest upon the He/you section (vv. 32-37) before them. But should we be too dense to see that, David carefully mixes in you-statements (vv. 40-41) with this I-section. David is crystal clear. All that he has been able to do has been done by Yahweh's power: 'You armed me with strength for battle' (v. 40a, NIV). David's kingdom rests on Yahweh's muscle. We will return to this point.

David also looks round and sees *the peoples that serve the kingdom* (vv. 44-50). His kingdom is, well, international:

People I do not know serve me;
foreigners come cringing to me;
as soon as they hear they submit to me.
Foreigners lose heart
and come trembling out of their hiding places   (vv. 44b-46).

That too is fuel for praise for it is God who 'brings down peoples under me' (v.48b). Hence David's praise must be international: 'Therefore I will praise you, Yahweh, among the nations' (v. 50a). Here is a glimpse of the scope of the kingdom. David was no more a Philistine vassal, reigning over a pint-sized section of Judean landscape. He was Yahweh's covenant king over Israel, and surrounding nations now acknowledged his authority, in which we have a preview and pledge of the day when all kings will bow down and all nations (will) serve David's royal Descendant (Ps. 72:11).

As David concludes his praise he alludes to *the promise that guarantees the kingdom,* when he praises Yahweh as

> The tower of deliverance for his king,
> the One who keeps acting with devoted love
>   toward his anointed,
> to David and to his seed for all time (v.51).

The mention of 'devoted love' (*ḥesed*), David's seed, and the phrase 'for all time' (*ad-'ôlām*) conjure up Yahweh's covenant promise to David in 7:12-16. This last verse reminds us that David's kingdom and its grand finale (cf. Ps. 72:8-11; Zech. 9:9-10) do not depend on the lucky breaks of history but on a decree that determines and shapes history. Because God's kingdom rests on God's promise it is sure. Such certainty is urgent for God's often battered people, for most of them can keep trudging through many dangers, toils, and snares so long as they know their kingdom is invincible and sure.

Let us return to the point that Yahweh's power establishes the kingdom. That, after all, is the dominant note of the whole section. Yahweh's promise (cf. v. 51) is sure but it is sure because Yahweh's power will bring it to pass. We must be careful to acknowledge this. W.G. Blaikie refers to an incident in English history, when after the English victory at the Battle of Agincourt (1415), Henry V of England ordered the singing of Psalm 115. Henry prostrated himself on the ground and caused his whole army to do the same, while the words pealed forth, 'Not unto us, O Lord, not unto us, but to thy name give glory.'[13] I fear this note may be absent in the church today – at least in the optimistic west. I think we sometimes

---

13. W.G. Blaikie, *The Second Book of Samuel,* The Expositor's Bible (Cincinnati: Jennings & Graham, n.d.), 353.

slip into the oxymoronic state of Christian cockiness, thinking that
our programs, our technology, our seminars, our activism, etc., will
get the kingdom established. We learn slowly. We will be repeatedly
disillusioned. We must get down with Henry V. We must confess,
'For thine is the kingdom and the power and the glory.' And it is
his power that guarantees the kingdom and the glory.

26. Last Words Look Forward
2 Samuel 23:1-7

Before Thomas Hog died in 1692 the Scot charged his congregation
at Kiltearn to dig his grave at the threshold of the church building
where he might act as a silent sentinel against any unworthy minister
coming into the charge. The inscription on Hog's tombstone read:

> This stone shall bear witness
> against the parishioners of Kiltearn
> if they bring ane [sic] ungodly minister
> in here.[1]

Those were, one might say, his last words on record, anticipating
what might come in the future. That is what we have in 2 Samuel
23:1-7: David's last words on record, last words with eyes not on
the past but the future, though with more confidence and less
forboding than Thomas Hog's.

David's 'last words' might be compared to the blessings of Isaac
(Gen. 27:2-4), Jacob (Gen. 49:1, 28), and Moses (Deut. 33:1) before
their deaths. But this text doesn't exactly fit that mould. It is not a
blessing on persons but a prophecy about the kingdom. This passage,
with chapter 22, stands at the center of 2 Samuel 21–24. The psalm
of chapter 22 looks back upon how Yahweh established the
kingdom; the prophecy of 23:1-7 looks forward to how Yahweh
will consummate the kingdom.[2]

Before moving to the teaching of this section I want to provide

---

1. Donald Beaton, *Some Noted Ministers of the Northern Highlands* (Glasgow:
Free Presbyterian, 1985), 10.
2. Obviously 23:1 does not mean to claim that these words were literally the
last words David breathed but that they are his last official words, or, as we
might say, his last words 'for the record'.

a working translation of it. The Hebrew text is sometimes terse in
its expression and teasing in its options. Since the text is short and
since I want to avoid making constant comparisons of English
versions, here is a fairly literal translation to use for our reference.

2 Samuel 23:1-7

1. And these are the last words of David:
   Oracle of David son of Jesse;
   Yes, oracle of the man who has been raised up high;
   the anointed one of the God of Jacob,
   and singer of Israel's songs.

2. The Spirit of Yahweh has spoken with me,
   and his word is upon my tongue;

3. The God of Israel has said,
   to me the Rock of Israel has spoken:

   > Ruler over mankind – righteous!
   > Ruler – fear of God!

4   And as the light of morning (when) the sun rises,
     morning without clouds,
     because of brightness, because of rain
         – grass from the earth.

5. Indeed, is not my house like this with God?
   For an everlasting covenant he ordained for me,
       a covenant fully stated and secured;
   for all my welfare and all (his) pleasure.
       – indeed, will he not make it spring up?

6. But the godless are like thorns,
   all of them tossed away;
   to be sure, they don't grab them with the hand,

7. but the man who approaches them arms himself
   with iron or a wooden spear,
   and they are totally burned up with fire on the spot.[3]

---

3. For discussion of matters of grammar and translation readers may consult
the commentaries of Driver, Gordon, Keil, and Kirkpatrick.

The theme of the text is the kingdom that is to come, and it teaches us that...

The Kingdom Is Certain (23:1-3a, 5)

David makes us wait for his actual prophecy, which comes in verses 3b-4. Before that we meet an extended introduction of eight or nine lines. The text is very deliberate; it is in no particular hurry.

This introduction (vv.1-3a) does what any decent introduction should do; it informs us about how we are to regard what it introduces. The message to come is a divine message, an 'oracle' (v.1). David claims that Yahweh has spoken with him and therefore David's tongue will be uttering Yahweh's word (v.2). What David will pass on is nothing but what the God and Rock of Israel has declared (v.3a). Such repetition suggests the hackneyed story of the young preacher who announced his text, 'Behold; I come!' His mind went blank; he couldn't conjure up what he had planned to say next. So he repeated his text – 'Behold! I come!' Still no light. In desperation he leaned against the pulpit and textualized with more gusto, 'Behold! I come!' At which point the pulpit gave way and the young man tumbled into the lap of a lady in the foremost pew. The embarrassed preacher apologized profusely, but the woman insisted on assuming the blame: 'No, no, I should have been prepared – you told me three times you were coming!' We too should pick up on David's insistent repetition. He wants us to understand unmistakably that what he announces is not David's guess but Yahweh's dogma, not a piece of human insight but a clip of divine decree. And if it is *God's* word, then it is a *sure* word and can be depended upon.

David sounds this note of certainty again in verse 5, immediately following the revelation proper. He knows that the hope of the future ruler (vv. 3b-4) is simply the fulfilment of the 'everlasting covenant' Yahweh had already instigated with him (7:12-16), 'a covenant fully stated and secured.'

How welcome this note of certainty should be for God's people. One could not look at the flux and flops of history and deduce that a righteous Ruler over mankind is coming to reign. Our world seems to be plunging to chaos rather than rising to civilization, wallowing in oppression rather than finding justice. And many of the Lord's own people walk through their personal lives riddled with uncertainties, wondering how their apparently senseless circumstances find a niche in divine wisdom. We could never infer kingdom hope from personal experience. David, however, tells us it is a matter of divine revelation. Hence the coming kingdom is not a political proposal but divine certainty.[4] God's people in this world seldom have circumstantial certainty but we have kingdom certainty. I don't think I could go on without it.

The Kingdom Is Attractive (23:3b-4)

Verses 3b-4 constitute the heart of David's prophetic revelation. The text is very clipped and abrupt. David sees a universal ruler (not merely over Israel but 'over mankind'); he is righteous, or legitimate; the fear of God infects his rule (v.3b). Verse 4 is not hopelessly obscure; it depicts via imagery of light, sun, rain, and grass the reviving, refreshing, renewing effects of this ruler's reign. Freshness and vitality ooze out of verse 4 no matter how one translates it. David points us to a coming universal Ruler, who rules righteously, and therefore renews and refreshes what and whom he rules.

I think David's 'ruler' refers to the Messiah. David certainly believes that the ruler is a 'Davidic' king, one from David's dynasty or 'house' (as v.5 clearly shows). But I do not think David in verses 3b-4 is merely holding up an ideal for Davidic kings. I think he speaks prophetically of the Final Representative of his dynasty, because the emphatic stress on divine inspiration in verses 1-3a is hardly compatible with a rather bland statement about what a king ought to be like.[5]

David speaks then of the last David:

> Ruler over mankind – righteous!
> Ruler – fear of God!

A Ruler who does not crush or milk his subjects but refreshes and

---

4. I understand that Jesus at his first advent already inaugurated the kingdom; but he has not yet consummated it with his second advent. Hence the future orientation of 2 Samuel 23:1-7 still pertains to the present people of God.

5. Cf. C.F. Keil, *Biblical Commentary on the Books of Samuel* (1875; reprint ed., Grand Rapids: Eerdmans, 1950), 487, and Gerard Van Groningen, *Messianic Revelation in the Old Testament* (Grand Rapids: Baker, 1990), 304-308.

nurtures them (v.4). The kingdom is attractive because the King is attractive!

Are we not drawn to this King precisely because we have seen so few of his kind? From my boyhood I recall sitting at the supper table on Sunday evenings after church. Cheese in some form was invariably part of the Sunday night fare. I remember seeing a last slice of cheese on a plate in the middle of the table. And I remember how my father, according to his practice, would 'stare down' that slice of cheese. He would not grab it impulsively. No, it had to be a thoughtful, contemplated process. So he would eye it for some time, almost oblivious to all else. At last, as though it were the climactic moment of an arduous gastro-rational debate, he would reach out his hand and apprehend the cheese. Once, in one of those rare revelatory moments, Pop explained his craving for cheese. He said, 'I never got enough cheese when I was a kid.' Deprivation stirred desire.

Does that principle not help us to explain the attraction we feel in this text? The kingdom is attractive because the King is attractive. And the King is attractive because we have seen so little of this kind of ruler. Where, from democracy to dictatorship, have we found a ruler so controlled by godly fear and personal righteousness that his tenure actually revives and renews his people? We are used to the leaders of this age – whether elected or imposed – being immoral, corrupt, oppressive, and power-grubbing. They decimate rather than relieve their people. At the time of writing I think, for example, of Liberia, where warring leaders and factions so rifle and mangle the land that citizens must emigrate to survive in safety. All of which should stir our appetite for the Final David and the imposition of his rule and goad us to pray for his kingdom to come.[6]

The Kingdom Is Exclusive (23:6-7)

Not everyone, however, wants that kingdom to come. Some want no part of a righteous Ruler's reign. It does not attract them, enamour them, draw them. These are the 'godless' (lit., Belial). If the messianic King is 'like light' (v.4), the godless are 'like thorns'

---

6. By my argument in this section I am not suggesting that Christ is not attractive in himself. He is (see Matt. 11:29-30). But, sadly enough, we often do not see that attraction until our flimsy idealisms and unfounded hopes are dashed to bits. The Lord must make us drink despair before we will thirst for salvation.

(v.6a); if he brings freshness (v.4), they inflict pain (vv. 6-7a). And they will be excluded from the regime they despise; they will be 'tossed away' and 'totally burned up with fire on the spot'.

The coming kingdom then involves both restoration and destruction, both salvation and judgment. Christ's new order will purge those who want no part in a righteous reign and who will not submit to the righteous king. It will all be clear at the end of the age:

> The Son of Man will send out his angels, and they will weed out of this kingdom everything that causes sin and all who do evil. They will throw them into the fiery furnace, where there will be weeping and gnashing of teeth (Matt. 13:41-42, NIV).

John the Baptist had already said so when Jesus was inaugurating his kingdom (Matt. 3:12). In one sense, then, the Messiah's kingdom has boundaries. The godless will be outside of it. In that sense the kingdom is exclusive.

This teaching is not in vogue today. The contemporary dogmas of tolerance and egalitarianism tar as heretical anyone who disputes the gospel of all-inclusiveness. Even the professing church sometimes loathes recognizing any distinctions between Christ's slaves and Belial's cronies. Some years ago an American denomination was sending a new missionary candidate to join their missionary force in an African country (even though this communion at that time was sending home career missionaries for lack of funds). He was a seminary graduate and was to serve as a 'frontier intern'. The field missionary, however, refused to seek a visa for the candidate since the candidate had indicated in writing that he did *not* wish to be classified as a professing Christian. Nevertheless, a church bureaucrat did not see this as an insurmountable difficulty. He wrote to the recalcitrant field missionary implying that this candidate was one of the 'younger generation, whose commitment is real but whose vocabulary and thought patterns are not traditional' and urging that 'in spite of his uncertainties' (which included an unwillingness to profess the Christian faith) the intern in question had a contribution to make.

The kingdom doctrine in the Bible, however, refuses to fuzzy such distinctions. Listen to David or to Jesus. They speak the same word: at the last the godless will stand outside the circle of Messiah's kingdom. Even at the end of the New Testament canon John refuses to budge on this point (Rev. 21:8, 27; 22:15). Even the great 'evangelical prophet' Isaiah closes his prophecy by forcing his reader to stand trembling on the edge of the abyss, gazing at the disaster within (Isa. 66:24). Doubtless for a reason: perhaps the sight will make you run into Christ's barn (cf. Matt. 13:30).

27. Hail to the Chiefs
2 Samuel 23:8-39

The breakdown of this passage is fairly simple. I prefer to view it, following Fokkelman,[1] in four divisions:

> The named trio, vv. 8-12
> The anonymous trio, vv. 13-17
> Two leaders, vv. 18-23
> Extended list, vv. 24-39

That overview should give us the lay of the land. The 'land,' however, is a minefield of textual problems. Readers comparing English versions (and/or their marginal notes) will observe that verses 8, 18-19, and 32-33 reflect uncertainty about the original text. I do not want to focus on these conundrums, because our task is not to explain the complexities but to hear the witness of the text, which is clear enough in spite of textual problems. Readers may look elsewhere to get a handle on the latter.[2]

A series of portraits hangs on the east wall in the faculty room at the seminary where I teach. These color portraits are of past or current faculty members who have served the seminary for at least ten years. It is the school's way of honoring those who have loyally and continually served the seminary over its thirty plus years. Second Samuel 23:8-39 is like that. It is primarily a list but is intended to recognize those warriors who loyally served David and

---

1. J.P. Fokkelman, *Narrative Art and Poetry in the Books of Samuel,* vol. 3, *Throne and City (II Sam. 2-8 & 21-24)* (Assen/Maastricht: Van Gorcum, 1990), 301.

2. A careful reading of Youngblood's comments would be a good place to start; see Ronald F. Youngblood, '1,2 Samuel,' *The Expositor's Bible Commentary,* 12 vols. (Grand Rapids: Zondervan, 1992), 3: 1085-94.

his kingdom over the years. It is an honor roll of kingdom servants. However, even though one may appreciate this fact, one must still confess that reading 'Helez the Paltite, Ira son of Ikkesh the Tekoite, Abiezer the Anathothite' (vv. 26-27a) fails to sweep us into devotional rapture. Hardly our idea of edification. But I propose there is more here than names and one-sentence stories. A patient look discovers more than first meets the eye. For example, there is...

The Secret That May Escape Us (23:8-12)

These verses describe an elite group of warriors (apparently, The Three), consisting of Josheb-basshebeth (v.8; or Jashobeam, 1 Chron. 11:11), Eleazar (vv. 9-10), and Shammah (vv. 11-12). Josheb-basshebeth notched up eight hundred fatalities during a single conflict ('at one time', v.8b). When the bulk of Israel retreated, Eleazar stood his ground and kept cutting down Philistines until his hand froze to his sword (vv.9-10).[3] And Shammah made some Israelite farmer very happy by defending a field of lentils from the pilfering Philistines. The Israelite troops had fled from the Philistines, but Shammah took his stand in that lentil patch and began whacking down all comers (vv. 11-12). All of these episodes seem to have been individual feats requiring massive doses of courage to stand alone and turn the tide in face of overwhelming odds. Hence one might think these vignettes were written in praise of the sheer audacity of human guts. But that would be wrong. Verses 10 and 12 uncover the secret behind it all (at least for the Eleazar and Shammah scenarios): 'And Yahweh brought about great victory' (lit., salvation).

In June 1948 Arab shellfire had been racking Jewish Jerusalem. The Jews could not answer with the same intensity for they were conserving their meagre supply of ammunition. The Arab

---

3. There are some interesting parallels to Eleazar's hand. 'A Highland sergeant at Waterloo had done such execution with his basket-handled sword, and so much blood had coagulated round his hand, that it had to be released by a blacksmith, so firmly were they glued together' (W.G. Blaikie, *The Second Book of Samuel*, The Expositor's Bible [Cincinnati: Jennings & Graham, n.d.], 346). 'At the close of the massacre of the Christians of Mount Lebanon by the Druses, in 1860, Sheikh Ali Amad's hand so clave to the handle of his sword that he could not open it until the muscles were relaxed by fomentation of hot water' (cited in A.F. Kirkpatrick, *The Second Book of Samuel*, The Cambridge Bible for Schools and Colleges [Cambridge: CUP, 1897], 216).

commander, Emile Jumean, suffered no such limitation. It was during this time that two shells hit the Church of the Holy Sepulchre and the Dome of the Rock. Anyone pondering that fact would likely chalk it up to the Jews. Who else – obviously – would want to shell the Dome of the Rock? But such thinking would be wrong. Jumean had ordered his Arabs to do the shelling; he was sure the Israeli army would be blamed for the outrage and he wanted to stir up worldwide antipathy toward the Jews. In this case, events were not what they appeared to be; one had to know the secret behind them to get to the truth.[4]

All this is not to negate the raw daring and trenchant courage of David's first three warriors. They displayed all that and more. (They were hardly humming 'Channels Only' during such forays!) And yet behind all such daring courage and dogged combat stands the fact that the victory was Yahweh's gift. He used courage and gall to bring his 'great salvation', but in the last analysis the deliverance was his doing. All God's servants must recognize this secret lest we fail to see our successes as gifts and turn them – or ourselves – into idols.

The Awe that Should Overcome Us (23:13-17)

David was flabbergasted. Overwhelmed. The goose bumps started coming out as he realized how seriously three of his warriors had taken his words. He remembered now: it was one of those passing bits of wishful thinking, a momentary outburst of nostalgia. 'O that someone might get me water from the cistern in Bethlehem...!' (v.15). And here it was. Why couldn't David stop shaking?

The incident passed on in verses 13-17 may have taken place in David's outlaw days during Saul's regime, for David frequented Adullam then (v.13; 1Sam. 22:1-2); or it could have occurred early in David's reign – some suggest 2 Samuel 5:17-21 as the setting. In any case, David was in the cave of Adullam and Philistines seemed to be everywhere; one detachment was southwest of Jerusalem in the Valley of Rephaim (v.13) and there was a garrison of them in David's hometown Bethlehem, six miles south of Jerusalem.[5] It

---

4. Larry Collins and Dominique Lapierre, *O Jerusalem!* (New York: Pocket Books, 1972), 619.

5. Adullam was about 12.5 miles west/southwest of Bethlehem; W.S. LaSor, 'Adullam,' ISBE, 1:58.

was in this setting David gave momentary vent to his homesickness, little realizing that three of his men would make his wish their agenda. And at great risk, for they did not secretly slither into Bethlehem under cover of night but cut their way through the Philistine lines.[6] They did not circle but fought Philistines to obtain their prize. Of course, the odds were not good, but they are not called mighty men for nothing. They are also durable men since the round trip covered twenty-five miles. But here it is – the elixir from Bethlehem!

And David refused to drink it. 'Then he poured it out to Yahweh' (v. 16b). David's response, however, would not incite their anger but their admiration, for it is not an act of waste but of worship. 'Far be it from me, O Yahweh,' David exclaims, 'that I should do this!' (v.17a), and adds, 'Isn't this the blood of the men who went at the cost of their lives?' (v.17b). He cannot believe the risk his men ran. It is the water of Bethlehem but to David it represents the blood of his men. 'Blood' belongs to Yahweh. Hence he dare not drink it. He poured it out, not because it was trash but because it was treasure – it belonged to Yahweh.[7]

Contemporary believers do not share David's status as covenant king, but we sometimes enjoy analogous experiences and are, therefore, obligated to make a similar response. On the day of my father's funeral in 1986, our family gathered at the church in the western Pennsylvania town where my parents lived. The mortician was about to lead the family into the church sanctuary to the pews reserved for us. Before we entered I caught a glimpse of the audience. I was stunned for, unless it was a ghost, there sat one of the elders from the church I served in Maryland. This – he – was completely unexpected. I cannot put into words the emotions that washed over me when I saw him there. To someone on the outside his presence might only connote an act of kindness and respect, appropriate at such a time. It was that, but it was more. Here was a

---

6. This is the sense of the verb *bāqa'* in verse 16a, as Fokkelman, *Throne and City,* 305, points out.

7. As Joyce Baldwin points out, David recognized that 'only the Lord was worthy of such sacrifice' (*1 & 2 Samuel,* Tyndale Old Testament Commentaries [Leicester: InterVarsity, 1988], 293). Cf. also H.W. Hertzberg: 'His conduct makes it easy to understand why his men went through fire for him' (*I & II Samuel,* The Old Testament Library [Philadelphia: Westminster, 1964], 405).

man who had driven three hundred miles to attend a funeral service, who had taken at least one day off work to do so. And I was shaken trying to take it all in; I could not comprehend that someone cared for me and my family like that. It was a goose bump situation. It was like someone snitching water from Bethlehem. In such awe-full moments we naturally owe our thanks to the human servant. But surely we are obligated to far more than that. Surely one can only 'pour it out to the Lord', who astonishes and melts us with his kindness.

The Honor That Might Encourage Us (23:18-39)

Abishai (v.18a) seems to lead us into a cafeteria of confusion as far as verses 18-19 go. Any reader can sense this textual uncertainty by checking English versions. Was Abishai chief of the thirty (NASB), or chief of the Three (NIV), or head of another three (NJPS)? The text is difficult and a very few Hebrew manuscripts offer alternate readings. I could spill several pages of ink on the problem and still not solve it. I propose that we pretend the NASB is correct and that we assume Abishai (v.18) and Benaiah (v.20) were premier leaders of the 'Thirty'. This may disappoint the tidy-minded, but we must move on.

What we have then are two types of entries. The first consists of these anecdotal briefs about Abishai (vv. 18-19) and Benaiah (vv. 20-23). Abishai's spear won him laurels by chalking up three hundred battle fatalities.[8] We are in the dark about Benaiah's first exploit (v.20b),[9] but the next two clearly earn our respect. It seems 'intimidation' was not in Benaiah's dictionary – unless it was something Benaiah himself did. He stalked lions not vice versa. Walked right through that snow and into that pit and had it out with that lion. Benaiah came out, the lion didn't (v.20c): an exploit David could appreciate (1 Sam. 17:34-37). Then, when packing only a club, Benaiah went one-on-one with a massive Egyptian armed

---

8. Fokkelman (Throne and City, 306) observes that Abishai's must have been a cumulative tally in contrast to Josheb-basshebeth whose feat was accomplished on a single occasion (v.8).

9. The problem is the word '$\bar{a}ri$'$\bar{e}l$. Should it be emended to a plural so that Benaiah struck down two heroes of Moab (David J.A. Clines, ed., The Dictionary of Classical Hebrew, 1:365)? Or should we follow LXX and assume he struck down two sons of a Moabite named Ariel?

with a spear.[10] Benaiah ripped the spear from the Egyptian's grip; the latter lost both his grip and his life (v.21).

The second type of entry is a much less exciting list of the 'Thirty' (vv. 24-39). No exploits; only an honor roll of David's elite: name plus lineage and/or home.[11] The 'Thirty' probably serves more as a general category than a precise figure. Over time some would fall in battle (e.g., Asahel, v.24; see 2 Sam. 2:18-23) and others would be added.[12] But their names are here – each of them one of David's most esteemed and loyal troops.

Their names are here because they excelled in their calling – fighting for David's kingdom. There are some true tales about liquidating lions and eliminating Egyptians. Usually, however, there is simply a name plus family or home connection (vv. 24-39). The name is in the list. That means they excelled in fighting for and in fidelity to the king. We needn't bellyache about their vocation or pilliorize them as being henchmen of David's ruthless power and violent force. No. They fought. They fought well. And since David

10. Note that the spear was a thrusting, not a hurling, weapon and was used by infantry in close combat. See Yigael Yadin, *The Art of Warfare in Biblical Lands,* 2 vols. (New York: McGraw-Hill, 1963), 1:80; and Mark J. Fretz, 'Weapons and Implements of Warfare', ABD, 6:894.

11. One might make some historical inferences from the list; cf. Robert P. Gordon *(I & II Samuel: A Commentary* [Grand Rapids: Zondervan, 1986], 314): 'K. Ellinger's study of these verses led him to conclude that the names are given in roughly the order in which the individuals concerned attached themselves to David. Most of the first dozen, for example, are Judahites. There is, indeed, a preponderance of Judahites throughout, from which B. Mazar deduces that the list reflects that period when David's rule was largely restricted to Judah.'

12. Verse 39 gives thirty-seven for the total names in vv. 8-39. Some account for this by adding the Three of vv. 8-12, plus two from vv. 18-23, plus thirty-two names from vv. 24-39 (if the text is amended; so Keil). Others calculate only thirty-one names in the list of Thirty (vv. 24-39) but add Joab, assuming that as overall chief he would be included in the tally though not explicitly noted (cf. Baldwin; cf. v. 37). D.G. Schley ('David's Champions,'ABD, 2:49-52) proposes that instead of 'thirty' (*šēlōšîm*) in, e.g., vv. 13, 23, and 24, we should read *šālîšîm* (cf. *šālîs,* adjutant, officer, according to BDB, 1026) and understand them as 'a special cadre of warriors, organized into three-man squads, who were attached directly to the king, and who carried out special assignments for him' (p. 51), or, more simply, 'a trusted body of retainers who carried out special assignments for the king' (p. 52). The proposal is attractive, but I am not yet convinced (see Fokkelman, *Throne and City,* 300-301).

was Yahweh's covenant king, their fighting really constituted fighting for the kingdom of God in this world. Through their arms Yahweh 'gave rest' to David and to Israel (2 Sam. 7:1, 10-11). They were, in that sense, kingdom servants. Because they fought well, they made the list. Their work was not forgotten.

We are also familiar with 'kingdom lists' in the New Testament. They are not lists of military elite since God's people existed under the Roman regime. But somehow the Scriptures can't get away from lists. I am tempted to say the Bible loves lists – maybe because God never tires of naming the names of his people. So we run into mini-notes about Epaphras (Col. 4:12-13) or Prisca and Aquila (Rom. 16:3-5a) – little samples of the Abishai-Benaiah genre. Sometimes little more than the name appears. 'Greet Mary,' the Romans are told, 'who worked very hard for you,' or 'Rufus, chosen in the Lord' (Rom. 16:6,13, NIV). This Bible phenomenon (Rom. 16; Phil. 2:19-30; Col.4; 2 Tim. 1:16-18; Phm. 23-24) simply reflects the Bible's Lord, who even watches servants slipping cups of water for him (Mark 9:41). Some of us find that mildly encouraging.

The Memories That Can Haunt Us (23:39)
When my father had occasion to become aggravated at me (or at one of my brothers) for stirring up havoc he would say, 'You're just like Walter _____ – trouble everywhere you go!' Walter what's-his-name (I withhold the surname to protect the living) was a preacher friend of my father's. And, according to my father, Walter had the knack of stirring up trouble in every church he pastored. So his very name conjured up memories of disasters. Hence his ultimate rebuke: 'You're just like Walter _____ ...'

Try another name. Uriah the Hittite (v.39). What memories, what associations come pouring in? Why, all of 2 Samuel 11–12; the whole nasty saga of David's lust, ruthlessness, perfidy, and cruelty. One name, the last in the list of 'The Thirty', punches our replay button and we see and hear the whole mess again. Is there no escape?

Not in 2 Samuel. There are about sixteen more names added to the (updated?) list in 1 Chronicles 11:26-47. Uriah is more or less lost in the list there. But in 2 Samuel the writer apparently uses an earlier form of the list – at least as early as David's reign in Hebron (note Asahel, v.24; see 2:12-32) in which, perhaps, Uriah's name

was the last entry to date. In any case, the list of the Thirty ends
with a thud. It's as if the writer had smeared bright yellow
highlighting across Uriah's name. No reader can fail to remember.

Yet I doubt that the writer intends Uriah's name as a signal for
us to relive the horror of 2 Samuel 11–12. I suspect rather that he
wants us to move beyond that. Hertzberg has argued in this direction:

> The mention of Uriah in the last place may be pure chance; we have
> the list up to the time when Uriah, as it were the novice, was accepted
> onto the order. But the final compiler and the audience will hardly
> have regarded it in this light. The name Uriah at the end of the list
> leads us to recall what is associated with his name. The list of the men
> who were David's 'bodyguard' ends with the name of one who did not
> betray the king, but was betrayed by him. The end of the list is meant
> to tell us, 'Do not forget the name of the last of David's mighty men'!
> We are thus prohibited from making heroes of David (and his men).
> Even here, history was not made by men, but by the grace of God,
> whose help and forgiveness were needed even by David and his time.[13]

'Uriah the Hittite' (v.39). That last name is loaded – with the
raunchiest memories. But Hertzberg has suggested that the
wickedness of David should lead us on to the grace of God. Our
rubric for this section was: 'The memories that can haunt us.' But
they need not. Not if they humble us instead. This is the testimony
of the chief of sinners in 1 Corinthians 15:9-10. There Paul asserts:
'For I am the least of the apostles, who am not worthy to be called
"apostle," because I persecuted the church of God; but by God's
grace I am what I am…' There it is, as lurid and sinister as 'Uriah
the Hittite' in 2 Samuel 23: 'Because I persecuted the church of
God.' An indelible memory, but Paul allows it to humble him, for
it is on the basis of this fact that he is (note the present tense) the
least of the apostles and unworthy to be called such. And in this
humility he moves beyond the despair of that memory to walk in
the grace of God (v.10a).[14] This is not just for kings and apostles.
When our most appalling memories are immersed in divine grace

---

13. Hertzberg, *I & II Samuel,* 408.
14. My colleague, Knox Chamblin, has put it well (commenting on 1 Cor.
15:9-10): 'Verse 9 is written by a man still broken under the weight of his
past sin: 'I *am*…the least…and *do* not deserve…'. Vital to Paul's effectiveness
as an apostle is that he never forgot his days as a persecutor. Yet it could

there is still a holy sadness, a godly grief, a broken heart, but the memories no longer haunt us.

Isn't 2 Samuel 23 simply vintage Bible? Even in a military list one runs into grace!

28. Senseless Census
2 Samuel 24

When I was a young lad in my father's house, the latter enforced a strange household rule. No one was to whistle in the house. Let one of us be touched with a stab of hilarity and begin to express such in that most natural mode and we would hear that raised voice reiterating the law: 'No whistling in the house!' Such dogma hardly seemed rational. I asked my mother the psychological question: *Why* can there be no whistling in the house? Why this lid on interior exuberance? She did not know. (Indeed, why should she care? She neither whistled nor was tempted to do so.) She wondered if per chance my father's father had not allowed his family to whistle in the house. But no one knew. Actually, I didn't need to know. If my father said not to whistle in the house, that was the law. I only needed to obey; I could whistle outdoors.

The census in 2 Samuel 24 is akin to my domestic perplexity. The census seems to be senseless – at least that's Joab's view (v.3). Not merely senseless but sinful – as David came to believe (v.10). Not only sinful but punishable – as Yahweh shows (v.15). The census is senseless and sinful, but why was the census senseless? Why was it sinful? Where was the wrong in it? Why was counting culpable?

There are two answers to these questions. The first is: it doesn't matter. The second is: there are four views. To slake curiosity let us develop the second answer.

Josephus (*Antiquities,* 7.13.1) reflects Jewish tradition, holding on the basis of Exodus 30:11-16 (note especially v.12) that David

---

hardly be said that the memory leaves him paralyzed. On the contrary, 15:10 testifies to his superlative achievements. The explanation lies in God's grace, by which Paul has been liberated from the guilt of his sins and energized for apostolic service. An ongoing awareness of grace reminds Paul of the appalling sin from which he had been delivered; an ongoing awareness of the sin keeps him dependent on grace' (*Paul and the Self,* [Grand Rapids, Baker, 1993], 24-25; emphasis his).

neglected to pay the per capita atonement money required whenever a census was taken.[1] If, however, the poll tax of Exodus 30 was a one-time requirement and did not become a precedent until long after David,[2] then there could be no fault on this score. Others infer (what else can one do?) that the offence must rest in David's motivation for the census, so that 'it is David's aspirations after self-sufficiency that are being censured'.[3] Still others, noting – as all do – the military nature of the census (see v.9), hold that the census was a preparation for additional military conquest that was either ill-conceived or beyond the limits of God's approval.[4] Finally, one can construe 1 Chronicles 27:23-24 to imply that at first David ordered Joab to include in his count those not yet subject to call up (i.e., those below twenty years of age). Perhaps David wanted to know the likely military capability for the coming years. Such action, however, was an implicit denial of God's promise to multiply Israel like the stars of the sky. Human planning replaced divine promise.[5]

None of these explanations can decisively carry the day. Second

---

1. See the helpful discussion in Robert P. Gordon, *I & II Samuel: A Commentary* (Grand Rapids: Zondervan, 1986), 316.

2. Nahum Sarna, *Exodus*, The JPS Torah Commentary (Philadelphia: Jewish Publication Society, 1991), 195; W.H. Gispen, *Exodus*, Bible Student's Commentary (Grand Rapids, Zondervan, 1982), 283.

3. Gordon, *I & II Samuel*, 316. Cf. Claus Schedl, *History of the Old Testament*, 5 vols. (Staten Island: Alba House, 1972), 3:262: 'Throughout the entire world of the Ancient Semite, knowing was equivalent to exercising power or dominion over a person or an object. Counting flocks or populations, "in order to know their number," was equivalent to a claim of absolute and unlimited dominion. Such dominion, however, was proper only and solely to God, the Lord of all. Accordingly, a census of the people must be regarded as an arrogation of the divine prerogative of dominion, and condemned as an act of sacrilege.'

4. See the argumentation of R. Laird Harris in TWOT, 2:731 (under $p\bar{a}qad$), and Raymond B. Dillard, 'David's Census: Perspectives on II Samuel 24 and I Chronicles 21,' in *Through Christ's Word: A Festschrift for Dr. Philip E. Hughes*, ed. W. Robert Godfrey and Jesse L. Boyd III (Phillipsburg, NJ: Presbyterian and Reformed, 1985), 105-106.

5. Matthew Henry was aware of this view in his day (*Commentary on the Whole Bible*, 6 vols. [New York: Revell, n.d]. 2:570); cf. also Dillard, 'David's Census', 105. On David's military organisation in 1 Chron. 27, see Yigael Yadin, *The Art of Warfare in Biblical Lands*, 2 vols. [New York: McGraw-Hill, 1963), 2:279-84.

Samuel 24 does not explicitly tell us why the census was wrong.[6] I
can only assume that this matter doesn't matter. It was wrong but
we needn't know why. 'No whistling in the house.' On to the teaching.

Our chapter breaks down into three major sections and can be
summarized in terms of the primary human characters David deals
with in each segment:

> David and Joab, vv. 2-9
> David and Gad, vv. 10-19
> David and Araunah, vv. 20-25

The digest may be a handy way to recall the content of the text, but
our primary interest centers on its theological witness. Each of the
segments above highlights an element of that witness.

The Mystery of Wrath (24:1-9)

One runs right into the thick of this mystery in verse 1: 'Then the
anger of Yahweh burned again against Israel, and [or: so that] he
incited David against them, saying, "Go, number Israel and
Judah."'[7] The 'again' may refer to the episode of 21:1-14. In any
case, David gave the order (v.2), Joab objected (v.3), David over-
ruled (v.4), and Joab & Co. canvassed the country (vv. 5-9).[8]

However, the mere quoting of verse 1 sets most people's minds
on the method rather than the mystery of Yahweh's wrath. How
can Yahweh stir up David to carry out an action for which he is
then held guilty? The situation is something like my view of a meal.
In my humble but real opinion, meals exist for dessert. I would

---

6. If the census bothered Joab (v. 3) there must have been something terribly
aruck with it; Joab was not famous for a tender conscience.

7. Some hold that the Hebrew construction means 'continued to burn' rather
than 'burned again'. See, e.g., Robert Polzin, *David and the Deuteronomist*
(Bloomington: Indiana University, 1993), 210, 232-33; Robert G. Boling,
Judges, The Anchor Bible (Garden City: Doubleday, 1975), 85; and Barry G.
Webb, *The Book of the Judges: An Integrated Reading* (Sheffield: JSOT,
1987), 221.

8. To trace Joab's circuit in verses 5-7, see the convenient map and explanation
in Yohanan Aharoni and Michael Avi-Yonah, *The Macmillan Bible Atlas*, 3rd
ed. (New York: Macmillan, 1993), 81. On the tallies of verse 9 and their
discrepancy with those of 1 Chronicles 21:5, see especially Ronald F.
Youngblood, '1,2 Samuel,' *The Expositor's Bible Commentary*, 12 vols.
(Grand Rapids: Zondervan, 1992), 3:1098-99.

almost say dessert *is* the meal. However, social convention (and, some
would say, nutritional wisdom) dictates that before one participates
in that only reason for eating in the first place one must muddle
through salad or vegetables or meat of some sort, items that have
mistakenly – again in my opinion – been dubbed 'the main course'.
Now I think the theological difficulty many feel over verse 1 is
wrongly made the 'main course' of attention in this passage. But
since it usually does grab readers' attention, we will turn aside to
deal with it before returning to the real difficulty of the text.

Some appeal to the parallel passage in 1 Chronicles 21:1 in
order to tone down the suggestion of our present text. There we are
told that 'Satan rose up against Israel and incited David to take a
census of Israel' (NIV).[9] One can then put the two texts together,
look at 2 Samuel 24:1 through 1 Chronicles 21:1, and hold that the
latter implies that in the former we are dealing with God's
permissive will; Satan was the real villain; Yahweh only permitted
it. I agree that both texts are true, but the appeal to God's permissive
will solves nothing. It may sound better, but God must *decide* to
permit. We cannot use Satan to avoid God.

There are some other recourses used to soften Yahweh's
responsibility in 2 Samuel 24:1. The *Modern Language Bible* takes
the verb *sût* (to incite, instigate, arouse) in an impersonal sense:
'One aroused David against them.' That is a possible but not a
natural rendering. We would normally assume the subject of the
preceding verb clause, viz., Yahweh or the wrath of Yahweh.

The NASB lightens Yahweh's direct involvement by translating,
'[I]t incited David against them to say, "Go, number Israel and
Judah." ' 'It' as the subject of the verb refers to 'anger' and not to
'Yahweh'. This, of course, is strictly correct, but since it is *Yahweh's*
anger he remains the essential subject of the verb. His anger is not
some third thing operating independently of him. Then NASB
renders the Hebrew infinitive *lē'mōr* as 'to say', which implies

---

9. I am aware of the view which does not take *śāṭān* in 1 Chronicles 21:1 as
a proper name but in its generic sense, viz., 'adversary'. Then the stimulus for
David's sin was the rise of a military opponent or, perhaps, even an insidious
domestic counsellor. For this view, argued especially by John Sailhamer, see
the summary in David M. Howard, Jr., *An Introduction to the Old Testament
Historical Books*, (Chicago: Moody, 1993), 245-48, and the cogent objections
of Youngblood, *Expositor's Bible Commentary*, 3:1096.

the following command quotes David's – and not so much Yahweh's – orders. This is a feasible translation. However, this infinitive in the vast majority of cases in traditional versions is rendered 'saying', implying that the words that follow come from the previous subject (in this case, Yahweh). The form is equivalent to our occasional expression, 'And I quote…'. It still seems to me that the more natural way to take the grammar leaves the impression that the words are Yahweh's.

How then could David be blamed for doing what Yahweh commanded? I don't know, but I don't want to fudge the text simply to escape a theological problem. Clearly, in verse 10 David realized he had sinned. Hence the writer casts Yahweh's role in the *form* of a command (v.1) and allows the developing narrative to qualify that by showing what the *reality* was (namely, David was responsible). Part of our problem also may be a failure to appreciate Hebrew thinking on such matters. While discussing the connection between 1 Chronicles 21:1 and 2 Samuel 24:1, Walter Kaiser put it this way:

> It is also true, according to the Hebrew thinking, that whatever God permits he commits. By allowing this census-taking, God is viewed as having brought about the act. The Hebrews were not very concerned with determining secondary causes and properly attributing them to the exact cause. Under the divine providence everything ultimately was attributed to him; why not say he did it in the first place?[10]

We come back now to verse 1 ('and the anger of Yahweh burned again against Israel, and he incited David against them') and to its main point, the mystery of wrath. There is a deeper mystery here than the obvious difficulty most readers see. Yahweh's wrath burns against Israel and he is going to use David's sin as the vehicle of his wrath upon Israel.[11] But why is Yahweh angry against Israel? We do not know. We are not told. De Graaf believes:

> The Lord brought this about because His anger was directed against the people on account of their misdeeds, for which they had not yet

---

10. Walter C. Kaiser, Jr., *Hard Sayings of the Old Testament* (Downers Grove: InterVarsity, 1988), 131.

11. 'The victorious and mighty ruler of Israel with his godless, overbearing deed is himself the instrument of the wrath with which God meets his people' (Karl Gutbrod, *Das Buch vom Reich,* Die Botschaft des Alten Testaments, 2nd ed. [Stuttgart: Calwer, 1973], 282).

been punished. Hadn't the people rejected David for Absalom and then for Sheba? They had rejected the *head* of the covenant – and thereby the Lord's covenant itself. For this the Lord now intended to punish them.[12]

This is a plausible explanation, an inference from the preceding chapters. But we simply don't know. The text itself is silent; it states the fact of, but not the reason for, Yahweh's wrath.

Does this bother us? Do we perhaps assume that God must always explain himself and justify his ways? If we cannot be content to accept the mystery of this text we may be revealing ourselves. If we are upset over a text that tells us Yahweh is angry but does not tell us why, are we not saying that we really don't trust him to be just? Is there not a strain within us that insists there must be no mysteries in God? Don't we sometimes subtly assume that God owes us an explanation? We can easily brandish an arrogance that does not worship, that comes into the presence of the Most High with a strut instead of a bow. Are we angry because God is not perfectly transparent?[13] Can we live – and worship – with mystery?

The Warmth of Mercy (24:10-19)
David apparently felt conviction apart from any prophetic intervention. Gad comes to give David direction after the king's confession and plea for forgiveness (v.10), not in order to bring him to repentance. Gad tells the king that Yahweh is laying three options before him and he must choose one (vv. 11-12): three years of famine, three months running from adversaries, or three days of plague (v.13).[14] We may understand David's reply ('Let us fall into the hand of Yahweh,' v.14) as eliminating the second option and leaving the remaining choice to Yahweh.[15] Yahweh brought

---

12. S.G. DeGraaf, *Promise and Deliverance*, 4 vols. (St. Catherines: Paideia, 1978), 2:188 (emphasis his). Keil makes a similar proposal.

13. Walter Brueggemann *(First and Second Samuel,* Interpretation [Louisville: John Knox, 1990], 351) has a stimulating, if perhaps overdrawn, exposition of this verse.

14. The Hebrew text of verse 13 reads 'seven years of famine'. This is often corrected to 'three' in line with LXX and 1 Chronicles 21:12. Note also the three years of famine in 2 Samuel 21:1. Pharaoh, however, faced seven years of it in Genesis 41:27. Josephus voted for seven here *(Antiquities,* 7.13.2).

15. So Hans Wilhelm Hertzberg, *I & II Samuel,* The Old Testament Library

the plague with 70,000 casualties (v.15), quite a dent in the proud tallies of verse 9.[16] But David was right about Yahweh's mercies: 'Yahweh was sorry about the disaster' and ordered the destroying angel to stop his work (v.16). Wrath stopped at Araunah's threshing-floor.

David made quite a point about Yahweh's mercies and I think we can appreciate his point better if we momentarily back away from the details of the text and look at the structure of the whole chapter:

Proposed Structure of Chapter 24

Wrath and orders, vv. 1-2
   Joab's objection & David's insistence, vv. 3-4
      Journey and tally, vv. 5-9
         David's contrition & Gad's direction, vv. 10-13
            Mercy trusted, v.14
               Wrath inflicted, v. 15
            Mercy displayed, v.16
         David's contrition & Gad's direction, vv.17-18
      Journey and purpose, vv. 19-21
   Araunah's objection & David's insistence, vv. 22-24
Sacrifice and wrath, v. 25

I am well aware that we need to be skeptical about seeing neatly-packaged structures in every text, but can I help it if – like Aaron's

---

(Philadelphia: Westminster, 1964), 413. For a differing view, cf. P. Kyle McCarter, Jr., *II Samuel,* The Anchor Bible (New York: Doubleday, 1984), 511. Of the three possible punishments Hertzberg also observes that 'the shortening of the duration (three years, three months, three days) corresponds with an intensification of their content'. Unlike David in the Hebrew text, LXX does not leave the choice to Yahweh but specifies that David chose the plague option. S.R. Driver thought the text of LXX was better here. I don't. I think the translators couldn't stand the suspense and so made David's decision for him!

16. There is a much-discussed phrase in verse 15: 'Yahweh set the plague in motion against Israel *from the morning until the appointed time.*' Suffice it to say that I agree with J.P. Fokkelman (*Narrative Art and Poetry in the Books of Samuel,* vol. 3, *Throne and City (II Sam. 2-8 & 21-24)* [Assen/Maastricht: Van Gorcum, 1990], 317, 323) that the phrase means the time appointed by God. The implication from verse 16 suggests that the appointed time was less than the full three days.

calf (Exod. 32:24) – it just came out this way? In any case, note that the very heart of the chapter focuses on Yahweh inflicting his wrath on Israel (v.15); and yet note that the segments immediately before and after verse 15 highlight Yahweh's mercy. I suggest that catches the tone of the whole chapter: *wrath wrapped in mercy.* For this reason we rightly hover over David's statement in verse 14.

This is at least the third time we have heard David make a statement of this sort (see 12:22 and 16:12 and our comments on each). 'I am in terrible distress,' David cries. 'Let us fall into the hand of Yahweh for his mercies are many.' David is about to meet Yahweh's wrath and yet is convinced of Yahweh's mercies. Somehow he imagines that the hand that strikes him will nevertheless spare him. David's assumptions are astounding! His words in verse 14 breathe not only necessary resignation but boundless consolation. See how well he knows his God! In his crises his theology seems to come out almost by reflex action. Is this not as it should be in believing experience? Must you not have your best theology for your darkest moments? And in the disasters and sins of life is there a kinder place to fall than 'into the hand of Yahweh'?

Not long ago newspapers told of an episode at the Brookfield (Illinois) Zoo. A three-year-old toddler fell eighteen feet into an area inhabited by seven gorillas. The lad would still be alert when taken to a hospital where he would be listed in critical condition. But how did he ever get out of gorilla-land? Binti, a seven-year-old female gorilla, picked up the child, cradled him in her arms, and put him down near a door where zoo keepers could get him. I suppose the story seems amazing to us because we do not customarily associate gorillas with kindness. We may be grateful to Binti but would prefer not to trust her with another child.

I wonder if in our gut-level thinking we don't have a gorilla view of God's mercies? We tend to look upon mercy as a divine exception rather than as the divine character. Not so David. Even in his wrath David knew he was not facing a gorilla-God. 'Let us fall into the hand of Yahweh for his mercies are many.' Here is a believer who has a grip on mercy. No. I'm wrong. Mercy has gripped him.

The Necessity Of Atonement (24:20-25)

Before we plod with David & Co. to Araunah's threshingfloor we need to back up to verse 16 and pick up the story. David was right about Yahweh's mercy. As the destroying angel turns to decimate Jerusalem Yahweh imposes a stay upon the disaster. It was mercy restraining wrath:

> But when the angel stretched his hand towards Jerusalem to destroy it, Yahweh felt sorry about the calamity and said to the angel who was destroying the people, 'Enough now! Hold your hand!' (v.16, NJB)[17]

The angel of Yahweh was at the threshingfloor of Araunah the Jebusite when he stopped the scourge. Gad then directed David to erect an altar to Yahweh at Araunah's threshingfloor (v.18); David obeyed Gad's order, which was also Yahweh's command (v.19).

If the altar on Araunah's threshingfloor was a matter of Yahweh's command (v.19), then the sacrifices offered there must have been imperative. This means that the situation was not resolved at the end of verse 16. There wrath was stayed but not satisfied. The scourge ceases in verse 16, but the wrath behind the scourge must not merely be curtailed or 'on hold' but must be dealt with, or, theologically, propitiated. Hence the altar and sacrifices of verse 25. And this is effected by atonement.

I do not think we can avoid this view of the matter. When Araunah peers down and sees David and his entourage approaching, goes out to meet him, and engages in the proper formalities, he asks why royalty is visiting his threshingfloor. David answers: 'To buy the threshingfloor from you to build an altar to Yahweh, that the plague may be held back from the people' (v.21b). There is a

---

17. Verse 17 is a flashback, reporting David's cry prior to Yahweh's restraining order. If we translate verse 17 following the order of the Hebrew text, the initial verb clearly requires a pluperfect sense: 'Now David had said to Yahweh when he saw the angel striking down the people – he said: "Look, I'm the one who has done wrong; but these sheep – what have they done? Let your hand be against me and my father's house." ' David confesses that he is guilty but assumes Israel is not. Here is a touch of irony (Fokkelman, *Throne and City*, 326), for we know in light of verse 1 that Israel is not innocent. David's anguish is completely proper but not fully informed. Oddly enough, we the readers have the same question: 'What have they done?' This we do not know, for verse 1 did not see fit to enlighten us on it.

clear connection between the anticipated sacrifices and a definitive restraining of the plague, the expression of Yahweh's wrath. Araunah seems to offer David all the paraphernalia (though perhaps not yet the site itself?) for sacrifice gratis (vv. 22-23).[18] But David insists on paying a full, fair price and weighs out fifty shekels of silver (v.24).[19] There he offers up burnt offerings and peace offerings. And things change. Then Yahweh 'answered prayer in behalf of the land' (v.25, NIV; see 21:14!). Then 'the plague on Israel was stopped' (NIV; the verb, *'āṣar*, is the same as in v. 21, which above I translated 'held back'). 'Tis mercy all, as Charles Wesley would sing. God in mercy restrains his wrath (v.16); and God in mercy provides the way for removing his wrath, through the atoning sacrifice (vv. 21, 25).

Do we really appreciate what it means to have a God-directed, God-provided atonement? By October 1944 Japan's sun was fast sinking in the war in the Pacific. Admiral Takijiro Onishi, soon to be vice chief of the Naval General Staff in Tokyo, realized that the time for desperate measures had come. At Mabalacat Field, Luzon, he disclosed his plan for turning the tide of the war: 'In my opinion, the enemy can be stopped only be crash-diving on their carrier flight decks with Zero fighters carrying 250-kilogram bombs.' Suicide attacks. Kamikaze pilots. These attacks proved far more successful than conventional air strikes. Admiral Onishi was convinced they must continue these inhuman tactics. By the time Japan surrendered Admiral Onishi's program had claimed the lives of 2,519 men and officers of the Imperial Japanese Navy. On August 15, 1945, came the Imperial proclamation calling for the immediate cessation of the war. That evening Admiral Onishi left a note thanking the souls of his late subordinates for their valiant deeds.

---

18. However, in the Near East one must often be cautious about whether 'give' (Heb., *nātan*, v. 23a) means give. In the wrangling of Genesis 23 it clearly meant 'offer' or 'sell'.

19. In 1 Chronicles 21:25 David pays six hundred shekels of gold. But that sum is for the whole site apparently and may well have been a separate transaction. See A.F. Kirkpatrick, *The Second Book of Samuel*, The Cambridge Bible for Schools and Colleges (Cambridge: CUP, 1897), 232. There is a different emphasis in the parallel story in Chronicles. Here in 2 Samuel 24 the stress is on what took place (turning away wrath), while in 1 Chronicles 21 there is more interest in *where* it took place, because Araunah's threshing-floor was to become the site of the future temple (1 Chron. 21:20–22:1).

'In death,' he wrote, 'I wish to apologize to these brave men and their families.' With that he plunged a samurai sword into his abdomen. He refused any medical aid, would allow no one to finish him off; he lingered in agony until six o'clock the next evening. The tellers of his story conclude: 'His choice to endure prolonged suffering was obviously made in expiation for his part in one of the most diabolical tactics of war the world has ever seen.' [20]

Is that the answer to divine wrath and human guilt? Or is there a *God who provides an altar* where his wrath can be quenched and our guilt atoned for? The witness of our text is that Yahweh is just such a God. The altar is not only for guilty David and sinful Israel, for 'we have an altar' (Heb. 13:10). It's not all that far from Araunah's threshingfloor. We know it is a place where Yahweh's wrath was let loose, for the altar is surrounded by the darkness of his judgment (Mark 15:33) and the cry of God-forsakenness pierces that darkness (Mark 15:34). Would that Admiral Onishi had known of it. There we have fallen into the hand of Yahweh and discovered that his mercies are many.

---

20. Rikihei Inoguchi and Tadashi Nakajima, 'Death on the Wing,' *Secrets and Spies: Behind-the-Scenes Stories of World War II* (Pleasantville, NY: Reader's Digest Association, 1964), 447-51 (quotations from pp. 447 and 451).

PERSONS INDEX

SUBJECT INDEX

STUDY GUIDE

Chapter 1

1. 'In Rousseau appearance and reality, publication and practice, did not mesh.' What about you and me?

2. It might seem as if the Amalekite was punished for a sin he did not in fact commit, but is this really so? Think about it.

3. A small child may cover his eyes in the belief that if he cannot see you, you cannot see him. Do we ever try to do something like that with God and is it just as ridiculous?

4. When confronted with the unbelief, apostasy and coldness of the visible church, do you always pray or do you remain content simply to analyse and criticise?

5 'Fear grounded in love' - think that through. How does it differ from fear grounded in sin? Which is your fear?

Chapter 2

1. When you write a letter of condolence to a bereaved friend whose grief you feel able to share, do you pen an expression of *thoughtful* grief as David did?

2. It is important to go back and sit with David in his day and in his circumstances if we want to hear God's word through this book of 2 Samuel as we should. Will you make the effort?

3. Modern Christian songs in our language often use the psalms of praise but rarely the psalms of lament. Does that tell us something about the church in our land today? If so, what?

4. 'Don't hesitate to carry on your mind the sufferings of God's people.' How deep is our identification with our Christian brothers and sisters who are going through deep valleys of suffering?

5. Jonathan was Saul's son and might have expected to succeed him as king and yet he rejoiced when David was honoured. Are you content to play second fiddle for the glory of God?

Chapter 3

1. Here we find that David would make no move before seeking direction from the Lord. Where most of all can we find God's guidance?

2. 2 Samuel 2:1-11 is a rebuke to our tendency to despise the day of small things. What other examples from God's dealings in Scripture and the church may rebuke us further in this regard?

3. Does your witness for Christ have the same union of challenge and winsomeness that characterised David - and even more the Lord Jesus Himself?

4. To know God's will and to choose to fly in the face of it, as Abner did, is a very serious sin. Can you think of other examples of it in Scripture?

5. When you get depressed at the apparent insignificance of some work for God in which you are involved, do you encourage yourself by all the Bible tells us about the certainty of Christ's return and the triumph of His kingdom?

Chapter 4

1. This chapter deals with a fairly large section of 2 Samuel. What particular value can you see in reading the Bible in large as well as in small portions?

2. To what extent do we, to whom God has revealed so much in Christ, actually live within that light in practical terms? If you do not, why not?

3. Abner quoted Scripture when it suited him but ignored it at other times. Did even the Devil do this? See Matthew 4.

4. Are you ever guilty of using the gospel as a means to an end - the end of your own reputation - when people praise you for what is in fact God's work in you?

5. What are the lessons of Joab's character for us as Christians?

Chapter 5

1. Baanah and Rechab decided to seize the hour. Can you distinguish between ungodly and godly opportunism?

2. 'We must see the real under the veneer of the apparent.' This is illustrated also in 1 Samuel 16:1-13 and most of all in the story of Jesus, who to some was apparently just a Carpenter who became a Preacher. How prone are you to judge by outward appearances?

3. How important is it that truth and love should be wedded together in the heart of a Christian man or woman?

4. How strong a motive for your actions is gratitude to Christ? If it is not your governing motive, do you spend enough time at the cross?

5. How concerned should Christians be about justice?

Chapter 6

1. How fundamental to the revelation of God in the Bible are the promises He has made?

2. 'His promises are not stamped with an expiration date in small print.' Ponder this wonderful fact in the light of another great fact stated in 2 Corinthians 1:20.

3. 'David is *over* Israel *for* Israel.' Is that the way you view your parenthood, your authority at work, your position as pastor, elder, deacon or whatever? How did Christ view His work?

4. The second time the Philistines came up and spread out in the Valley of Rephaim, David might have reasoned that he had guidance

the first time, so did not need it now. How wrong he would have been! Ponder the implications of this for your own life.

5 We must not tone down vigorous images of Yahweh's power such as the Leveller and the Warrior. Are there other images of Him that embarrass you and are you prepared to face what they tell us about Him?

Chapter 7

1. If the ark represented the Lord's presence among His people and it emphasised His rulership, reconciliation and revelation, what can the Christian church learn from this in terms of its own privileged task of representing Him in the world?

2. If the real question is not 'Who is against us?' but 'Who is among us?' is it any wonder that we sometimes find ourselves depressed when we fail to realise this?

3. Do you agree that it is often the difficult stories in the Bible that most assure us of its inspiration because they cut across so much of our thinking? What other examples of this can you find?

4. A Christian touring Britain after a long absence abroad said he was glad to find many churches with bright, attractive services, but was disturbed that he was rarely aware of God's people being filled with awe by His holy presence among them. Is this true of you?

5. 'Rejoice with trembling!' (Ps. 2:11). Could this sum up what worship is to you?

Chapter 8

1. When you get 'a good idea' that you think will further God's kingdom, do you wait in the presence of God to ask Him if it really came from Him or if it is nothing more than your own thinking?

2. It was said of an eminent man of God that the only criticism of him his friends could recall was that he would never go through a

door before somebody else but always insisted that person went first! Would you be happy if that was the main 'fault' people could discern in you?

3. 'Humility – the most surprising of all God's wonderful attributes.' Do you agree?

4. In the matter of a house, David was to be a passive recipient rather than an active initiator. Do you think there is a place for both in the Christian life, and which would you reckon to be primary?

5. 'How firm a foundation, you saints of the Lord, is laid for your faith in His excellent word.' Think of how 2 Samuel 7 and countless other Scriptures underscore the faithfulness of God so that it becomes the firmest possible ground for your faith.

Chapter 9

1. 'Yahweh's declarations stirred David's devotions; his promises ignited David's praises and prayers. That's how it should be.' Does God's word stir that kind of response in you?

2. In the light of what you have seen so far in 2 Samuel do you agree with the idea sometimes put forward that there is little of the grace of God in the Old Testament?

3. If you sometimes forget to act as one who has Christ as his Master, is this because you over-emphasise the freedom He has given you, or is it rather that you do not think enough about the cost to Him of that freedom?

4. 'Redeemed, preserved, privileged' – do you give full weight to each of these wonderful truths in your devotions and in your everyday living?

5. 'Prayer pleads promises.' Such a thought as this could revolutionise your prayer-life, so spend some time reflecting on it.

Chapter 10

1. 1. If there is a clear continuity between the kingdom teaching of a passage like 2 Samuel 8 and later kingdom doctrine, do you think we sometimes drive too thick a wedge between the Testaments?

2. Do you think the fact that the Second Advent and judgement to come are so often played down is because of a sentimentalised, unbiblical view of Jesus?

3. Christ is your rightful King. Are you fully submitted to Him?

4. What will doing just and right involve in the particular circumstances of your life?

5. How much in 2 Samuel 8 reminds you of the nature of Christ's coming triumph?

Chapter 11

1. What past promises – to God and other people – have you forgotten to keep, and will you determine by God's grace to fulfil them?

2. If you are a Christian, what does it mean to you that you are in a covenant relationship with God?

3. BB Warfield was Princeton's Professor of 'Polemic Theology', which sounds very stern and exacting, and yet he showed great tenderness towards his invalid wife. Are concern for truth and tender love combined in your character?

4. The story of David and Mephibosheth shows that a person's character is best seen in his or her relations with somebody who is weaker. How do you figure in this regard?

5. Christ's love for us, like David's for Mephibosheth, is so unexpected, so incredible. Have you become so used to it that it no longer causes you to be amazed?

Chapter 12

1. David showed courtesy to the Ammonite king in conveying condolences to him over the death of his father. Do you think courtesy is important in our witness for Christ?

2. 2 Samuel 10 looks like a regionalised version of Psalm 2:1-3. Can you think of more modern events that have seemed like that too?

3. Do you show kindness not only to your fellow-Christians but to all with whom God brings you into contact?

4. George Macdonald once wrote, 'Truth is truth, whether from the lips of Jesus or Balaam.' Are you unwilling to hear God speak through those you find unattractive, or do you recognise His sovereign freedom in such matters?

5. Romans 8:28 affirms that God always works for the good of His people. Does the context there tell us anything which helps us to see what His own view of 'good' is?

Chapter 13

1. In what ways does the writer seem to be suggesting in 2 Samuel 11:1,2 that David was in a somewhat self-indulgent frame of mind when temptation came to him?

2. Do you agree that you need not only to grasp the important truth that in Christ there is great strength to overcome temptation, but also the companion truth that in yourself you are utterly weak?

3. Most of us have some position, some status, even if we are not in the same league as a king like David. Are you ever guilty of abusing power and so sinning against the God who loves you?

4. David's act was evil in Yahweh's eyes. Do you sometimes forget how all-seeing those eyes are?

5. Those who commit adultery today do not normally find themselves committing murder as well, but does this make the adultery itself any the less serious?

Chapter 14

1. Francis Thompson called God, in His pursuit of the sinner, 'the Hound of heaven'. How grateful are you when He catches up with you and makes you confront your sin? Do you recognise that there is amazing grace in that?

2. David was convicted out of his own mouth. Do you think that subsequently he regretted this or do you think he was really thankful for it?

3. Can you think of events in your own life when you have sensed the ingenuity of God's grace?

4. 'Grace is not merely favor; it is also the fury that precedes the favor.' Is that a new thought to you? Explore it a little and give praise to God for it if you discover it in His dealings with you.

5. On his deathbed, Heinrich Heine said, 'God will pardon me. It is His trade.' Do you agree or do you see something wrong with these words?

Chapter 15

1. If you do not hate sin – especially your own sin – enough, where should you go? What about a hill outside Jerusalem?

2. Do you think rape victims get sufficiently compassionate treatment in today's society?

3. Do you think 'love' badly needs Biblical definition in today's world?

4. 'Skill without scruple, wisdom without ethics, insight without integrity.' This summary of the character of Jonadab prompts the

thought that skill, wisdom and insight may be the qualities we look for in church leaders, but do we remember the other three qualities too?

5. Calvin asserts that prudence without integrity and sincerity produces craftiness. Do you think that every virtue needs companions, even holiness and love needing each other?

Chapter 16

1. How very important it is to be able to discern the difference between God's wisdom and the various types of human wisdom! Are there tests we can apply?

2. Likewise with apparent providence. Can it be applied equally to a legacy a godly receiver uses to the glory of God and one that an ungodly man squanders on his own pleasures?

3. Can manipulation ever really serve the purposes of God? Do you see it sometimes in the context of a local church?

4. 'Physical presence before men without internal submission to God makes for leadership disaster.' No doubt we can all think of modern examples of this – but is it not more important to ask questions about one's own outward demeanour and inner attitude?

5. How far short does the modern church – made up of people like you and me- fall short of Christ's ideal for it?

Chapter 17

1. Absalom added a little religious veneer when talking to people. Did Saul ever do the same? What consequences might this bring in your own character, in your relations with others, and, most of all, in your relations with God?

2. For another example of a wicked act fulfilling God's word, see Isaiah 10. Can you think of others?

3. 'Ittai is an island of fidelity in a sea of treachery.' Fidelity from such a man when David's fortunes were so low was a great virtue. How high to you rate it in the scale of virtues with which you operate?

4. 'Let go and let God ...' Is this an attitude of faith or a prescription for spiritual idleness?

5. Can you recall surprising ways in which God has answered your prayers? Such reflection will undoubtedly strengthen faith and lead to praise.

Chapter 18

1. 'David must not be viewed as an individual but in terms of his office.' Does this help you to come to terms with passages in the psalms where he asks God to destroy his enemies?

2. If the pressure of the moment requires a quick decision, what should we do? Perhaps several passages in the Book of Nehemiah may point to an answer.

3. To what extent does concern that others recognise you as a spiritual person play a part in your life?

4. Compare 2 Samuel 16:12 (as the commentary understands it) with Hosea 11:8, 9 and reflect particularly on the wonderful words, 'for I am God and not man', there.

5. Sometimes Satan's activities actually fulfil God's purposes. Consider 2 Corinthians 12:7-10 as an example of this in the life of Paul. Can you see examples in your own life?

Chapter 19

1. As you look back on your life as a Christian (if you are one), can you discern the hidden sovereignty of God in some of its events?

2. Suppose Job had known the behind-the-scenes drama of chapters 1 and 2 of the book that features him, would the trial of his faith

have been as testing, and would the lesson of the book be as powerful?

3. What little providences have functioned as grand encouragements for you?

4. Add to the sentence that begins, 'the Ahithophels and Adolfs' as many other names as seem appropriate. Every name aptly added will strengthen your faith in the ultimate triumph of God's kingdom.

5. In what ways may your loyalty to Christ be tested and how can you prepare for such tests?

Chapter 20

1. If David's troops would not allow him to risk himself on the field of battle, why was Peter wrong in what he said to Jesus, as recorded in Matthew 16:22? Think about the difference in the two situations.

2. If there are twists of irony in the story of Absalom, how much more is this true of the story of the cross. Read that story, e.g. in Mark, and see, for instance, how the enemies of Jesus actually testified to who He really was even though they had no intention of doing so.

3. Reflect on the fact that because God is God, the punishment of the wicked is completely inevitable.

4. Do you think that Christians in general and you in particular are realistic enough today?
    Are our views about sin and about judgement determined wholly by Scripture or partly by sentiment?

5. In David's reaction to Absalom's death, we see how guilt has aggravated grief. Do you see how in Christ's death in our place it is our guilt, not His, that brought Him such deep sorrow and suffering?

Chapter 21

1. Do you see any parallel between the inter-tribal bickering in David's day and the party-spirit in the Corinthian church attacked by Paul in 1 Corinthians 1–4?

2. Shimei's submission to David was simply a matter of policy. How radical is your personal submission to Christ?

3. Do you think Mephibosheth could be compared with Joseph of Arimathaea (see Luke 23:51-54) or were there important differences in their situations?

4. Godly contentment and godly discontent? Is there a place for both in your life and mine?

5. God gave Solomon the gift of wisdom. Do you think David, his father, showed wisdom or its opposite (or, perhaps something of both) in the events recorded in this section of 2 Samuel?

Chapter 22

1. The element of repetition we encounter when we come to Chapter 20 perhaps reminds us of Judges 2. What does this teach us about human nature and about human society?

2. How seriously – not in theory only but also in practice – do you take the authority of Scripture?

3. Joab was extremely loyal to David but essentially unsubmissive to him. Could this be true of a true Christian in relation to Christ? If so, what do you make of Matthew 7:21?

4. In the light of what we have so far seen in this Bible book, how would you distinguish between worldly and godly wisdom?

5. 'Apparently fragile but always standing.' Do you think that is true for the individual Christian as well as for the church?

Chapter 23

1. Are there ways in which we may take the Lord's name in vain without actually swearing an oath? What about claiming to be guided by Him when we are doing something that is clearly unbiblical?

2. Is a promise always important, no matter how long ago it was made or how inconvenient or costly it now is to fulfil it?

3. This section deals with a very difficult passage. A Bible teacher once said, 'I am not too bothered about Bible passages I don't understand, although I continue to seek light on them. There is quite enough challenge for me in the passages I do understand.' Consider this.

4. Do you think the cross round the neck or even the beautiful, polished cross on a communion table may be giving us a wrong view of Calvary? Can you combine wonder and horror in your attitude to it?

5. Do you think we lose something if we spend much time thinking about the theology of the cross in the Epistles, but rarely stand at the actual scene as depicted in the Gospels?

Chapter 24

1. Can you think of times when an apparently dull passage of Scripture has begun to shine with a new light as the Holy Spirit has shown you its relevance to Christ or to your own life?

2. Most Christians would not recognise the name Ishbi-benob, yet it was so important that God saved David from him. Can you think of apparently minor but actually important incidents in God's dealings with you?

3. Is there a midway between giving God's servants the honour due to Him alone and giving no recognition at all to their service?

4. What promises of God have meant much to you throughout the years you have had so far as a Christian? – if, of course, you are one.

5. The Books of Samuel show us clearly that it is not mere size or strength that really counts in the warfare between the forces of God and those of Satan. What other illustrations of this can you find in the Bible?

Chapter 25

1. Does it encourage you to see in Chapter 22 how the Lord really 'pulled out all the stops' to rescue just one man?

2. When you see from the language of the psalm that it was the God of creation, of the Exodus and of Sinai who did this for David, does this give meaning to Revelation 15:3, 'They ... sang the song of Moses ... and the song of the Lamb'? Your God is all He has ever shown Himself to be in the history of His people.

3. We cannot over-emphasise the righteousness God gives us through Christ's work for us, but do we under-emphasise the importance of actual righteous living?

4. Do you spend enough time thinking about the many evidences in Scripture that show how invincible and sure the kingdom of God is?

5. Can you think of events in your own life when God's good purpose for you was forwarded quite independently of human planning, either yours or that of others?

Chapter 26

1. Why do you think David lays such stress on his inspiration by God in 2 Samuel 23:1-7? What gives this passage such importance?

2. What does it mean to you that the future is the subject of Divine revelation so that all human attempts to discern it, from the deep

thoughts of the intellectual to the banal 'forecasts' of the horoscopes, are not only fruitless but quite unnecessary?

3. Like David, Isaiah was given prophecies of the great King of the future. He lived in the reigns of several kings, varying from the imperfect to the utterly evil. To what extent does experience of human imperfection, including your own, increase your longing for Christ's return and reign?

4. The kingdom is attractive because the King is attractive. Should this be true also of you if you are a servant of this King in His kingdom?

5. Somebody has said that, as far as the kingdom of God is concerned, the outsiders are simply those who have not yet seen that they are really insiders. Can you see the danger of this outlook?

Chapter 27

1. Can you think of times when you, or somebody you know, has been given courage beyond the normal to face a particular situation which could only be faced in God's power?

2. If David's men loved him so much that they would risk their own lives to get him water, what effect should love of Christ have, not just in inspiring an exceptional act, but in even the routine duties of our lives?

3. What answer would you give to any who told you that Sunday worship was simply a waste, a waste of time?

4. Read the 'kingdom list' in Romans 16. Do you think that, like Paul here, we should emulate God in not forgetting the work of His servants, no matter how humble they are?

5. Is there a Uriah in your life that saddens you but nevertheless recalls to you the wonderful grace that forgave you and that encourages you still?

Chapter 28

1. For another incident connected with the *per capita* atonement money see Matthew 17: 24-27, where Jesus makes it clear that He did not have to pay it and yet that He would. What can we learn from that story?

2. There have been attempts, for the New Testament, as well as the Old, to treat the wrath that comes on impenitent sinners, as impersonal, 'the inevitable operation of the law of cause and effect in a moral universe.' Can you see how inadequate that view is?

3. 'Wrath wrapped in mercy.' The profound saying of Paul in Galatians 3:13 shows this in a most wonderful sense, for in Christ's cross the wrath of God against sin is clearly revealed, but wrapped in mercy because borne by Christ in our place. Does that fill you with gratitude?

4. Does it strike you as significant that the last story in the Books of Samuel makes us think about Calvary? Does that remind you of the purpose of God in the Old Testament as a whole?

5. Take a little time to think about and write down the main lessons you have learned from 2 Samuel and reflect on these prayerfully.

MENTOR COMMENTARIES

1 and 2 Chronicles
Richard Pratt
(hardback, 512 pages)
The author is professor of Old Testament at Reformed Theological Seminary, Orlando, USA. In this commentary he gives attention to the structure of Chronicles as well as the Chronicler's reasons for his different emphases from that of 1 and 2 Kings.

Psalms
Alan Harman
(hardback, 456 pages)
The author, a professor of Old Testament, lives in Australia. His commentary includes a comprehensive introduction to the psalms as well as a commentary on each psalm.

Amos
Gray Smith
(hardback, 400 pages)
Gary Smith, a professor of Old Testament in Bethel Seminary, Minneapolis, USA, exegetes the text of Amos by considering issues of textual criticism, structure, historical and literary background, and the theological significance of the book.

Other forthcoming volumes

Joel/Obadiah: Irvin A. Busenitz, The Master's Seminary, California

Gospel of Matthew: Knox Chamblin, Reformed Theological Seminary, Jackson, Mississippi

Gospel of John: Steve Motyer, London Bible College